stop walking on eggshells

taking your life back when
someone you care about has borderline
personality disorder

PAUL T. MASON, MS
RANDI KREGER

New Harbinger Publications, Inc.

Publisher's Note

Care has been taken to confirm the accuracy of the information presented and to describe generally accepted practices. However, the authors, editors, and publisher are not responsible for errors or omissions or for any consequences from application of the information in this book and make no warranty, express or implied, with respect to the contents of the publication.

The authors, editors, and publisher have exerted every effort to ensure that any drug selection and dosage set forth in this text are in accordance with current recommendations and practice at the time of publication. However, in view of ongoing research, changes in government regulations, and the constant flow of information relating to drug therapy and drug reactions, the reader is urged to check the package insert for each drug for any change in indications and dosage and for added warnings and precautions. This is particularly important when the recommended agent is a new or infrequently employed drug.

Some drugs and medical devices presented in this publication may have Food and Drug Administration (FDA) clearance for limited use in restricted research settings. It is the responsibility of the health care provider to ascertain the FDA status of each drug or device planned for use in their clinical practice.

Distributed in Canada by Raincoast Books

Copyright © 2010 by Paul T. Mason & Randi Kreger
New Harbinger Publications, Inc.
5674 Shattuck Avenue
Oakland, CA 94609
www.newharbinger.com

Acquired by Catharine Sutker; Cover design by Amy Shoup; Edited by Kimberlee Roth

Library of Congress Cataloging-in-Publication Data

Mason, Paul T., M.S.
  Stop walking on eggshells : taking your life back when someone you care about has borderline personality disorder / Paul T. Mason and Randi Kreger. -- 2nd ed.
     p. cm.
  Includes bibliographical references.
  ISBN-13: 978-1-57224-690-4 (pbk. : alk. paper)
  ISBN-10: 1-57224-690-1 (pbk. : alk. paper)
  ISBN-13: 978-1-57224-770-3 (pdf ebook)
  ISBN-10: 1-57224-770-3 (pdf ebook)
  1. Borderline personality disorder--Popular works. 2. Borderline personality disorder--Patients--Family relationships. I. Kreger, Randi. II. Title.
  RC569.5.B67M365 2009
  616.85'852--dc22

                                        2009044345

15 14 13

15 14 13 12 11 10 9

"*Stop Walking on Eggshells* makes good on its promise to restore the lives of people in close relationships with someone diagnosed with borderline personality disorder (BPD). It is a rich guide to understanding and coping with the reactions aroused in others by troubling BPD behaviors that negatively impact relationships. Readers will find this book very useful and beneficial."

—Nina W. Brown, Ed.D., professor and Eminent Scholar at Old Dominion University in Norfolk, VA, author of *Children of the Self-Absorbed*

"This book is the absolute go-to guide for my clients who are dealing with a loved one with borderline personality disorder. Readable and thorough, it strikes a perfect balance of practical advice and emotional sensitivity. This book has helped so many people break through their sense of confusion and isolation by helping them to name, understand, and respond to the difficulties of this complex and misunderstood disorder."

—Daniel E. Mattila, M.Div., LCSW

"This book is urgently needed now that a National Institutes of Health study shows that 6 percent of the general population has borderline personality disorder (BPD). I constantly get requests from families needing resources on BPD, and I recommend *Stop Walking On Eggshells* almost every time. This second edition is really easy to read and packed with even more useful tips for family members in distress."

—Bill Eddy, LCSW, attorney, mediator, clinical social worker, and author of *High Conflict People in Legal Disputes* and *Splitting*

"Amazingly, *Stop Walking On Eggshells* not only teaches readers how to recognize the signs of borderline personality disorder, it also shows how they can make life and relationship decisions based on what they want and need instead of decisions controlled by the illness."

—Julie A. Fast, author of *Loving Someone with Bipolar Disorder*

Fasten your seatbelts. It's going to be a bumpy night.

—Bette Davis, *All About Eve*

No matter how confused, self-doubting, or ambivalent we are about what's happening in our interactions with other people, we can never entirely silence the inner voice that always tells us the truth. We may not like the sound of the truth, and we often let it murmur just outside our consciousness, not stopping long enough to listen. But when we pay attention to it, it leads us toward wisdom, health, and clarity. That voice is the guardian of our integrity.

—Susan Forward, Ph.D.

This book is for the children, young and old, whose lives have been affected by borderline personality disorder. And to our teachers: the hundreds of people who told us their stories, shared their tears, and offered us their insight. You made this book possible.

contents

acknowledgments

First and foremost, I would like to thank the two men in my life who made this book possible: my husband, Robert Burko, and my good friend and literary agent, Scott Edelstein.

Robert made countless emotional and financial concessions during the three long years of research and writing. Without his quiet faith, generous nature, and profound love, this book would have been a dream deferred.

Scott was more than my agent: he was my mentor, my coach, my emergency hotline, my chief cheerleader, my number-one believer. When I doubted this book would ever get published, he assured me that it would. When I felt like quitting because the sacrifices were too great, he reminded me of the people whose lives I had changed. His sense of humor and unwavering support sustained me and helped me believe in myself.

I was accompanied on this three-year journey by an incredible group of people whom I have met only electronically. They literally saved people's lives by creating a caring Internet community that freed them from their isolation and gave them hope. Without their hard work and devotion to this cause, there would be no Internet-based support groups, no BPD Central website, and no "Walking on Eggshells" booklet. Special thanks to A. J. Mahari, Alyssa (Alyfac), David Anders, Harwijn B., Anita F., Martin Cleaver, Edith Cracchiolo, Sharon Harshman, Patty Johnson, Lee Meinhardt, Daniel Norton, Rachel Russo, Kieu Vu, Kristin Wallio, and Mark Weinstock.

My Welcome to Oz online community for people with a borderline loved one made its debut in January, 1996. When the twelve list members shared their experiences of living with someone with borderline personality disorder (BPD) traits, they found they were not alone. Since then, the group has grown to 16,000 and spawned a handful of other groups for family members. While each member of Welcome to Oz is special, I must single out clinician Elyce M. Benham, MS, who has been our "ship's counselor" since the beginning. Her gentle humor, compassion, and professional insights have brought hope to many grieving and confused list members.

The Welcome to Oz list has also been blessed with a handful of members who are recovering from BPD. Even though they had reason to feel unwelcome at times, they cared enough to stay and educate us about the true cost of living within the grips of this disorder. When needed, they reminded us diplomatically that both borderlines and family members and others must accept responsibility for their part in the relationship. Their courage is an inspiration; their grace and compassion provided light along the path to understanding, forgiveness, and healing.

Dozens of clinicians and BPD advocates from all over the globe contributed their insights to this book. Mike Chase, FNP, analyzed and organized hundreds of Internet postings for the chapter on children with BPD.

Clinicians interviewed for this book include Elyce M. Benham, MS; Joseph T. Bergs, MD; Mari E. Bernhardt, ACSW; Lori Beth Bisbey, Ph.D.; Barbara Blanton, MSN; James Claiborn, Ph.D.; Kenneth A. Dachman, Ph.D.; Jane G. Dresser, RN; Bruce Fischer, Ph.D.; MaryBelle Fisher, Ph.D.; John M. Grohol, Psy.D.; John Gunderson, MD; Paul Hannig, Ph.D.; Perry Hoffman, Ph.D.; Janet R. Johnston, Ph.D.; Ikar J. Kalogjera, MD; Otto Kernberg, MD; Jerold J. Kreisman, MD; Marsha M. Linehan, Ph.D.; Richard A. Moskovitz, MD; Thomas Meacham, MD; Susan B. Morse, Ph.D.; Cory F. Newman, Ph.D.; Andrew T. Pickens, MD; Margaret Pofahl, ACSW; Joseph Santoro, Ph.D.; Larry J. Siever, MD; and Howard I. Weinberg, Ph.D.

Many books not related to BPD were also influential in my thinking. Chief among them was *The Dance of Anger* (1985) by Harriet Goldhor Lerner, Ph.D. Its fundamental concepts are interwoven into every page of this book. When I first read it many years ago, it changed my life. I feel honored to be able to pass along Lerner's wisdom, and I am indebted to her for her inspiration. Books by Susan Forward, Ph.D., also influenced this work, chiefly *Emotional Blackmail* (1997) and *Toxic Parents* (1989). I highly recommend all three books.

Finally, I would like to thank my coauthor, Paul Mason, MS, for being such a delight to work with; my publisher, New Harbinger Publications, for the same reason; my stepdaughter, Tara Gerard, for her working title; my mother, Janet Kreger, for supporting my writing efforts since grade school; and Edith Cracchiolo, my guardian angel throughout this project.

And to you, dear reader: We wrote this book so that your own journey would be easier. Knowing that you would benefit gave meaning to the often painful experiences of the borderlines and nonborderlines interviewed for this book.

—R. K.

Many people have encouraged me and supported me in the writing of this book. I wish to thank them all and am especially grateful to the following people:

- Monica, my wife, whose unconditional faith and belief in me throughout the three years of this project was unmatched. Despite the long hours, she was always supportive and encouraging while working full-time as a stay-at-home mom. And thanks to my children, Zachary, Jacob, and Hannah, who, in their own ways, consistently remind me of the important things in life.

- My parents, Thomas and Jean Mason, whose love, values, and persistence throughout life's struggles have been a cornerstone on which I continue to build.

- My colleagues at All Saints Health Care System, Inc. and Psychiatric Services, for providing a challenging and supportive clinical environment in which to practice and try new things. Their willingness to risk thinking outside the box has helped shape my career and direction as a mental health professional.

- My graduate school mentor, Kathleen Rusch, Ph.D., who nurtured and supported my earliest interests in borderline personality disorder. In the main, without her early support and confidence, it is highly likely that my clinical and professional interests would have turned elsewhere.

I would like to similarly acknowledge all the clinicians and advocates who contributed their insights, experiences, and knowledge to this book, as well as Dr. Marlena Larson for the outstanding work that she has done at Wheaton Franciscan Healthcare–All Saints in service to patients with BPD and their families.

Finally, I would like to thank my coauthor, Randi Kreger, and our literary agent, Scott Edelstein, who approached me with the idea to write this book more than three years ago. Without their persistence and efforts, I would still be just considering it.

—P. M.

prologue

More than 400,000 copies—that's how many *Stop Walking on Eggshells* copies have been purchased since it was published in 1998. At the rate it's selling, the benchmark of half a million copies is well within sight. Not only that, this book has been translated into so many languages, I have trouble remembering which they are.

When Paul Mason and I were writing this book, we had to struggle to find information of use to family members. A few people were talking about borderline personality disorder (BPD) on AOL and a personality newsgroup. We found just two books for laypeople. Now, the Internet is teeming with information, and you'd need an entire bookshelf to hold the mainstream books about BPD—not to mention all the self-published books and e-books by people who have struggled with this disorder from the inside or the outside.

So what happened? Many things. Researchers started to have the ability to scan the brain and actually see the differences between the normal brain and the brains of people with BPD. New medications followed, and research continues to reveal data that explain why people with BPD think, feel, and act the way they do. Forward-thinking clinicians developed novel approaches that started showing results. Advocates started their own organizations and began pressuring for more visibility and research dollars.

But that's not all. *Stop Walking on Eggshells*, along with my website and my Welcome to Oz online community, was a potent force in increasing awareness of BPD. Readers went online and started to talk to each other on the Internet; people with BPD and their families started websites and formed communities because they had something to say and they didn't feel heard in other arenas. Formerly isolated, people started reaching out to each other.

Between 1995 and 2008, my online Welcome to Oz family group grew from twelve members to sixteen thousand.

The success of *Stop Walking on Eggshells* (and later, the *Stop Walking on Eggshells Workbook*) also showed publishers that books about BPD *could* succeed, hence the proliferation of titles. The foreign editions started information flowing in other countries. In 2008, I (Randi Kreger) gave a series of presentations to BPD family members in Tokyo on the invitation of the Japanese publisher of *Stop Walking on Eggshells*.

But not everything is rosy. Most clinicians still lack essential knowledge—especially about how to assess and treat children and adolescents with symptoms of BPD. Another problem is the fundamental lack of understanding that borderline behavior can be expressed in a multitude of ways that don't necessarily get noticed by, or detected as, signs of BPD by clinicians in the mental health system.

On a more personal level, just as the world has moved on, so have my coauthor and I. A few years after this book was first published, I wrote *The Stop Walking on Eggshells Workbook: Practical Strategies for Living with Someone Who Has Borderline Personality Disorder*. The workbook format allows for lots of examples and description, and the interactive elements help readers understand themselves and apply the information to their own lives.

In 2008, I came out with another major book, *The Essential Family Guide to Borderline Personality Disorder: New Tools and Techniques to Stop Walking on Eggshells*. It contains a clear-cut system with five skill sets to help family members move beyond blame and use concrete solutions to feel better, get unstuck, be heard, and set limits with confidence. As you'll see, I've sprinkled some items from the book in this new edition; both books complement each other and offer different perspectives. Family members need all the help they can get!

Paul Mason, my coauthor, took a different path. He is now the vice-president of clinical services at Wheaton Franciscan Healthcare–All Saints in Racine, Wisconsin. In his role, Paul has executive and administrative oversight of the Mental Health and Addiction Care service line, which includes three inpatient programs and six outpatient clinics serving the needs of adults, children, and families in southeast Wisconsin.

His three children, who were just entering grade school when this book first appeared in bookstores, are now ages thirteen, seventeen, and eighteen. He continues to be happily married to Monica, who, when not taking care of all of the family needs, maintains a small therapy practice serving adults and couples in Racine.

We hope you'll enjoy this new edition.

intimate strangers: how this book came to be

I must be defective.

That was the only explanation I could think of for his behavior. Why did he act so loving one moment and then rip me to shreds the next? Why did he tell me I was talented and wonderful and then scream at me that I was contemptible and the cause of all his problems? If he loved me as much as he said he did, why did I feel so manipulated and powerless? And how could someone so intelligent and educated sometimes act so completely irrational?

On a conscious level, I knew I hadn't done anything to deserve this treatment. But over several years, I came to accept his view of reality—that I was flawed and everything really was my fault. Even after the relationship ended, my feelings of distrust and low self-esteem remained. So I began seeing a therapist.

After several months, she revealed something to me about my former friend that would radically change my life—and those of many others: "The behavior you describe is very characteristic of someone with borderline personality disorder," she said. "I can't make a diagnosis since I've never met him. But from what you've said, he certainly seems to fit the criteria."

Borderline personality disorder? I had never heard of it. She recommended that I read *I Hate You—Don't Leave Me* by Jerold Kreisman, MD

(1989). I did—and discovered that my friend's confusing behavior matched seven out of the nine traits for borderline personality disorder (BPD) listed in the clinician's "bible," the *Diagnostic and Statistical Manual*. Just five traits are needed for a diagnosis.

I wanted to learn more about how the disorder had affected me. I needed to know how to heal. But I could find just two books about BPD for consumers, and they were more like popular explanations of BPD than practical self-help books for family members.

So I decided to write my own self-help book. Because BPD affects six million people in North America, I figured that at least eighteen million family members, partners, and friends—like me—were blaming themselves for behavior that had little to do with them.

A friend who knew I wanted to write the book with a credentialed mental health professional suggested that I contact a colleague of hers, Paul Mason. A psychotherapist, Paul had worked with borderlines and their families in inpatient and outpatient settings for ten years. A respected journal had published his research on the subtypes of BPD. He had also given several professional and community presentations on the subject.

Like me, Paul strongly believed that friends, partners, and family members of those with BPD desperately needed to know they were not alone. "Family members tell me that they're in an emotional combat zone, and they just don't know how to react anymore," he said.

Paul began researching the book, searching the professional literature for relevant studies. Many articles discussed the difficulties of treating borderline clients, whom some practitioners view as being needy, challenging, and slow to improve—if they get better at all. But although the articles outlined coping techniques for trained professionals who see borderline patients one hour a week, most glossed over the needs of the untrained family members who interact with the person seven days a week.

In the studies that did discuss "the family," the term almost always referred to the family of origin of the person with BPD. The focus was to determine the role the early family environment played in the development of the disorder. In other words, the studies looked at behavior directed toward the person with BPD rather than the behavior of that person toward others.

While Paul buried himself in professional journals, I began interviewing dozens of mental health professionals about what the "non-borderline," or non-BP (the partner, friend, or family member of a person with BPD or BPD traits), can do to take control of their own lives and stop "walking on eggshells," while remaining supportive of the person they care about. Some of these clinicians were well-known BPD researchers. Others were local professionals recommended by friends.

I was in for a surprise. Although BPD by definition negatively affects those in relationships with borderlines (BPs), most mental health professionals I spoke with—with a few notable exceptions—were so overwhelmed by the needs of their borderline patients that their advice for non-BPs was quite limited. But as I continued interviewing, the body of knowledge grew.

Paul and I had uncovered essential information for people who care about someone with BPD. But we didn't have a book yet—not the detailed, supportive guide we wanted to write. Enter the Internet.

My new computer, which I had purchased for my public relations, marketing, and writing business, came with a disk for America Online (AOL). Curious to see the Internet firsthand, I installed the program.

I discovered an entire world that I didn't know existed. Internet newsgroups and message boards on AOL are like colossal recovery support groups in the biggest church basement in the world. The "netizens" I met there— both BPs and non-BPs—weren't waiting for professionals to come up with the answers. They were sharing coping strategies, exchanging technical information, and offering emotional support to intimate strangers who understood exactly what they were going through.

I started by reading the years of accumulated postings of hundreds of BPs and non-BPs on America Online. I sent e-mail messages to the recent posters, asking them to participate in our research. Most did, delighted that someone was finally addressing the need for more information about BPD.

As we conversed back and forth via e-mail, I began identifying the primary concerns of family members, partners, and friends. Then I asked people with BPD for their perspectives. For example, when the non-BPs spoke of their helplessness in the face of borderline rage, I asked the BPs to articulate what they were thinking and feeling during a rampage and how others could best respond.

Initially, the people with BPD distrusted me. But over the months, as their confidence in me grew, they revealed their deepest feelings about themselves and described the incredible devastation wrought by the disorder. Many told me horrific stories of sexual abuse, self-mutilation, depression, and suicide attempts. "Being a borderline feels like eternal hell—nothing less," wrote one woman. "Pain, anger, confusion, hurt. Never knowing how I am going to feel from one minute to the next. Sadness because I damage those I love. Once in a great while I'll get too happy and then feel anxious because of that. Then I cut myself. Then I feel ashamed that I cut myself. I feel like my life is an endless 'Hotel California' and the only way to leave is to check out permanently."

Some of the therapists didn't have much hope that people could actually recover from BPD. But on AOL and the Internet, I met many people who had greatly improved through a combination of therapy, medication, and emotional support. Their joy in feeling normal for the first time in their lives sometimes brought me to tears. And, for the first time, I understood how my own BP must have suffered. Behavior that had seemed incomprehensible to me now made sense. For the first time, I understood on a gut level that those years of unprovoked emotional assaults weren't really about me. They probably resulted from his own sense of shame and his intense fears of being abandoned. The discovery that he was a victim, too, turned some of my anger into compassion.

The stories from the family members on the Internet were just as horrifying. Partners told me about spouses who told damaging and embarrassing lies about them—or even filed false charges of abuse. Loving, bewildered parents of children diagnosed with BPD traits spent their entire life savings trying to help their children, only to be implicitly or explicitly accused of child abuse.

Adult children of BPs talked about their nightmarish childhoods. One man said, "Even my body functions were criticized. My borderline mother claimed that I didn't eat, walk, talk, think, sit, run, urinate, cry, sneeze, cough, laugh, bleed, or hear correctly." Siblings of borderlines spoke of having to fight for their parents' attention and worrying that their own children might develop the disorder.

With the assistance of volunteers I met on the message boards, I established a website about BPD (www.BPDCentral.com) and organized an online community for non-BPs called Welcome to Oz. Most were flabbergasted to discover that so many other people shared an experience they thought was unique. For example, three members of Welcome to Oz reported that major arguments had taken place at airports. Four members said that the borderline in their life had been furious at them for days because of something they did in the BP's dreams.

Paul and I began to organize this mass of information very slowly. We developed a system: I would come up with ideas and suggestions based on Internet discussions and give them to Paul, who would revise them, expand on them, and put them into a theoretical framework.

Other times, Paul would develop recommendations based on his research that I would fine-tune and distribute to Welcome to Oz members for their "real world" observations. We both marveled at the technology: with just a stroke of a key, the Internet made it possible to obtain feedback from hundreds of people across the globe.

When we were both satisfied with our work, we shared it with Paul's colleagues, other mental health professionals, and well-known BPD researchers who had spent years working with borderline patients and their families. They confirmed that their patients and family members had the same kinds of concerns as our Internet corespondents. To further ensure the accuracy of our data, we asked Edith Cracchiolo, MA, a professor of psychology at Cerritos College in Norwalk, California, to conduct a survey of the non-BPs in our Internet support group.

Of course, we weren't able to satisfy everyone. When I first considered writing the book, I couldn't figure out why it had never been done before. Several months into the project, the reasons became quite clear. Borderline personality disorder is a controversial, complex topic. Just defining it is like trying to catch a fish with your bare hands, blindfolded, and in the rain. Theories on what causes BPD are plentiful but inconclusive. Treatment is hotly disputed by reputable researchers.

Most frustrating of all was the lack of recognition of BPD by the mental health community, and, consequently, the general public. According to the American Psychiatric Association (APA), the incidence of BPD is nearly that of schizophrenia and bipolar disorder combined. Yet most professionals we interviewed acknowledged that their training did not adequately prepare them to diagnose and treat this challenging disorder. Some had heard only one or two lectures on the subject.

Writing this book proved to be as emotionally difficult as it was intellectually challenging. Many people with BPD included veiled or explicit suicide threats in their responses to my questions. Each day, I received at least one desperate letter from someone who had just discovered the existence of BPD from www.BPDCentral.com and wanted guidance about what to do next.

The result of our three years of effort is the book you now hold in your hands. It is not the last word on the subject. It is only the beginning. We hope that it sparks interest in new research, helps clinicians educate their clients, provides support and comfort to family and friends, and offers hope that people with BPD can get better. Most of all, we hope it will help you—and countless others like you—get off the emotional roller coaster you've been riding since someone with BPD came into your life.

—Randi Kreger

PART 1

understanding
BPD behavior

CHAPTER 1

walking on eggshells: does someone you care about have BPD?

After fifteen years of marriage, I still couldn't figure out what I was doing wrong. I researched in libraries, talked to doctors, spoke to counselors, read articles, and chatted with friends. I spent fifteen years wondering, worrying, and believing too much of what she was telling me about myself. I doubted myself and hurt so much without knowing why.

Then one day, I finally found the answers on the Internet. I started crying with relief. Although I can't get my borderline significant other to admit she needs help, at least I finally understand what's going on. It's not my fault. Now I know the truth.

—From the Welcome to Oz online
community, www.BPDCentral.com

is this book for you?

- Is someone you care about causing you a great deal of pain?

- Do you find yourself concealing what you think or feel because you're afraid of the other person's reaction or because it just doesn't seem worth the horrible fight or hurt feelings that will follow?

- Do you feel that anything you say or do will be twisted and used against you? Are you blamed and criticized for everything wrong in the relationship—even when it makes no logical sense?

- Are you the focus of intense, violent, or irrational rages, alternating with perfectly normal and loving behavior? Does no one believe you when you explain that this is going on?

Do you feel manipulated, controlled, or even lied to sometimes? Do you feel like you're the victim of emotional blackmail?

- Do you feel like the person you care about sees you as either all good or all bad, with nothing in between? Is there sometimes no rational reason for the switch?

- Are you afraid to ask for things in the relationship because you will be told that you're too demanding or that there is something wrong with you? Do you feel that your needs are not important?

- Does the other person denigrate or deny your point of view? Do you feel that their expectations are constantly changing, so you can never do anything right?

- Are you accused of doing things you never did and saying things you never said? Do you feel misunderstood and, when you try to explain, do you find that the other person doesn't believe you?

- Are you often put down? If you try to leave the relationship, does the other person try to prevent you, using anything from declarations of love and promises to change to implicit or explicit threats? Do you make excuses for their behavior or try to convince yourself that everything is okay?

If you answered yes to many of these questions, we have good news for you: You're not going crazy. It's not your fault. And you're not alone. You may share these experiences because someone close to you has traits associated with borderline personality disorder (BPD).

Following are three true stories of people who discovered that someone they care about had the disorder. As with all examples in this book, the stories are based on those shared in Internet support groups, though we have changed many details to conceal the authors' identities.

Jon's Story: Married to BPD

Being married to someone with BPD is heaven one minute, hell the next. My wife's moods change by the second. I'm walking on eggshells trying to please her and avoid a fight for speaking too soon, too quickly, in the wrong tone, or with the wrong facial motions.

Even when I do exactly as she asks, she gets mad at me. One day she ordered me to take the kids somewhere because she wanted time alone. But as we were leaving, she threw the keys at my head and accused me of hating her so much I couldn't stand to be in the house with her. When the kids and I got back from the movie, she acted like nothing had happened. She wondered why I was still upset and told me that I have problems letting go of my anger.

Right now, are you thinking, "I had no idea that anyone else was going through this!"?

It wasn't always like this. Before we got married, we had a whirlwind, fantasy courtship. She idolized me—said I was perfect for her in so many ways. The sex was incredible. I wrote her love poems and bought her expensive gifts. We got engaged after four months, and a year later we were married and on a ten-thousand-dollar dream honeymoon. But right after the wedding she began taking meaningless little things and turning them into mountains of criticism, interrogation, and pain. She accused me of wanting other women constantly and would point out imaginary "examples" to substantiate her claims. She became threatened by my friends and began cutting them down. She said bad things about my business, my past, my values, my pride—anything connected to me.

Still, every once in a while the "old" her comes back—the one who loved me and thought I was the greatest guy in the universe. She's still the smartest, funniest, and sexiest woman I know, and I'm still very much in love. The marriage counselor thinks that my wife might have BPD, but my wife insists I'm the one who is screwing up our relationship. She thinks that the counselor is a quack, and she won't go back. How can I make her get the help she desperately needs?

You're not going crazy. It's not your fault. And you're not alone.

Larry's Story: Parenting a Child with BPD

We knew something was wrong with our adopted son, Richard, when he was eighteen months old. He was cranky, cried a lot, and would scream for three hours straight. At age two, he began having several tantrums a day—some lasting for hours. Our doctor simply said, "Boys will be boys."

When Rich was seven, we found a note in his room saying he was going to kill himself when he turned eight. His elementary school teacher referred us to a local psychiatrist, who told us he needed more structure and consistency. We tried positive reinforcement, tough love, and even diet modification. But nothing worked.

By the time Rich was in junior high, he was lying, stealing, skipping school, and raging out of control. The police became involved when he attempted suicide, started cutting himself, and threatened to kill us. He would dial the child abuse hotline each time we disciplined him by sending him to his room. Our son manipulated his teachers, his family, and even the police. He could be very sharp and charm people with his wit, good looks, and sense of humor. Every counselor was convinced that his behavior was our fault. By the time they saw through his deception, he would refuse to go back. And each new therapist never took the time to read through his chart, which by now was several inches thick.

Finally, after threatening a teacher at school, he wound up in a short-term treatment center. At various times we were told that he had attention deficit disorder or suffered from post-traumatic stress disorder from some unknown trauma. One psychiatrist said he was suffering from "depression with psychotic disorder." Lots of people told us he was just a bad kid. After four hospitalizations, our insurance company told us they would no longer pay. The hospital said he was too sick to come home. And the local psychiatrists were advising us to go to court and have ourselves declared unfit parents. Somehow, we found a state-subsidized inpatient hospital where he received his first BPD diagnosis. They put him on various meds but said that there was little hope of him getting better.

Rich did manage to graduate from high school and start college, which ultimately was a disaster. His maturity level now is about age eighteen, although he's twenty-three. Reaching adulthood has helped some, but he still fears abandonment, can't sustain a long-term relationship, and has quit four jobs in two years. His friends come and go because he can be overbearing, obnoxious, manipulative, and opinionated. So he depends on us for money and emotional support. We're all he has left.

Ken's Story: Living with a Parent with BPD

My mother's love for me was conditional. When I didn't do what I was supposed to—chores or whatever—she would rage, cut me down, and say I was a horrible kid who would never have any friends. But when she needed love, she would become affectionate, hug me, and talk about how close we were. There was never any way to predict which mood she would be in.

My mother got resentful if she felt someone else was taking up too much of my time and energy. She was even jealous of our dog, Snoopy. I always thought I had done something wrong—or that there was something wrong with me.

She took it upon herself to improve me by constantly telling me how I needed to change. She saw something wrong with my hair, my friends, my table manners, and my attitude. She seemed to exaggerate and lie to justify her assertions. When my father protested, she dismissed him with a wave of her hand. She always had to be right. Over the years, I tried to meet her expectations. But whenever I did, they changed. Despite years of stinging criticism, I never became accustomed to it. Today, I have trouble getting close to people. I can't trust anyone completely—not even my wife. When I feel especially close to her, I brace myself for the inevitable rejection I know will come. If she doesn't do something I can label "rejecting," I rebuff her in some way—like getting mad at her for something stupid. Intellectually I know what's happening. But I feel powerless to stop it.

the intensity of BPD behavior

People with BPD feel the same emotions other people do. They do many of the same things that other people do. The difference is that they:

- feel things more intensely

- act in ways that seem more extreme

- have difficulty regulating their emotions and behavior

BPD does not cause fundamentally different behavior but behavior that is very far to one side of the continuum.

> Researchers coined the term "borderline" in the first half of the twentieth century, when they thought people who exhibited behaviors we now associate with BPD were on the border between neurosis and psychosis. Although this concept was discarded in the 1970s, the name stuck.

if you learn it's BPD

People who care about someone with borderline personality disorder are usually flabbergasted when they learn that BPD may be at the root of this person's erratic, hurtful, and confusing behavior. They often wonder why they haven't heard of BPD before—especially if they've sought help from the mental health system.

why don't we hear much about BPD?

Unfortunately, BPD is not always recognized, even by mental health professionals. Several factors may explain why.

1. The American Psychiatric Association didn't formally recognize BPD in its *Diagnostic and Statistical Manual* (*DSM* 1994), a standard reference for the diagnosis and treatment of psychiatric illnesses, until 1980. Many mental health professionals miss signs of BPD in their patients simply because they're not educated enough about the disorder.

2. Some clinicians disagree with the information in the *DSM*; a few do not believe that BPD exists. Some professionals dismiss the diagnosis as a catchall designation or a "wastebasket diagnosis" to describe difficult patients. (This is becoming less common as the research has mounted over the years; BPD is the most researched of all personality disorders.)

3. Some clinicians believe that BPD is so stigmatizing that they will not label patients with the diagnosis for fear they will become outcasts within the mental health system. Many clinicians make a formal diagnosis of BPD on patients' charts but choose to not to discuss it with the patient. Or they mention it briefly but do not explain it.

to tell or not to tell?

As you read this book, you may be eager to talk about BPD with the person you think has it. This is understandable. Learning about the disorder can be a powerful, transformational experience. The fantasy goes like this: the person will be grateful to you and will rush into therapy to conquer their demons.

Unfortunately, the reality differs. Family members repeatedly told us that their loved one instead responded with rage, denial, and a torrent of criticism. Frequently, the person with BPD traits accused the family member of being the one with the disorder.

No celebrity has ever admitted to having the disorder (although tabloids and biographies speculate widely), but many show the traits. Issues like eating disorders, domestic violence, AIDS, and cancer often do not move to the forefront of our national consciousness until they affect someone famous.

Other scenarios are possible, too: The person with BPD traits may feel such shame and despair that they attempt to hurt themselves. Or they may use the information to deny responsibility for their behavior—"I can't help it; I'm borderline."

seek help from a qualified therapist

The issues here are complex. Don't rush into anything. Discuss your thoughts with a qualified therapist who is experienced in treating people with BPD. Generally, it's preferable that the person learn about BPD from a therapist—not from you. If the person is an adult and is currently seeing a therapist, the therapist probably will not discuss BPD with you because of confidentiality laws. You can, however, share your concerns with the counselor.

You cannot force someone to want to change their behavior. After all, they are not just "behaviors" to the person suffering from the disorder—they are coping mechanisms they have used all their life.
— John M. Grohol, Psy.D.

It's likely that other people in the person's life may also respond with denial and accusations, especially the borderline's family of origin: his or her mother, father, and siblings. Keep in mind that it is not your job to convince anyone of anything. People have to be ready and willing to learn.

The Exception

There are some situations when you might carefully discuss BPD with someone you think has the disorder:

- if they are actively looking for answers as to why they feel the way they do

- if the two of you are not playing the "blame game"

- if you can do so in a caring, loving way and assure the person that you plan on sticking with them through years of treatment. (Do not make this promise lightly. Making it and breaking it can be worse than not making the promise at all.)

---

when you know and they don't

The eggshells get more fragile when you are aware of a possible BPD diagnosis and the other person is not. Sam, for example, says that because he can't discuss BPD with his possibly borderline wife, Anita, she won't take responsibility for her actions and complains that she's always the "victim." Talking about treatment, obviously, is not an option. He also feels like he's being dishonest because he uses a separate mailing address to receive information about BPD.

Since finding out about BPD, my interactions have become softer and more compassionate—but certainly just as frustrating. At times, it feels like the tremendous volume of information I have gained has been killing me.

—Wesley

Only you, in consultation with a trained mental health professional with experience treating BPD, can decide how to proceed. We offer suggestions for choosing a therapist in Appendix A.

---

don't get stuck on the diagnosis

Rather than dwell on the diagnosis per se, help the person see that in any relationship, both people bear responsibility for the way things are. (You may feel that the BP is responsible for all the problems, but set this aside for now.) Your message should be that when there are problems in relationships, both people need to work on them together.

If the person with BPD cannot seem to take a cooperative approach to working on the relationship, you may wish to simply focus on setting limits (chapter 6). As we'll discuss, asking the person to observe your limits doesn't depend on their awareness of, or willingness to admit having, the disorder.

> Your message should be that when there are problems in relationships, both people need to work on them together.

Remember, the other person may or may not have BPD. And even if they do, that may not completely explain their behavior. Switch the focus from wondering about the possible causes of their actions to solving problems that result from those actions and behaviors.

how to use this book

This book is packed with information. Read slowly and don't try to absorb it all at once. It is meant to be digested in small bites.

go step by step

We suggest you read this book in order rather than skipping around. The knowledge you gain in each chapter serves as the foundation for the next. This is especially true in part 2. We reiterate some fundamental concepts in several chapters; this is to help you integrate them into a new way of thinking about yourself and your relationship.

understand terms

We have created some new terms and definitions in order to make this book more readable.

Non-Borderline (non-BP)

The term "non-borderline" (non-BP) does not mean "person who doesn't have BPD." Rather, it is shorthand for "relative, partner, friend, or other individual who is affected by the behavior of someone with BPD." Non-BPs can be in any type of relationship with someone who has BPD. Non-BPs we interviewed included aunts, cousins, and coworkers of people with BPD.

Non-BPs are a diverse group of people who are affected by people with BPD in a variety of ways. Some non-BPs are very supportive of the people with BPD in their lives; some may be verbally or physically abusive. Non-BPs may have mental health concerns of their own, such as depression, substance abuse, attention deficit disorder, and borderline personality disorder.

> Some people with BPD were sexually, physically, and emotionally abused by their parents or other caretakers. Others had very good parents who have dedicated their lives to getting treatment for their children. The parents we interviewed fall into the latter category. They were not perfect parents (who among us can claim perfection?). But their behavior was not abusive. When we discuss parents we mean ordinary parents who make ordinary mistakes.

Borderline (BP)

We use the term "borderline" (BP) to mean "a person who has been diagnosed with borderline personality disorder or who seems to fit the definition for BPD in the *Diagnostic and Statistical Manual IV-TR* (*DSM* 2004), published by the American Psychiatric Association."

> BPD is often misdiagnosed and frequently coexists with other mental health conditions. If your BP has been under the care of several mental health professionals, it's quite possible that there are differing opinions about the diagnosis. In the absence of a formal diagnosis, you may feel uncomfortable calling this person borderline. Don't let that stop you from getting vital information you need to make your life better.

You should not diagnose people based on information in a book. A diagnosis can only be made by a professional who is experienced in assessing and treating people with BPD. You may never know for sure if the person you care about really has BPD. The person may refuse to be evaluated by a mental health professional—in fact, that person may deny that he or she is having difficulties. Or he or she may be seeing a therapist but choose not to share the diagnosis with you.

> Remember, this book is about you, not the BP. You have the right to seek help. And if you are being confronted with behavior patterns like those listed on the previous pages, you will be able to benefit from the strategies in this book—regardless of the presence or absence of a BPD diagnosis.

"Borderline" Versus "Person with BPD"

Some professionals prefer the phrase "person with BPD." They believe that calling someone a "borderline" implies that the diagnosis defines the person. These clinicians assert that the longer phrase "person with BPD" should always be used.

While we agree that the term "person with BPD" is less stigmatizing than the noun "borderline," our goal is to produce a book that is readable and succinct, as well as respectful to people with mental disorders. To examine the complex interactions between BPs and non-BPs, we must often differentiate between them—sometimes several times in the same sentence. Using the longer phrase would make this book too hard to read, so we have chosen to use "borderline" or "BP" instead. More importantly, "BP" is inclusive of people who have not been formally diagnosed, but show the traits.

remember our focus

As you read, it may seem as if we are holding the person with BPD responsible for all the problems in the relationship. But actually, we are not discussing the relationship as a whole at all. Our focus is very narrow: coping with BPD behavior.

Even reading this book may seem like a betrayal of the person you care about. It's not.

19

In real life, relationships are multifaceted. Hundreds of factors unrelated to BPD affect them. We do not address these factors because they are beyond the scope of this book.

> The BP is responsible for 50 percent of the relationship, and the non-BP is responsible for the other half. At the same time, each person is responsible for 100 percent of their own 50 percent.

know there is hope

BPD is probably the most misunderstood psychiatric diagnosis. And the biggest misperception is that people with BPD never get any better. In reality, medications can help reduce depression, moodiness, and impulsivity. Certain treatments have been shown to be effective in empirical research. We have met many recovered borderlines who no longer feel compelling urges to hurt themselves, who feel good about themselves, and who give and receive love joyfully.

The biggest misperception is that people with BPD never get any better.

What if the BP refuses help and treatment? There's still hope. Although you can't change the person with BPD, you can change yourself. By examining your own behavior and modifying your actions, you can get off the emotional roller coaster and reclaim your life.

CHAPTER 2

the inner world
of the borderline:
defining BPD

Trying to define BPD is like staring into a lava lamp: what you see is con-
stantly changing. The illness not only causes instability but symbolizes it.

—Janice Cauwels, *Imbroglio: Rising to the*
Challenges of Borderline Personality Disorder

Understanding Personality Disorders

According to the *DSM-IV-TR* (2004), a personality disorder is:

- an enduring pattern of inner experience and behavior that devi-
  ates markedly from the expectation of the individual's culture

- pervasive and inflexible (unlikely to change)

- stable over time

- leads to distress or impairment in interpersonal relationships

The very definition of a personality disorder is that it causes distress for both the person who has the disorder and those who interact with him or her. Since the description of BPD seems so negative, people diagnosed with it often feel stigmatized. It's crucial to keep in mind that borderline personality disorder and the person who has it are not one and the same.

> Borderline personality disorder is something people have, not something they are.

When you're living with someone with BPD, however, it can be difficult to separate BPD from the person who suffers from it. Borderlines recover.

Ultimately, the only person who can control the thoughts, feelings, and behaviors of the person with BPD is the borderline him- or herself. Understanding this is vital for the BP's recovery—and your own.

The Criteria for BPD

The *DSM-IV-TR* (2004) diagnostic criteria for borderline personality disorder reads as follows:

> A pervasive pattern of instability of interpersonal relationships, self-image, and affects [moods], and marked impulsivity beginning by early adulthood and present in a variety of contexts, as indicated by five (or more) of the following:
>
> 1. Frantic efforts to avoid real or imagined abandonment. Note: Do not include suicidal or self-mutilating behavior covered in (5).
>
> 2. A pattern of unstable and intense interpersonal relationships characterized by alternating between extremes of idealization and devaluation.
>
> a 3. Identity disturbance: Markedly and persistently unstable self-image or sense of self.
>
> 4. Impulsivity in at least two areas that are potentially self-damaging (e.g., spending, sex, substance abuse, shoplifting, reckless driving, binge eating). Note: Do not include suicidal or self-mutilating behavior covered in (5).

5. Recurrent suicidal behavior, gestures, or threats, or self-mutilating behavior.

6. Affective instability due to a marked reactivity of mood (e.g., intense episodic dysphoria, irritability, or anxiety usually lasting a few hours and only rarely more than a few days).

7. Chronic feelings of emptiness.

8. Inappropriate, intense anger or difficulty controlling anger (e.g., frequent displays of temper, constant anger, recurrent physical fights).

9. Transient, stress-related paranoid ideation or severe dissociative symptoms.

We'll explain more about the criteria, as well as provide examples from people with BPD and their family members. In this text, we've grouped lack of identity and feelings of emptiness (3 and 7) in the same section because we believe they are related. We've also separated suicide and self-mutilation (5) because we believe that the motivations for each are very different.

Dysphoria is the opposite of euphoria. It's a mixture of depression, anxiety, rage, and despair.

---

1. *frantic efforts to avoid real or imagined abandonment*

— calling multiple times; panic over Bolivia

Imagine the terror that you would feel if you were a child lost and alone in the middle of Times Square in New York City. Your mom was there a second ago, holding your hand. Suddenly the crowd swept her away. You look around, frantically, trying to find her.

This is how people with BPD feel nearly all the time: isolated, anxious, terrified at the thought of being alone. Caring, supportive people are like friendly faces in the middle of the crowd. But the moment they do something that the BP interprets as a signal they're about to leave, the BP panics and reacts. The person may burst into rage or beg the loved one to stay.

It takes little to trigger fear of abandonment—one borderline woman refused to let her roommate leave their apartment to do laundry. The fear of abandonment can be so strong that it can overwhelm the BP. For example, when one man told his BP wife that he had a potentially fatal illness, she raged at him for seeing the doctor.

If your BP was neglected as a child or raised in a severely dysfunctional household, he may have learned to cope by denying or suppressing his terror at being abandoned. After many years of practice, he no longer feels the original emotion. When your BP becomes upset or angry, it may help to think about whether anything has happened that might be triggering fears of abandonment.

Armin (non-BP)

If I'm five minutes late coming home from work, my wife will call to find out where I am. She pages me constantly. I can't go out by myself with friends anymore because she reacts so strongly—she'll even page me while I'm watching a movie. It's so stressful that I've stopped going out with friends unless she feels like coming along.

Tess (BP)

When I feel abandoned I feel a combination of isolation, terror, and alienation. I panic. I feel betrayed and used. I think I'm going to die.

One night I called my boyfriend, and he said he would call me back because he was watching TV. So I did my ironing to pass the time. He didn't call. I waited. He didn't call. This terrible feeling of being abandoned came over me again. It hurt so bad because the day before, I had started to believe that he really loved me.

By the time the phone rang at 10 P.M., I had decided to break up with him—get rid of him before he could get rid of me. He had still been watching the movie. I felt so ridiculous, but the pain, the fear, and the poker in my gut were very real.

Sometimes the person with BPD will tell you outright that they are afraid of being abandoned. But just as frequently, this fear will be expressed in other ways—rage, for example. Feeling vulnerable and out of control can provoke anger.

2. a pattern of unstable and intense interpersonal relationships characterized by alternating between extremes of idealization and devaluation (splitting)

People with BPD look to others to provide things they find difficult to supply for themselves, such as self-esteem, approval, and a sense of identity. Most of all, they are searching for a nurturing caregiver whose never-ending love and compassion will fill the black hole of emptiness and despair inside them.

Beverly (BP)

I used to approach every friendly looking person with a deep hope that they would take care of me. Then I began to realize that none of them were able to nurture me the way that I wanted because although I felt like a child inside, I looked like an adult on the outside.

The intense need of people with BPD can put a strain on any relationship—even when the non-BP is a parent and the BP is a child.

Roberta (non-BP)

Parenting my eighteen-year-old daughter with BPD has always been a twenty-four-hour-a-day job. She is depressed and needs to be comforted. She needs help in thinking through solutions to everyday problems. She cries and bleeds from self-inflicted cuts. I love her very much, but I don't know what to do. All of my time and energy goes to her, and my other children resent it.

People with BPD look to others to provide things they find difficult to supply for themselves, such as self-esteem, approval, and a sense of identity.

For people with BPD, the potential loss of a relationship can be like facing the loss of an arm or leg—or even death. At the same time, their sense of self-esteem is so low that they really don't understand why anyone would want to be with them. People with BPD are hypervigilant, looking for any cues that might reveal that the person they care about doesn't really love them after all and is about to desert them. When their fears seem to be confirmed, they may:

- erupt into a rage
- make accusations
- sob
- seek revenge
- mutilate themselves
- have an affair
- do other destructive things

This leads us to the central irony of borderline personality disorder: People who suffer from it desperately want closeness and intimacy. But the things they do to get it often drive people away. As torturous as this can be for you, imagine what it's like for the person who has the disorder. You can take a break and get away from it for awhile—go to a party, read a book, take a walk on the beach. But the BP lives with the fear and panic twenty-four hours a day.

Understanding Splitting

Many BPs fluctuate between extremes of idealization and devaluation. This is called "splitting."

> People with BPD often perceive other people as either the wicked witch or fairy godmother, a saint or a demon. When you seem to be meeting their needs, they cast you in the role of superhero. But when they perceive that you've failed them, you become the villain.

People who suffer from BPD desperately want closeness and intimacy. But the things they do to get it often drive people away.

Because people with BPD have a hard time integrating a person's good and bad traits, their current opinion of someone is often based on their last interaction with them—like someone who lacks a short-term memory.

Jerold J. Kreisman, author of *I Hate You—Don't Leave Me: Understanding the Borderline Personality* (1989) and *Sometimes I Act Crazy* (2006), explains splitting this way:

Normal persons are ambivalent and can experience two contradictory states at one time; borderlines characteristically shift back and forth, entirely unaware of one feeling state while in another.... A child emotionally, the borderline cannot tolerate human inconsistencies and ambiguities; he cannot reconcile another's good and bad qualities into a constant coherent understanding of another person. At any particular moment, one is either "good" or "evil"; there is no in-between, no gray area. Nuances and shadings are grasped with great difficulty, if at all.

> When there is a problem, some people with BPD may feel as if there is only one solution.

All-or-nothing thinking may appear in other areas of the BP's life—not just relationships. When there is a problem, some people with BPD may feel as if there is only one solution. Once action is taken, there's no turning back. For example, when one borderline woman was given new work duties she disliked, her solution was to quit her job. A BP's effort may be all or nothing. For example, a borderline college student became so involved with a political campaign that he flunked all his classes but then dropped his political activities in favor of school the next semester.

Difficulty Defining Relationships. People with BPD may feel that relationships must be clearly defined. Someone is either their friend or their enemy, their passionate lover or a platonic buddy. This is one reason why people with BPD may have a hard time being platonic friends after a romance ends. This need for definition does not just apply to others; people with BPD also see themselves in black and white. In his self-help book for borderlines, *Lost in the Mirror: An Inside Look at Borderline Personality Disorder*, Richard Moskovitz (1996) writes:

> You [the person with BPD] may strive valiantly for perfection and feel, at times, that you have achieved it, only to condemn yourself when the smallest flaw appears. When you are good, you may feel entitled to special treatment and live outside the rules made for others. You may feel entitled to take whatever you wish and have everything good for yourself.

Dealing with Splitting. It is impossible to fulfill all your borderline's needs and expectations. Once you take steps to meet the borderline's needs, he may decide he wants something else. Your role may change from hero to villain several times in one day, or it can take years for the person with BPD to cycle through the saint/sinner pattern. Sometimes the BP may find a new "love object" once the old one has proven to be "flawed," only to repeat the cycle with someone else.

> People with BPD are fully convinced their skewed feelings and beliefs— be they positive or negative—are unquestionably true. Therefore, your mission is to maintain a consistent, balanced view of yourself despite their ups, downs, and sideways.

Partially because of their habit of splitting, people with BPD—especially those who were abused as children—find it extremely difficult to trust others. This lack of trust causes a great deal of turbulence in relationships; for example, while they are seeing you as a villain, they may accuse you of not loving them or of having an affair.

Non-BPs in this situation often try *harder* to show their trustworthiness, but often to no effect. That's because the feelings of mistrust lie within the person with BPD and have nothing to do with the specific actions of the non-BP.

Rachel Reiland, author of *Get Me Out of Here: My Recovery From Borderline Personality Disorder* (Hazelden, 2004) wrote in an email:

> *I always had this insatiable hunger for something I couldn't define, except to call it the bottomless pit of need. Something that made me scared to get close to anybody for fear they'd discover I was rotten and disturbed. So I diversified. I had lots of friends and didn't get too close to any of them. If I let my guard down and one friend found out how weird I was and they backed off—well, I had fifty-nine others.*
>
> *But now a romantic relationship has kicked in. The stakes are high, with one person meaning so much. This is different—the guy needs me, too. So maybe it's safe here. Be with me, please. Every day and every night. Look at me, listen to me. I'm here. See me? I'm here! I'm here... Oh, this is incredible! Finally, the one person who can take all of this need! What a relief!*
>
> *Hey... wait a minute! He's resisting this—says he wants to watch TV in peace, says he's got something else to do. What the hell do I do now? Ooohhh, am I frustrated . . . Damn it. I hate this guy! I let my guard down— doesn't he know how hard it was for me to do that? How dare he rather watch TV*

than talk to me? How dare he rather be out with his friends than be right here? How dare he find out what kind of a completely disturbed person I am? I'm furious. And I'm embarrassed as hell. I've been caught with my pants down— he's seen the bottomless pit of need.

Embarrassed, I lash out. Let him have it! Hey, guess what buddy—I don't care about you. Take this—take that! I rage, I scream until I collapse in exhaustion. And then I wake up and I see how much I've hurt him. And I despise myself more than I could ever imagine. I'm scared to death. Because I just know he's gonna walk. I'm so vulnerable. I'm not tough. Please don't leave. I do need you! How can I show you?

I cry, I beg, I tell him what an incredible man he is, how patient he is. I just know you hate me! You should hate me! I'd be better off dead. You'd be better off without me! No, I mean it—I wish I were dead . . . He's relenting a bit. Oh, please, let me make it up to you. Let's make incredible love anywhere, anytime! Let me show you the best side of my passion. Whew! He's back. He's still around. Thank God I didn't blow it permanently. It feels so good to be with him. He cares. I need him.

When I realize that I've caused irrevocable damage—when the cycle has repeated itself so often I'm convinced that I've irrevocably blown it—whether or not he has reached this conclusion—I cut the cord and find somebody else. And go through the whole damned thing again.

3. identity disturbance: markedly and persistently unstable self-image or sense of self and 7. chronic feelings of emptiness

By the time people reach their twenties and thirties, their self-image is usually fairly consistent. Some people also go through a midlife crisis in their forties, when they question the choices they've made. But most of us take certain things for granted, such as our likes and dislikes, our values, our religious beliefs, our positions on important issues, and our career preferences.

Lacking a Sense of Self

But the searching never ends for people with BPD. They lack an essential sense of themselves, just like they lack a consistent sense of others. Without a sense of self to cling to, they are like passengers on the deck of a ship during a typhoon, getting tossed about and battered. They frantically look around, searching for something to hold onto. But all they see are other passengers wearing life jackets, lashed to poles for security. As another wave roars over the deck, they grab onto someone else's pole and hang on for dear life. But the life jacket is only big enough for one person. And the pole can't withstand the combined weight and is starting to crack.

In his book *The Role of Psychodynamic Concepts in the Diagnosis of Borderline Personality Disorder*, Robert J. Waldinger (1993) discusses the issue of identity diffusion, a characteristic that leads to feelings of emptiness:

> Identity diffusion refers to borderline patients' profound and often terrifying sense that they do not know who they are. Normally, we experience ourselves consistently through time in different settings and with different people. This continuity of self is not experienced by the person with BPD.

Instead, borderline patients are filled with contradictory images of themselves that they cannot integrate. Patients commonly report:

- feeling empty inside

- feeling there is "nothing to me"

- feeling that they are different people depending on whom they are with

- being dependent on others for cues about how to behave, what to think, and how to be

- feeling that being alone leaves them without a sense of who they are or with the feeling that they do not exist

- feeling panicked and bored when alone

A sense of inner emptiness and chaos renders borderline patients dependent on others for cues about how to behave, what to think, and how to be; whereas being alone leaves them without a sense of who they are or with the feeling that they do not exist. This, in part, accounts for these patients' frantic and often impulsive effort to avoid being alone, as well as their descriptions of panic, crushing boredom, and dissociation.

Never Good Enough. While a BP may have difficulty with self-definition, he may also feel that, no matter what his identity, he's never good enough.

Some people with BPD become extremely successful at what they do. They become known for their achievements at work, in their community, or at home. But they often feel like actors reciting their lines. When the audience goes home, they cease to exist.

People with BPD:

- base their self-worth on their latest achievement—or lack of it

- judge themselves as harshly as they judge others, so whatever they do is never good enough

- see themselves as helpless victims of other people—even when their own behavior has affected the outcome of a particular situation

The Role of Victim. For example, during group therapy, a borderline man complained that his landlord had evicted him and he had no place to live. After twenty minutes of commiseration, group members began asking him why this had happened. It turned out that the man had violated many apartment rules, including parking in the landlord's space. Another borderline woman repeatedly battered her husband, had numerous affairs, and had her husband falsely arrested for possession of drugs after she planted them in his suitcase. Eventually, she filed for divorce. Her ex-husband began dating a woman he worked with. Yet, when the woman described the breakup to her friends, she told them that her husband deserted her for a coworker. These two BPs refused to recognize their role in the situations.

Why Do They Do It?

- Some people with BPD may play the role of victim because it draws sympathetic attention.

- Some people with BPD may feel being the victim supplies an identity.

- The victim role gives people with BPD the illusion that they are not responsible for their own actions.

- Borderlines with abusive backgrounds may be replaying scripts from the past.

31

✓**The Role of Caretaker.** Another role common among people with BPD is that of helper or caretaker. This more positive role may help provide them with an identity, heighten feelings of control, and lessen feelings of emptiness.

Salia (BP)

I have a chameleon-like ability to take on the coloring of the individual I am with. But the act is done more to fool me than to fool them. For the time being, I have become who I'd like to be.

I am not some kind of a Machiavellian manipulator with nothing better to do than ruin lives. The process isn't even really conscious. It's been going on for so long now that I don't even know who I really am. I feel unreal—like a phony. If I had any true control over it, I would simply revert back to "myself" whenever I felt threatened. But I don't know who that is.

4. impulsivity in at least two areas that are potentially self-damaging (e.g., spending, sex, substance abuse, shoplifting, reckless driving, binge eating)

Everyone has urges they would love to indulge if they could: eat every chocolate in the box, buy a great new sweater in every color, or drink one last glass of champagne to toast in the New Year. Most people have varying abilities to control impulses and delay immediate gratification. They're aware of the long-term consequences—in this case, weight gain, a massive credit card bill, or a nasty hangover.

But people with BPD are characterized by impulsivity—even recklessness.

> People with BPD may also try to fill the emptiness and create an identity for themselves through impulsive behaviors such as bingeing and purging, indiscriminate sexual activity, shoplifting, compulsive shopping, drinking, or substance abuse.

BPD and substance abuse disorders often go hand in hand (Oldham et al. 1995). Another study (Links, Steiner, and Offord 1988) reported that about 23 percent of borderline patients had a diagnosis of substance abuse. Borderline substance abusers:

- are likely to abuse more than one drug (a frequent combination is drug and alcohol abuse)

- are more likely to be depressed

- have more frequent suicide attempts and accidents

- have less impulse control

- seem to have more antisocial tendencies (Nance, Saxon, and Shore 1983; Links et al. 1995)

If the BP in your life is actively abusing drugs and alcohol, it can be difficult to determine what behavior is related to BPD and what is related to substance abuse.

5. recurrent suicidal behavior, gestures, or threats

Suicide

According to the *DSM-IV* (2004) about 8–10 percent of all people with BPD commit suicide. This does not include BPs who engage in risky behavior that results in death, such as drinking and driving. Marsha M. Linehan (1993a) explains that suicide and other impulsive, dysfunctional behaviors are seen as solutions to overwhelming, uncontrollable emotional pain:

> Suicide, of course, is the ultimate way to change one's [moods].... Other, less lethal behaviors can also be quite effective [in changing the borderline's mood]. Overdosing, for example, usually leads to long periods of sleep; sleep in turn, has an important influence on regulating emotional vulnerability.... Suicidal behavior, including suicidal threats, is also very effective in eliciting behaviors from the environment—help that may be effective in reducing the emotional pain. In many instances, such behavior is the only way an individual can get others to pay attention to and try to ameliorate her emotional pain.

Tony (non-BP)

My wife came home crying, desperate because her boyfriend had dumped her. Incredibly, she felt that I shouldn't be angry about the affair, and that I should support her because of the pain she was feeling. When I wasn't supportive enough, she started threatening suicide in front of our ten-year-old son.

Self-Mutilating Behavior

Self-mutilation, without suicidal intent, is another BPD behavior that is very difficult for family members to understand. Examples include:

- cutting

- burning

- breaking bones

- head banging

- needle poking

- skin scratching

- pulling out hairs

- ripping off scabs

Sometimes, dangerous or compulsive behavior can be a type of self-mutilation—overeating to the point of obesity, for example, or provoking physical fights with others.

Self-injury is a coping mechanism that BPs use to release or manage overwhelming emotional pain—usually feelings of shame, anger, sadness, and abandonment. Self-mutilation may release the body's own opiates, known as beta-endorphins. These chemicals lead to a general feeling of well-being.

Borderlines' reasons for self-mutilation vary tremendously and include:

- to feel alive, less numb, and empty

- to feel more numb

- to express anger at others

- to punish themselves or express self-loathing (probably more frequent among BPs who have been abused)

- to somehow prove that they are not as "bad" as they think they are

- to relieve stress or anxiety

- to feel in control of their pain

- to bring back a sense of reality

- to feel "real"

- to seek relief from emotional pain, frustration, and other negative feelings by focusing on physical pain

- to communicate emotional pain to others or ask for help

Here are some words from BPs on self-mutilation:

- "To tell you the truth, I think I did it so someone would notice that in fact I needed help."

- "When I cut, I don't have to try to explain how bad I am feeling. I can show it."

- "When I get angry at someone, I want to destroy, hurt, or kill them. But I know that I can't really hurt that person. So I take out the anger by cutting myself or pulling out my hair. It makes me feel better at the time, but later on I am ashamed of myself and I wish that I had not done it."

- "When my father stopped abusing me, I had to make up for the hurt that suddenly disappeared."

- "For me, the scars were just outside paintings of what my parents did."

Self-harm may be planned in advance or done impulsively. It may be performed intentionally or unconsciously—almost as if the

Self-mutilation can become addictive, much like smoking, and the urge to do it can be just as powerful as a smoker's urge for another cigarette.

person is in a haze and doesn't realize what they're doing. People who mutilate themselves may or may not feel pain while they're doing it. Some people hide their self-mutilation, only disfiguring areas normally hidden by clothing. Some people learn to sew up their wounds so they won't have to seek medical attention and reveal their secret. Other people are more open about the results of their self-injury—perhaps because it's a way of asking for help or a method of communicating their pain.

People with BPD are often very aware of their own reasons for self-injury. But an intellectual understanding doesn't make it any easier to stop. Self-mutilation can become an addiction, much like smoking, and the urge to do it can be just as powerful as a smoker's urge for another cigarette.

There is a misperception that all people with BPD harm themselves or are suicidal. Many high-functioning BPs do not. BPs who hurt themselves, however, may seek professional help more often than those who don't.

6. affective instability due to a marked reactivity of mood (e.g., intense episodic dysphoria, irritability, or anxiety usually lasting a few hours and only rarely more than a few days)

When most people feel bad, they can take steps to feel better. They can also control, to some extent, how much their moods affect their relationships with others. People with BPD have a hard time doing this. Their mood may swing from intense anger to depression, depression to irritability, and irritability to anxiety within a few hours. Non-BPs often find this unpredictability exhausting.

Dina (non-BP)

Living with my borderline husband is heaven one minute and hell the next. I call his personalities Jovial Jekyll and Horrible Hyde. I walk on eggshells trying to please someone who blows up just because I spoke too soon, too quickly, in the wrong tone, with the wrong facial motions.

7. chronic feelings of emptiness (see number 3 on page 29)

8. inappropriate, intense anger or difficulty controlling anger (e.g., frequent displays of temper, constant anger, recurrent physical fights)

If you care about someone with BPD, you are probably very familiar with this trait.

Borderline rage is usually intense, unpredictable, and unaffected by logical argument. It is like a torrential flash flood, a sudden earthquake, or a bolt of lightning on a sunny day. And it can disappear as quickly as it appears.

Some borderlines, however, have the opposite problem: they feel unable to express their anger at all. In her text, Marsha M. Linehan (1993a) writes that borderline individuals who under-express anger "fear they will lose control if they express even the slightest anger, and at other times they fear that targets of even minor anger expression will retaliate."

Jane G. Dresser, RN, who specializes in BPD, told us in an interview that she believes that people with BPD feel all emotions intensely, not just anger. She theorizes that anger was highlighted in the *DSM* criteria because anger is typically the feeling that causes the most problems for people close to the borderline. Linehan echoes this belief, often saying that people with BPD are like people with third-degree burns over 90 percent of their body. Lacking emotional skin, they feel agony at the slightest touch or movement."

> If you are being attacked verbally or physically by someone with BPD, keep in mind that even experienced mental health professionals may, at times, take borderline rage personally and become upset. We explain how to take steps to protect yourself in chapter 8.

Jeremy (BP)

When I can't control my surroundings, I become nervous and angry. It gets much worse when I am under stress. When triggered, I can go from perfectly calm to full-blown, white-hot rage within a fraction of a second.

I think that my temper comes from the abuse I suffered when I was a child. At some point, I decided that I didn't have to take my parents' abuse anymore. Raging back became a matter of survival.

So now, it's hard for me to feel concerned about the other person's feelings—in fact, I want them to hurt because they've hurt me. I know this sounds bad, but that's the way I feel when I'm in the middle of an outburst. I'm just trying to survive the best way I know how.

Laura (BP)

I think that borderlines are concerned with only one thing: losing love. When cornered, I get very scared and I show that by getting angry. Anger is easier to feel than fear and makes me feel less vulnerable. I strike before being struck.

When I'm mad, all the intellectual understanding in the world doesn't help. The only thing that helps is when my husband says to me, "I know you are scared and not angry." At that moment my anger melts away and I can feel my fear again.

Real anger—the anger normal people feel when they've been treated unjustly—I don't feel at all. That would require a self. Since I don't have a self—or since I put away my own self so deep that I can't reach it anymore—I can't get angry.

9. transient, stress-related paranoid ideation or severe dissociative symptoms

Have you ever arrived home from work without remembering how you got there? You've traveled the route so many times that your brain let your eyes and reflexes do the driving. This "out of it" feeling is a mild type of dissociation.

People who are severely dissociating, however, feel unreal, strange, numb, or detached. They may or may not remember exactly what happened while they were "gone." The degree of dissociation can vary from the car-trip-home variety to the extreme dissociation characterized by multiple personality disorder, now called "dissociative identity disorder."

> The more stressful the situation, the more likely it is that the person will dissociate.

People with BPD may dissociate to different degrees to escape from painful feelings or situations. The more stressful the situation, the more likely it is that the person will dissociate. In extreme cases, people with BPD may even lose all contact with reality for a brief period of time. If the borderline in your life reports memories of shared situations quite differently from you, dissociation may be one possible explanation.

Karen (BP)

Sometimes I feel like a robot going through the motions. Nothing seems real. My eyes cloud over, and it's like there's a movie going on all around me. My therapist says I look lost, like I am off in a place where even she can't reach me. When I come back, people tell me that I did or said certain things that I can't remember.

additional BPD traits

People with BPD may have other attributes that are not part of the *DSM* definition but that researchers believe are common to the disorder. Many of these may be related to sexual or physical abuse the BP might have experienced earlier in life.

pervasive shame

John Bradshaw's book *Healing the Shame That Binds You* (1998) is not about borderline personality disorder, yet his explanation of toxic shame and the resulting feelings and behaviors epitomizes BPD. Bradshaw writes:

Toxic shame is experienced as the all-pervasive sense that I am flawed and defective as a human being. It is no longer an emotion that signals our limits; it is a state of being, a core identity. Toxic shame gives you a sense of worthlessness, the feeling of being isolated, empty, and alone in a complete sense. Exposure to oneself lies at the heart of toxic shame. A shame-based person will guard against exposing his inner self to others, but more significantly, he will guard against exposing himself to himself.

Bradshaw sees shame as the root of issues such as:

- rage
- criticism and blame
- caretaking and helping
- codependency
- addictive behavior

- excessive people pleasing

- eating disorders

In their typical all-or-nothing way, people with BPD may either become consumed by their shame or deny to themselves and others that it even exists. Shame is also a core issue for many non-BPs—especially those who remain in abusive relationships.

undefined boundaries

People with BPD have difficulty setting and maintaining personal limits—both their own and those of others.

Tom (BP)

I was brought up thinking that the perfect intimate relationship had no boundaries. Boundaries only meant a rift between people. Boundaries meant I had to be alone, separate, have an identity. I didn't feel good enough to have a separate identity. I needed either total enmeshment or total isolation.

We will further discuss boundary issues in chapter 6.

control issues

Borderlines may need to feel in control of other people because they feel so out of control with themselves. In addition, they may be trying to make their own world more predictable and manageable. People with BPD may unconsciously try to control others by putting them in no-win situations, creating chaos that no one else can figure out, or accusing others of trying to control them.

Conversely, some people with BPD may cope with feeling out of control by giving up their own power; for example, they may choose a lifestyle where all choices are made for them, such as the military or a cult, or they may align themselves with abusive people who try to control them through fear.

Bradshaw believes that shame also leads to over-steering:

Those who must control everything fear being vulnerable. Why? Because to be vulnerable opens up one to be shamed. Control is a way to insure that no one can ever shame us again. It involves controlling our own thoughts, expressions, feelings, and actions. And it involves attempting to control other people's thoughts, feelings, and actions. (Bradshaw 1998)

lack of object constancy

When we're lonely, most of us can soothe ourselves by remembering the love that others have for us. This is very comforting even if these people are far away—sometimes, even if they're no longer living. This ability is known as object constancy.

Some people with BPD, however, find it difficult to evoke an image of a loved one to soothe them when they feel upset or anxious. If that person is not physically present, they don't exist on an emotional level. The BP may call you frequently just to make sure you're still there and still care about them.

> To help the BP understand and better cope with fears of abandonment, the person may keep a photo of you nearby or carry something you gave them to remind them of you, in the same way that children use teddy bears and blankets to remind them of their parents' love. Letters, pictures, colognes (scents that remind the BP of their partner) are typically used. These strategies help the BP, often reducing their anxieties and fears. Usually the result is less clinging behavior, which can bring some relief to the non-BP.

interpersonal sensitivity

Some people with BPD have an amazing ability to read others and uncover their triggers and vulnerabilities. One clinician jokingly called people with BPD "psychic."

BPs often have an astute ability to identify and use social and nonverbal cues of others. BPs can empathize well with others and often understand and respect how others feel, and they can use these skills to "see through others."

As adults, BPs continue to use their social antennae to uncover triggers and vulnerabilities in others that they can use to their advantage in various situations. Therapists who work with BPs can attest that BPs have a "gift" for knowing how their therapist is doing that day (for example, tired, worried, sad, angry) and will often bring this up during the session.

situational competence

Some people with BPD are competent and in control in some situations. For example, many perform very well at work and are high achievers. Many are very intelligent, creative, and artistic. This can be very confusing for family members who don't understand why the person can act so self-assured in one situation and fall apart in another. This ability to have competence in difficult situations while being incompetent in seemingly equal or easier tasks is known as situational competence.

One borderline woman says, "We know deep within that we are defective. So we try so hard to act normal because we want so much to please everybody and keep the people in our lives from abandoning us." But this competence is a double-edged sword. Because they can appear so normal, high-functioning borderlines often don't get the help they need.

> BPs can empathize well with others and often understand and respect how others feel.

narcissistic demands

Some people with BPD frequently bring the focus of attention back to themselves. They may react to most things based solely on how it affects them. Some people with BPD draw attention to themselves by complaining of illness; others may act inappropriately in public. These self-involved characteristics are defining components of narcissism; narcissistic behavior can be especially taxing on non-BPs, as the BP may not even consider how their actions affect others. About 25% of people with BPD also have narcissistic personality disorder.

Jack (non-BP)

My mother's perception of me, my brother, and my father were as an extension of her. All my relationships were perceived to be about her, affecting her either by creating a reflection of her (good or bad) as a mother or by threatening my availability to provide her with emotional support and validation.

My mom also saw all of my friends as threats to her. She did everything she could to sabotage my friendships. The only "acceptable" people were ones who could never be really close friends, such as those who weren't of our faith (we were a very religiously conservative family).

manipulation or desperation?

It's no secret that non-BPs often feel manipulated and lied to by their borderline loved ones. In other words, they feel controlled or taken advantage of through means such as threats, no-win situations, the "silent treatment," rages, and other methods they view as unfair. We believe that, in most cases, the BP's behavior is not intentionally manipulative. Rather, this kind of behavior can be seen as desperate attempts to cope with painful feelings or to get their needs met—without the aim of harming others.

The Non-BP Point of View

In her book *Emotional Blackmail: When the People in Your Life Use Fear, Obligation, and Guilt to Manipulate You* (Forward and Frazier 1997), Susan Forward defines emotional blackmail as a direct or indirect threat by someone to punish someone if they don't do what the person wants. "At the heart of [emotional blackmail] is one basic threat, which can be expressed in many different ways: if you don't behave the way I want you to, you will suffer."

Forward explains that people who use this technique—widely used by all types of people, not just BPs—can skillfully mask the pressure they're applying to people, who often experience it in ways that make them question their perception of what's happening.

Almost universally, non-BPs say they feel manipulated by the BPs in their lives. If the non-BP doesn't do what the BP wants them to do, the BP may threaten to break off the relationship, call the police, or even kill him- or herself.

The BP Point of View

The terms "manipulation" and "emotional blackmail" imply some sort of devious, planned intent. While this may be true for some people, borderlines who appear to be manipulative usually act impulsively out of fear, loneliness, desperation, and hopelessness—not maliciousness. Marsha Linehan (1993a) writes:

> People with BPD do influence others, such as through the threat of impending suicide or through communications of intense pain and agony. But this, by itself, is not evidence of manipulation. Otherwise, we would have to say that people in pain or crises are "manipulating" us if we respond to them.

In our interview with psychiatrist Larry J. Siever, he said:

Although [people with BPD] can be apparently manipulative, they don't think about the behavior as such. They're trying to meet their needs in the only way they know how. Somebody has to relieve their anger or anxiety or distress or sense of impending annihilation right now. They are trying to elicit a response to soothe them, to help them feel better.

Degrees of Awareness

In our experience, people with BPD have varying degrees of conscious awareness that their behavior could be perceived as manipulative—just like most people do.

A. J. Mahari (recovered-BP)

My days and thoughts are not consumed by plans of how to push which button in whom. My actions are about survival and preserving my identity; they are not some preplanned sporting activity.

Rachel Reiland (BP)

Often I realize my motivations only after the incident is over. Once, I was so upset that my husband was ignoring me at Christmas that, right in front of him, I began destroying all the gifts he had just given me. My husband stopped me as I was about to rip apart the gift I loved most: a book of love poetry. When I saw the book, it dawned on me that I never would have ruined it. I was more interested in seeing my husband try to stop me. If I had been living alone, the whole episode would never have happened. So why did I do it? The answer was ugly and harsh, shameful and disgusting. Manipulation. I felt deeply ashamed.

Laurey (BP)

While others might feel manipulative, I feel powerless. Sometimes I just hurt so bad from the mean things that people do to me, real or perceived, or I'm so desperately feeling abandoned, that I withdraw and pout and go silent. At some point people get pissed off and fed up with that crap and they go away and then I'm left with nothing all over again.

It is important that you understand the differences between manipulation and desperation. The BP's behavior is more about them than you. For example, it may help to be able to look at a self-mutilating BPs behavior as self-punishment rather than as a way to "trap" the non-BP into a relationship.

---

real-world types of BPD

People with BPD vary a great deal in their ability to work inside or outside the home, cope with everyday problems, interact with others, and so on. This variation is one reason why BPD befuddles those trying to define it scientifically.

In *The Essential Family Guide to Borderline Personality Disorder: New Tools and Techniques to Stop Walking on Eggshells* (2008), Randi Kreger, coauthor of this book, developed a real-world, way of looking at these differences. She writes that there are three general categories of people with BPD: lower-functioning, "conventional" BPs, higher-functioning, "invisible" BPs, and those with characteristics of both. The challenges family members face can be very different.

mostly lower-functioning, conventional BPs

Lower-functioning, conventional BPs tend to have the following characteristics:

1. Under stress, they cope through self-destructive behaviors, such as self-injury and suicidality. The term for this is "acting in"—as opposed to "acting out," which we'll get to shortly.

2. They may spend a lot of time in the hospital because of self-mutilation, severe eating disorders, substance abuse, or suicide attempts. For this reason, they may be well known to treatment providers and fit the more conventional stereotype of someone with BPD.

3. They may be incapacitated by their illness and unable to work. Some BPs are on disability.

4. They often have overlapping, or co-occurring, disorders, such as eating disorders.

5. People who are close to low-functioning, conventional borderlines often find themselves living from crisis to crisis. They may feel manipulated by self-mutilation and suicide attempts. However, because the borderline is obviously ill, non-BPs usually receive understanding and support from family and friends.

mostly higher-functioning, invisible BPs

Higher-functioning, invisible BPs, in contrast, tend to have these characteristics:

1. High functioning, invisible borderlines act perfectly normal much of the time—at least to people outside the family. They hold jobs and appear to have no trouble with the usual activities of daily living, which makes them "high functioning." They usually show their other side only to people they know very well. That's why family members say these people bring to mind Dr. Jekyll and Mr. Hyde.

2. They cope with their pain by acting out, projecting it onto someone else—for example, by raging, blaming, criticizing, making accusations, becoming physically violent, and engaging in verbal abuse. Unlike conventional BPs, they usually don't project vulnerability (think Marilyn Monroe or Princess Diana).

3. Although these borderlines may feel the same shame and fear as their less-functional, more conventional counterparts, their denial is so complete that when they say, "There's nothing wrong with me; there's something wrong with you," they truly believe it.

4. These BPs may fiercely refuse to seek help unless someone threatens to end the relationship. That's why they are "invisible" to the mental health community. They're not included in the statistics about the number of people with BPD, perhaps drastically lowering the actual figure.

5. If they do go to counseling, it may well be because someone has given them an ultimatum. Couples therapy is often not productive because they use it to try to prove they're "right" and their partner is "wrong."

6. Non-borderlines involved with this type of BP need to have their perceptions and feelings validated. Friends and family members who don't know the borderline very well may not believe stories of rage and verbal abuse. Many non-BPs told us that even their therapists refused to believe them when they described the BP's out-of-control behavior.

BPs with overlapping characteristics

Of course, there's a lot of room in between high-functioning—sometimes referred to as the "borderline" borderline—and low-functioning BPs. Stressful life events are most likely to trigger dysfunctional coping mechanisms in all BPs (and in others who don't have the disorder, too).

	Mostly Lower-Functioning Conventional BPs	Mostly Higher-Functioning Invisible BPs
Coping Techniques	*Acting In*: Mostly self-destructive acts such as self-harm.	*Acting Out*: Uncontrolled and impulsive rages, criticism, and blame. These may result less from a lack of interpersonal skills (more typical of conventional BPs) than from an unconscious projection of their own pain onto others.
Willingness to Obtain Help	Self-harm and suicidal tendencies often bring these BPs into the mental health system (both as inpatients and out-patients). High interest in therapy.	A state of denial much like an untreated alcoholic. Disavows responsibility for relationship difficulties, refuses treatment; when confronted, accuses others of having BPD. May see a therapist if threatened but rarely takes it seriously or stays long.
Co-occurring (Concurrent) Mental Health Issues	Mental conditions such as bipolar and eating disorders require medical intervention and contribute to low functioning.	Concurrent illness most commonly a substance use disorder or another personality disorder, especially narcissistic personality disorder.

Functioning	BPD and associated conditions make it difficult to live independently, hold a job, manage finances, and so on. Families often step in to help.	Appears normal, even charismatic, to outsiders but exhibits BP traits behind closed doors. May have a career and be successful.
Impact on Family Members	Major family focus on practical issues such as finding treatment, preventing/reducing BP's self-destructive behavior, and providing practical and emotional support. Parents feel extreme guilt and are emotionally overwhelmed.	Without an obvious illness, family members blame themselves for relationship problems and try to get their emotional needs met. They make fruitless efforts to persuade their BP to get professional help. Major issues include high-conflict divorce and custody cases.

From *The Essential Family Guide to Borderline Personality Disorder* by Randi Kreger. Copyright 2008 by HAZELDEN FOUNDATION. Reprinted by permission of Hazelden Foundation, Center City, MN.

BPD is pervasive: it impacts the way the sufferer feels, thinks, and behaves. But BPD doesn't exist in a vacuum. In the next chapter, we'll discuss what happens when you enter the picture.

CHAPTER 3

making sense of chaos: understanding BPD behavior

Borderlines and non-borderlines live in two different worlds that coexist in the same space, but not always in the same time. Comprehending the "real" world, for me, is as formidable as the task of understanding the borderline world is for you.

—A. J. Mahari (recovered-BP) from the Welcome to Oz support community at www.BPDCentral.com

Each person with BPD is unique. If something you read rings true for you, consider it carefully. If it doesn't seem to apply in your situation, don't try to make it fit.

Remember that people with BPD, like everyone else, will sometimes have reactions that are either greatly exaggerated or seem to have no basis in reality. However, don't blame everything on BPD.

Ask yourself if there is any truth to what the person with BPD is saying. People with BPD can be very intuitive. Many are extremely sensitive to tone of voice and body language. They may even pick up something you are feeling before you are aware of it. Acknowledging and owning up to what is truly your responsibility can often defuse a potentially explosive situation.

> Before concluding that BPD is responsible for your loved one's strong response, ask yourself if your behavior triggered a natural human reaction. Let's say you cope with BPD behavior by spending as much time as possible away from home. You work late, and when you come home, you barely speak to the person with BPD. You may be trying to protect yourself, which is understandable. However, if your distancing triggers abandonment fears and acting out, you may need to take a look at how your own actions are affecting the situation.

the BP world

Most people find it hard to understand BPD behavior because they assume that people with BPD think and feel the way they do. It's an understandable mistake. High-functioning borderlines can act quite normal when their BPD behaviors are not being triggered. They don't look or sound like they have a disorder.

Some people with BPD—usually those in therapy—can have an excellent intellectual understanding of BPD. They can recite the *DSM* criteria and pinpoint which traits describe them. When not overcome by intense emotions, they may understand that their feelings don't always reflect reality as others see it.

But that knowledge doesn't fill the aching hole inside them. Understanding the causes of their pain doesn't necessarily make them feel any better, and it may not make it any easier for them to change their behavior. It also doesn't prevent them from feeling hopelessly misunderstood when exasperated non-BPs tell them, "Just pull yourself together."

> To understand borderline behavior, you have to leave your own world and journey into theirs. And you should, since you're asking the BP in your life to come into yours. As you read, keep in mind that these behaviors are usually unconscious. They are designed to shield the person with BPD from intense emotional pain—not to hurt you.

Common BP Thinking

When you travel to another country, it's important to know the local customs. When you're interacting with someone with BPD, it's crucial to understand that their unconscious assumptions may be very different from yours. They may include:

- I must be loved by all the important people in my life at all times or else I am worthless. I must be completely competent in all ways to be a worthwhile person.

- Some people are good and everything about them is perfect. Other people are thoroughly bad and should be blamed and punished for it.

- My feelings are caused by external events. I have no control over my emotions or the things I do in reaction to them.

- Nobody cares about me as much as I care about them, so I lose everyone I care about—despite the desperate things I do to stop them from leaving me.

- If someone treats me badly, then I become bad.

- When I am alone, I become nobody and nothing.

- I will be happy only when I can find an all-giving, perfect person to love me and take care of me no matter what. But if someone close to this loves me, then something must be wrong with them.

> To understand borderline behavior, you have to leave your own comfortable world and journey into theirs.

- I can't stand the frustration that I feel when I need something from someone and I can't get it. I've got to do something to make it go away.

feelings create facts

In general, emotionally healthy people base their feelings on facts. If your dad came home drunk every night (fact), you might feel worried or concerned (feeling). If your boss complimented you on a big project (fact), you would feel proud and happy (feeling).

People with BPD, however, may do the opposite. When their feelings don't fit the facts, they may unconsciously revise the facts to fit their feelings. This may be one reason why their perception of events is different from yours.

> People with BPD may unconsciously revise the facts to fit their feelings. This may be one reason why their perception of events is different from yours.

Let's look at Minuet (BP) and her husband Will. One Friday afternoon, Will calls his wife to say he'll be home late because he's having a beer with the guys after work. Minuet feels anxious, rejected, and jealous. Minuet's emotions are confusing and overwhelming to her. To make sense of them, she concludes that Will must be doing something to bring them on. She might accuse Will of having a drinking problem. She might tell him that he's a terrible person for wanting to be with friends instead of her after a hard work week. She unconsciously revises the facts so that her feelings make sense.

rationalization

Rationalization is another common defense mechanism. You know you should exercise, but it seems like too much trouble. So you tell yourself that you're too busy to work out—even though you always have enough time to watch your favorite TV shows. Some family members use rationalization to explain a BPs behavior—for example, "He's just acting this way because he's so stressed out at work."

tag, you're it: a game of projection

Some people with BPD who act out may use a game we call "Tag, You're It" to relieve their anxiety, pain, and feelings of shame. It's complex because it combines shame, splitting, denial, and projection.

Tag is a fun game for a child. But it's not a game for people with BPD. Lacking a clear sense of who they are, and feeling empty and inherently defective, people with BPD feel like "it" all the time. Others seem to run away from them, which is lonely and excruciatingly painful. So borderlines cope by trying to "tag" someone else. This is called projection.

Projection is denying one's own unpleasant traits, behaviors, or feelings by attributing them—often in an accusing way—to someone else. In our interview with Elyce M. Benham, MS, she explained that projection is like gazing at yourself in a hand-held mirror. When you think you look ugly, you turn the mirror around. Voila! Now the homely face in the mirror belongs to somebody else.

Understanding Projection

Sometimes the projection is an exaggeration of something that has a basis in reality. For example, the borderline may accuse you of "hating" them when you just feel irritated. Sometimes the projection may come entirely from their imagination. For example, they accuse you of flirting with a salesclerk when you were just asking for directions to the shoe department.

The BPs unconscious hope is that by projecting this unpleasant stuff onto another person—by tagging someone else and making them "it"—the person with BPD will feel better about themselves. And they do feel better, for a little while. But the pain comes back. So the game is played again and again.

> Lacking a clear sense of who they are, and feeling empty and inherently defective, people with BPD feel like "it" all the time.

Projection's Other Purpose: Redirection

Projection also has another purpose: your loved one unconsciously fears that if you find out they're not perfect, you will abandon them. Like in the Wizard of Oz, they live in constant terror that you'll discover the person behind the curtain. Projecting the negative traits and feelings onto you is a way to keep the curtain closed and redirect your attention to the perfect image they've tried to create for themselves.

Your task is to examine what the person with BPD is saying and determine whether they have an accurate point. Remember, not everything is projection. But if the borderline is projecting, you need to stop playing the game and decline to be "it" in a respectful way. We'll explain how to do this in the second part of this book.

How the Game Is Played

When someone with BPD tags you, they're unconsciously trying to transfer their own behaviors, feelings, or perceived traits onto you. When projecting their traits onto you, the person with BPD thinks they're defective, so they accuse you of having something wrong with you. Sometimes the flaw they see in others is the identical flaw they fail to see in themselves. Sometimes it's not.

Sharon (BP)

I hate myself so much I can barely see straight. When I am drowning in hate, it floods over everyone and everything, and I feel so justified for feeling such loathing toward everyone—mostly my husband. He seems so utterly disgusting, so pitifully stupid.

Projection Statements and Unconscious Thoughts/Feelings

Projection Statement	Unconscious Thought/ Feeling
You're a horrible person. No one will ever love you but me.	I am such a rotten person that anyone who would love me must be defective, too.
You're such a suck up, it's no wonder Mom loved you best.	I feel so flawed that not even my own mother loves me.
You are such a terrible parent that you shouldn't even be around our kids.	I feel like a terrible parent.
You two are the worst parents in the world. It's no wonder I have BPD.	I feel like the worst kid in the world.
I do not have BPD. You do!	The thought that I might have BPD terrifies me.
You made me have this affair and get pregnant because you're such a lousy husband.	I had this affair because I think I'm a lousy wife and don't deserve to be loved.

When projecting behaviors, the BP may accuse you of doing something that they are actually doing. Or they may use your real or imagined behavior to absolve themselves of responsibility for their own actions or keep themselves from feeling shame for having engaged in the behaviors.

Typical Behavioral Projections and Unconscious Thoughts/Feelings

Behavioral Projections	Unconscious Thoughts/ Feelings
You made me do it.	I did it for reasons I don't understand.
You think I'm controlling? You're the one who's so controlling!	I feel like I'm losing control right now, and it scares me.
Stop screaming at me!	I am so angry that I need to scream at you right now.
You never consider my needs. You're always thinking about yourself.	My needs are so overwhelming to me that I can't think about yours.
You're the one who left this marriage. You're not the person I fell in love with anymore.	I've shown you my real, flawed self and it scares me so much that I have to reject you before you reject me.
If you had taken my calls at work, I wouldn't have had to call you at three o'clock in the morning at home.	I need to talk with you so badly that I'll do anything to reach you.

The other way a person with BPD can project onto you is to accuse you of having feelings and thoughts that really belong to them.

Ellen (BP)

When I accused my psychiatrist of hating me and telling me to "snap out of it," it was because I hated myself and I wished that I could snap out of it. My deepest fears and feelings of self-hatred were those I would project onto someone else because they were too frightening and disturbing to acknowledge within myself.

More BP Projections

Projection	Unconscious Thoughts/Feelings
You hate me.	I hate myself.
You don't think I'm good enough.	I don't think I'm good enough.

Projection	Unconscious Thoughts/Feelings
When you said "it's cold outside," you really meant to criticize the way I dressed the children for school this morning.	I have such a low opinion of myself that I question my parenting abilities.
You spend so much time at work because you don't want to be around me.	I don't want to be around myself, so why would anyone else want to be around me?

How can people with BPD deny that they are projecting when it is so obvious to everyone else? The answer is that shame and splitting may combine with projection and denial to make the "Tag, You're It" defense mechanism a more powerful way of denying ownership of unpleasant thoughts and feelings.

The Process of Projection

The BPD logic goes like this: There seems to be a problem. It's not my fault. Therefore, the problem must be yours.

How does this process, which can take place in only a few seconds, work? Some people with BPD feel shame—defective at the core of their being. Like everyone else, people with BPD have negative feelings, behaviors, and traits. But because of splitting—black-and-white thinking—they often deny any flaws, because that would make them less than perfect. And if they're not perfect, they're worthless. Projection then completes the picture. The BPD logic goes like this: There seems to be a problem. It's not my fault. Therefore, the problem must be yours.

Projective Identification

There's one more piece of "Tag, You're It" that's important to understand. After many games of tag, you may actually come to believe the accusations of the person with BPD. You may even start to behave in such as way as to make the accusations true. This is called projective identification.

Let's say that in order to cope with her own feelings of shame and worthlessness, Edith (BP) constantly tells her five-year-old daughter, Joanie, that she's a horrible person and she'll never have any friends. Eventually, Joanie concludes that she is a horrible person. Convinced that she is innately flawed, she avoids contact with other people. When they reach out to her, she rejects them before they reject her.

A Self-Fulfilling Prophecy. Projective identification brings to mind the political cliché, "If you repeat a lie often enough, people will believe you." It's also a bit like a self-fulfilling prophesy: Edith's prediction has come true: Joanie has no friends, not because she's a loathsome person but because she feels like she is.

Children are especially vulnerable to projective identification because they're still forming their own identities. In fact, on a subconscious level they may feel that they may lose their parent's love if they don't do whatever mom or dad seemingly expects of them—including act badly. (See chapter 9 for more discussion about the effects of BPD behavior on children.) Projective identification also may have more of an impact on those adults whose self-esteem is low and whose own identities are weak.

In our interview with Elyce Benham, MS, she explained, "Even as adults, we give credence to what others tell us about ourselves. If we find ourselves in an important relationship with someone who constantly undermines what we know or believe about ourselves, we'll start to believe it."

For Example...

Here are some adult examples of projection and projective identification:

- Your BP girlfriend accuses you again and again of not loving her and wanting to abandon her. For years, you try to get her to see that this isn't true, but nothing works. Exhausted, you realize that the relationship is over and you need to get on with your life—thereby "abandoning" her.

- Your teenage borderline son accuses you of not loving him enough to let him live at home. When he comes home for a visit from the residential facility, he's physically violent. He brings drug-dealing friends into the house and threatens his sister with a knife. You lie awake at night, vowing to never let him live at home again—thereby seeming to fulfill your son's belief.

- Your borderline sister accuses you of "sucking up" to Mom and Dad, who always "loved you best." You spend more time with your folks because you enjoy being with them and they enjoy being with you. They love your sister, but rescuing her from her reckless behavior has put a terrible strain on them. As time goes on, you wonder if your parents do indeed prefer being with you.

What Projective Identification Offers the BP

Some adults who enter into relationships with borderlines feel brainwashed by the BPs accusations and criticisms. Says Benham: "The techniques of brainwashing are simple: isolate the victim, expose them to consistent messages, mix with sleep deprivation, add some form of abuse, get the person to doubt what they know and feel, keep them on their toes, wear them down, and stir well."

everything is your fault

Continual blame and criticism are other defense mechanisms people with BPD who act out use. The criticism may be based on a real issue that the person with BPD has exaggerated, or it may be a pure fantasy on the borderline's part. Family members we interviewed have been raged at and castigated for such things as carrying a grocery bag the wrong way, having bedsheets that weighed too heavily on the BP's toes, and reading a book the BP demanded they read. One exasperated non-BP said that if by some chance he didn't make an unforgivable error one day, his wife would probably rage at him for being too perfect. Another family member asked, "If a non-BP is standing out in the woods making a statement—and their borderline partner isn't around to hear it—is the non-BP still wrong?"

Like "Tag, You're It," this defense mechanism may really be about abandonment. The borderline's unconscious thinking process may go like this: "If there is just one thing wrong with me, then everything is wrong with me. If everything is wrong with me, I really am as defective as I feel. And when people find out I'm defective, they will abandon me. So there just can't be anything wrong with me—it has to be someone else's fault!" Often, what seems like angry, impulsive, and manipulative behavior is really a misguided attempt to elicit involvement and caring.

Patty (BP)

Sometimes I criticize my fiancé's every move, telling him that if he loved me, he wouldn't do that. When I belittle and blame him, I feel that I might be abandoned or embarrassed or that he is somehow not showing me love. I feel fearful. I am so upset that I yell and scream and knock over objects. My decision making is poor. Just yesterday I threw my engagement ring in the garbage during my rage at him. Today, I realized I would be lost without him. He cannot tell me he loves me enough. I expect him to cheat on me though I have no logical reason to. I look through his pockets and his bankbook. I surprise him at work to make sure he's there. When I find things are fine, I feel very reassured and embarrassed and swear to myself I won't ever feel that way again. But I always do.

If you object to the criticism or try to defend yourself, your loved one may accuse you of being defensive, too sensitive, or unable to accept constructive criticism. Since their very survival seems to be at stake, they may defend themselves with the ferociousness of a mother bear protecting her cubs.

> What seems like angry, impulsive, and manipulative behavior is really a misguided attempt to elicit involvement and caring.

When the crisis has passed and the person with BPD seems to have won, they may act surprised that you're still upset. From their point of view, their response has prevented you from seeing their hollow inner core. They may think that this should draw you closer to them or at least prevent you from withdrawing. They may also have been dissociating, which would make them genuinely remember things differently.

You, of course, feel worse. Only now, you also feel baffled because the person with BPD doesn't seem to understand the impact of what they've done. You may also feel frustrated because they never seem to accept responsibility for their own behavior. This cycle happens again and again.

When Blaming Becomes Verbal Abuse

When the person with BPD lashes out at you, he's consumed with his own needs. He may also be displacing rage and anger onto you that are the result of abuse suffered in the past. If he seems controlling, he may be trying to gain control over his own life—not yours.

And even when they seem to have won an argument, they've really lost. For one thing, they've damaged their relationship with you—someone they're terrified will leave them. When things calm down, the person with BPD may feel ashamed of the way he or she behaved toward you. This adds to the downward spiral of shame, guilt, and low self-esteem. BPs may apologize and beg for your forgiveness, then deny that they ever admitted that their behavior was out of line.

But even though their behavior is not really about you, excessive criticizing and blaming can cross the line and become verbal abuse. Beverly Engel, in *The Emotionally Abused Woman: Overcoming Destructive Patterns and Reclaiming Yourself* (1990), writes:

> Emotional abuse is any behavior that is designed to control another person through the use of fear, humiliation, and verbal or physical assaults. It can include verbal abuse and constant criticism to more subtle tactics like intimidation, manipulation, and refusal to ever be pleased. Emotional abuse is like brainwashing in that it systematically wears away at the victim's self-confidence, sense of self-worth, trust in her perceptions, and self-concept. Whether it be by constant berating and belittling, by intimidation, or under the guise of "guidance" or teaching, the results are similar. Eventually, the recipient loses all sense of self and all remnants of personal value.

> When your family member lashes out at you, he is consumed with his own needs.

Defining Verbal Abuse

Engel categorizes verbal abuse in several ways. Some of these definitions read like the criteria for BPD from the *DSM,* although Engel's book never refers to the disorder. Keep in mind that we are not discussing the intentions of the person with BPD. We are talking about the effects of their coping strategies on you.

- **Domination:** The person resorts to threats to get their own way.

- **Verbal assaults:** This includes reprimanding, humiliating, criticizing, name calling, screaming, threatening, excessive blaming, and using sarcasm in a cutting way. It also involves exaggerating your faults and making fun of you in front of others. Over time, this type of abuse erodes your sense of self-confidence and self-worth.

- **Abusive expectations:** The other person makes unreasonable demands and expects that you will be their first priority—no matter what. This includes denouncing your needs for attention and support.

- **Unpredictable responses:** This includes drastic mood changes or sudden emotional outbursts. Living with someone like this is extremely anxiety provoking. You may feel frightened, unsettled, and off balance.

- **Gaslighting:** The other person denies your perceptions of events and conversations.

- **Constant chaos:** The BP may deliberately start arguments and is in constant conflict with others. They also may be addicted to drama, since it creates excitement. (Many non-BPs may be addicted to drama.)

BPD behavioral patterns

no-win situations

Most family members we've interviewed say they feel like the person with BPD puts them in no-win situations.

Jack (non-BP)

If I asked her about her unhappiness, she told me I was too sensitive and paranoid. If I ignored the unhappiness, she said I didn't care about her. If I praised her, she thought I was up to something. If I criticized her, I was trying to hurt her. If I spent time talking to her four-year-old, she wanted to know what I was asking him. If I played a simple game with him, she criticized me if I won. If I wanted to have sex, she wanted it to be her idea—later. If I didn't want to have sex, I was a homosexual. If I spent time alone, I was up to something. If I spent too much time with her, I was needy. If I wasn't thirty minutes early, I was late. If she wasn't ready and I sat down to read, I was rushing her.

Some of the people with BPD we've interviewed gave possible reasons for this behavior. Paige (BP) suggested that it may be a variation of "Everything Is Your Fault," saying, "Putting other people in no-win situations allows me to self-validate, when validation has been in short supply in my life. So maybe it's a way to grab something I've felt I haven't gotten before, even though it alienates others and harms me in the long run."

Another possible explanation for no-win situations is that the person with BPD may be dissociating. Someone who is dissociating or under a great deal of emotional stress may not remember what they have said or done previously.

People with BPD may be inconsistent, thus causing seemingly no-win situations, because they have an inconsistent sense of self. In order to state their preferences, people must be able to clearly identify their feelings and beliefs. Only then can they communicate these to others. But as you know, some people with BPD have an inconsistent sense of self. When BPs tell you what they want, it probably is what they want—at that moment. Later, they may want something else. But because of shame and splitting they may not be able to admit to you—or to themselves—that they're being inconsistent. They may even try to portray you as the one who's hopelessly mixed up.

fear of abandonment, fear of engulfment

Sometimes it may seem as if the BP is wanting you to "keep your distance a little closer." This impossible request is not like "Tag, You're It" and "Everything Is Your Fault." Rather, it is a behavior pattern that results from two primary and conflicting fears: the fear of being abandoned and the fear of being engulfed or controlled by others.

Fear of Abandonment

As infants, all people experience fear of abandonment. Babies have two primary needs: to feel safe and secure and to develop a sense of trust in their caregivers. When they cry, they need to know that someone will respond with love, food, or a diaper change. When mommy or daddy leave, they need to know a parent will return.

As people grow up, they balance their dependency needs with another objective: becoming independent and venturing away from the protective womb of the family. You can see this in the two-year-old who proudly runs on the playground, falls, and comes crying to mommy and daddy. As time goes by, the need to run back to parents diminishes and the need to establish a separate identity gains importance. The teen years are the most distinct time of testing, as adolescents try out new adult roles under the steadily decreasing guidance of school and family. Ideally, adulthood brings an independence that is neither dominated by fears of abandonment nor engulfment.

People with BPD struggle daily with the issues of engulfment and abandonment. Torn between the urge to merge and the desire for independence, they may feel—and look—like a walking contradiction. Their actions may not make sense because at times they seek closeness and nurturing and, at other times, seem compelled to drive you away.

Afraid of Losing Control

Borderlines may begin to feel engulfed or afraid of losing control when people get too close to them. They don't know how to set healthy personal limits, and genuine intimacy may make them feel vulnerable. They may be afraid you might see the "real" them, be repulsed, and leave them. So they begin to distance themselves to avoid feeling vulnerable or controlled. They may pick a fight with you, "forget" to do something important, or do something dramatic or explosive. But then the distance makes them feel alone. Feelings of emptiness worsen, and their fear of abandonment become stronger. So they make frantic efforts to get close again. And the cycle repeats.

Their actions may not make sense because at times they seek closeness and nurturing and, at other times, seem compelled to drive you away.

During an argument, it might take your loved one only seconds to bounce from feelings of abandonment to engulfment. Or the cycle might take days, weeks, months, or years. External events often play a part; for example, going off to college could easily trigger abandonment fears in an adolescent borderline, while an ill, elderly borderline parent moving in with an adult child might feel engulfed.

As the level of intimacy rises, so does the degree of the abandonment or engulfment issues, which results in more dramatic behaviors. This is one reason why people who don't know a borderline as well as you do may not believe your accounts of their behavior.

testing your love

The back and forth dance of "keep your distance a little closer" is incredibly frustrating for friends and family.

Beth (non-BP)

> As the level of intimacy rises, so does the degree of the abandonment or engulfment issues, which results in more dramatic behaviors.

The harder I try to placate my borderline husband, the fiercer his reaction becomes. The moment I give up and start to walk away, he turns into a clinging vine. It's like that old burlesque routine of the clown trying to pick up his hat. Every time he bends to grab it, he accidentally kicks it further away. Finally, he gives up in disgust. And as he walks away, the wind blows his hat after him.

Herein lies yet another seeming contradiction of BPD: From your point of view, the person with BPD is in control. They're the choreographer of the abandonment/engulfment dance, and you're just being whirled around, getting dizzier and dizzier. But from the BP's point of view, you're the one with all the power.

The BP can't predict how you're going to react to his behavior. Not knowing may make them feel even more unsafe and insecure than they usually do.

Remember, to people with BPD, everything is "all or nothing." If the dance stops, it stops forever. And once you're gone, they cease to exist because they have no identity of their own. Feeling helpless in the face of both their own emotions and your unpredictable reactions, they may try to grab control in the only way they know how: by acting out in ways that, to you, feel intensely manipulative. They may threaten suicide. Then, once you've capitulated, the music starts and the dance begins anew.

Testing Your Love

> To people with BPD, everything is "all or nothing."

Some people with BPD may also try to gain control of the dance by testing you to see how much you really care. The logic goes like this: if you really love them, you should be willing to put aside all your own desires and concentrate on fulfilling their needs.

For example, if you and the BP have agreed to meet at a certain time and place, he may show up an hour late. If you "fail" the test by becoming irritated or giving up and going home, the person with BPD may feel his unworthiness has been confirmed. This makes the world more predictable and therefore safer.

If you "pass" the test by tolerating his actions, he may escalate the behavior (perhaps by showing up many hours late next time), until you finally blow up in anger. Then you become the bad guy, and the BP becomes the victim.

You may be wondering, "What kind of test is this? No matter what happens, we both fail!" You're right. It doesn't make any sense in your world. But it does in the borderline world.

a childlike world view

Many adult borderlines—especially those with young children—have noticed that their view of the world can be very childlike. Splitting, object constancy problems, abandonment and engulfment issues, identity issues, narcissistic demands, seeming lack of empathy, and seeming manipulation are all borderline thinking patterns that correspond to developmental stages in children.

Laura (BP)

When my two-year-old wants something, she wants it now. When I am shopping, I can't tell myself no, so I buy it, even though I'm in debt. To a child, the most important thing is security and safety. For me, safety means being what others want me to be so they won't reject me. The inside stays hidden—even to me. But under all the politeness hides an angry, frightened toddler. My husband wants the damaged little girl inside me to set priorities by saying, "Yes, I'm angry, but when I talk to you I'm going to try to be reasonable." You wouldn't ask that from a real two-year-old, so don't ask that from me, either. It's not that I don't want to. I just can't.

Some people with BPD feel patronized or insulted when people point out these similarities.

> You may be wondering, "What kind of test is this? No matter what happens, we both fail!"

Janet (BP)

I definitely feel like a child! People say to me, "Grow up."
They accuse me of being a crybaby and having temper tantrums. Do they

think I want to act this way? Do they think it's fun to have your emotions rule you? Do they really believe I can mature twenty years in minutes?

The borderline world may differ markedly from your own in several ways:

- People with BPD may unconsciously revise facts in order to justify their feelings.

- Some people with BPD use extreme defense mechanisms to manage their painful feelings.

- People with BPD may feel alternatively abandoned and engulfed, which may cause them to intermittently change their behavior 180 degrees.

- Finally, some people with BPD see the world through the eyes of a child. But they have the ability to affect the world in more serious, adult ways.

In chapter 4, we'll explain the effects of BPD behavior on you.

You wouldn't ask that from a real two-year-old, so don't ask that from me, either. It's not that I don't want to. I just can't.

CHAPTER 4

living in a pressure cooker: how BPD behavior affects non-BPs

Living with a BP is like living in a pressure cooker with thin walls and a faulty safety valve.

Living with a BP is like living in a perpetual oxymoron. It's a seemingly endless host of contradictions.

I feel like I've been through the spin cycle on a washing machine. The world is whirling around, and I have no idea which way is up, down, or sideways.

—From the Welcome to Oz family member
support community at www.BPDCentral.com

Filled with self-loathing, people with BPD may:

- accuse others of hating them

- become so critical and easily enraged that people eventually want to leave them

- blame others and put themselves in the role of victim

> Meanwhile, the borderline's unhealthy behaviors are reinforced because the non-BP accepts responsibility for the feelings and actions that belong to the borderline.

BPD is not infectious. It is not like the measles. But people who are exposed to these behaviors can unwittingly become an integral part of the dynamics. Friends, partners, and family members usually take these behaviors personally and feel trapped in a toxic cycle of guilt, self-blame, depression, rage, denial, isolation, and confusion. They try to cope in ways that do not work long-term or that even make the situation worse.

Meanwhile, the borderline's unhealthy behaviors are reinforced because the non-BP accepts responsibility for the feelings and actions that belong to the borderline.

In this chapter, we'll discuss some common ways non-BPs react to BPD behavior. Then we will provide you with questions to help you determine how BPD behavior might affect you personally.

common non-BP thinking

These beliefs do not reflect the thinking of every person with a borderline in their life. You must judge what is pertinent in your circumstances.

beliefs and facts

BELIEF: I am responsible for all the problems in this relationship.

FACT: Each person is responsible for 50 percent of the relationship.

BELIEF: The actions of the person with BPD are all about me.

FACT: The BP's actions result from a complex disorder caused by a combination of biology and environment.

BELIEF: It's my responsibility to solve this person's problems, and if I don't do it, no one else will.

FACT: By trying to take charge of the borderline's life, you may be giving them the message that they can't take care of themselves. You're also avoiding the opportunity to change the relationship by focusing on yourself.

BELIEF: If I can convince the person with BPD I am right, these problems will disappear.

FACT: BPD is a serious disorder that profoundly affects the way people think, feel, and behave. You can't talk someone out of it no matter how persuasive you are.

BELIEF: If I can prove that their accusations are false, they will trust me again.

FACT: Lack of trust is a hallmark of BPD. It has nothing to do with your behavior; it has to do with the way people with BPD view the world.

BELIEF: If you really love someone, you should take their physical or emotional abuse.

FACT: If you love yourself, you won't let people abuse you.

BELIEF: This person can't help having BPD, so I should not hold them accountable for their behavior.

FACT: It's true the borderline in your life didn't ask to have BPD. But with help, they can learn to control their behavior toward others.

BELIEF: Setting personal limits hurts the person with BPD.

FACT: Setting personal limits is essential for *all* relationships—especially those in which one or both people have BP.

BELIEF: When I try to do something to help my situation and it doesn't work, I shouldn't give up until it does work.

FACT: You can learn from what hasn't worked and try something new.

BELIEF: No matter what my BP does, I should offer them my love, understanding, support, and unconditional acceptance.

FACT: There is a big difference between loving, supporting, and accepting the person and loving, supporting, and accepting their behavior. In fact, if you support and accept unhealthy behavior, you may be encouraging it to continue and perpetuating your own suffering.

non-BP grief over borderline behavior

Non-BPs being devalued by someone with BPD cherish clear and powerful memories of the times when the borderline thought they could do no wrong. Some family members say they feel like the person who loved them has died and that someone they do not know has taken over the BP's body.

One non-BP said, "If I had cancer, at least I would die just once. This emotional abuse ensures that I die many, many times and that I will always live on the edge."

Elisabeth Kübler-Ross, author of *Death: The Final Stage of Growth* (1975), outlined five stages of grief, which are appropriate for people who care about someone with BPD. We have adapted these stages to directly address BPD issues.

denial

Non-BPs make excuses for the BPs' behavior or refuse to believe that their behavior is unusual. The more isolated the non-BP, the greater the chances they will be in denial. This is because without outside input, non-BPs lose their sense of perspective about what is normal. People with BPD can be skillful at convincing others that their behavior is the non-BP's fault. This keeps non-BPs in a continual state of denial.

anger

Some non-BPs respond to angry attacks by fighting back. This is like adding gasoline to a fire.

Other non-BPs maintain that anger is an inappropriate response to borderline behavior. Some say, "You wouldn't get mad at someone for having diabetes—why would you be angry when they have BPD?"

Feelings don't have IQs. They just are. Sadness, anger, guilt, confusion, hostility, annoyance, frustration—all are normal, and to be expected by people faced with borderline behavior. This is true no matter what your relationship is to the person with BPD. This doesn't mean that you should respond to the BP with anger. But it does mean that you need a safe place to vent your emotions and feel accepted, not judged.

> People with BPD can be skillful at convincing others that their behavior is the non-BP's fault. This keeps non-BPs in a continual state of denial.

bargaining

This stage is characterized by the non-BP making concessions in order to bring back the "normal" behavior of the person they love. The thinking goes, "If I do what this person wants, I will get what I need in this relationship." We all make compromises in relationships. But the sacrifices that people make to satisfy the borderlines they care about can be very costly. And the concessions may never be enough. Before long, more proof of love is needed and another bargain must be struck.

> You need a safe place to vent your emotions and feel accepted, not judged.

depression

Depression sets in when non-BPs realize the true cost of the bargains they've made: loss of friends, family, self-respect, and hobbies. The person with BPD hasn't changed. But the non-BP has.

Sarah (non-BP)

For three years he told me the problem was me—that my shortcomings ruined everything. And I believed him. I turned my back on some of my good friends because he didn't like them. I rushed home after work because he said he needed me. Then we had a big fight, and now I'm lonely and depressed because I don't have anybody else to turn to.

Dreams die very hard. The child of a borderline parent may spend decades trying to win that parent's love and approval. When nothing seems good enough, it may take years for them to mourn the loss of unconditional parental love they never really had.

Fran (non-BP)

> Acceptance comes when non-BPs integrate the "good" and "bad" aspects of the borderlines they care about and realize that the BPs are not one or the other, but both.

I spent many years grieving for my borderline son when I realized the dreams I had for him might never come true. I began mourning in earnest when my son's therapist asked me what I would do if my son needed to live in a residential facility for the rest of his life. I just started sobbing. The therapist explained that the child I thought I had had died, along with the future I had pictured for him. But when I was done grieving, I would have a new child, and I would have new aspirations for him.

acceptance

Acceptance comes when non-BPs integrate the "good" and "bad" aspects of the borderlines they care about and realize that the BPs are not one or the other, but both. Non-BPs in this stage have learned to accept responsibility for their own choices and hold other people accountable for their choices as well. Each can then make their own decisions about the relationship with a clearer understanding of themselves and the person with BPD.

non-BP responses to borderline behavior

Borderline behavior causes many reactions in non-BPs. Some of the more common responses are addressed here.

bewilderment

Phil (non-BP)

At first everything looks and sounds normal. Then, unexpectedly, strange twists and reversals of reality occur; off-kilter shifts in the time-space continuum hurl me onto the floor as my wife suddenly roars at me for something I can't begin to understand. Suddenly, I realize I've crossed into the Borderline Zone!

Phil is baffled because of a reaction called "impulsive aggression," a core feature of borderline personality disorder.

According to *The Essential Family Guide to Borderline Personality Disorder* (2008) by Randi Kreger, coauthor of this book, impulsive aggression is an impulsive, hostile, even violent reaction, triggered by immediate threats of rejection or abandonment paired with frustration. The source of these feelings may be obvious or triggered by something unseen (as it probably was in Phil's case).

Kreger's colloquial term for impulsive aggression is "border-lion," because it's like a ferocious beast that is spontaneously uncaged when BPs' emotions are so strong and overwhelming they can no longer be contained. The border-lion's "claws" can be turned outward (raging, abusive language, actual physical violence) or inward (self-harm, suicide attempt) (Kreger 2008).

loss of self-esteem

Beverly Engel, in *The Emotionally Abused Woman* (1990), describes the effect of emotional abuse on self-esteem:

Emotional abuse cuts to the very core of a person, creating scars that may be longer-lasting than physical ones. With emotional abuse, the insults, insinuations, criticism, and accusations slowly eat away at the victim's self-esteem until she is incapable of judging the situation realistically. She has become so beaten down emotionally that she blames herself for the abuse. Emotional abuse victims can become so convinced that they are worthless that they believe that no one else could want them. They stay in abusive situations because they believe they have nowhere else to go. Their ultimate fear is being all alone.

feeling trapped and helpless

The borderline's behaviors cause a great deal of anguish, but leaving seems impossible or improbable. Non-BPs may believe they are trapped in the relationship because they either feel overly responsible for the safety of the BP or they feel overly guilty for perhaps "causing" the BP to feel and behave the way they do. The BP's threat of suicide or threat to harm others can paralyze the non-BP and make him or her feel as if leaving the relationship is too risky.

withdrawal

The non-BP may leave the situation, either emotionally or physically. This could include working long hours, remaining silent for fear of saying something wrong, or terminating the relationship. This may result in the person with BPD feeling abandoned and acting out more intensely. The non-BP may leave children alone with the BP for longer periods of time. If the BP acts abusively toward the children, the non-BP isn't there to protect them.

> "Emotional abuse cuts to the very core of a person, creating scars that may be longer-lasting than physical ones."

guilt and shame

Over time, accusations can have a brainwashing effect. Non-BPs may come to believe they are the source of all the problems. This is extremely damaging when it happens to children, who look up to their parents and who do not have the capacity to question an adult borderline's accusations or assumptions.

Parents of people with BPD are also vulnerable to this. They believe that they have been horrible parents when they simply made the same mistakes most parents make. Some parents we interviewed berate themselves endlessly, trying to figure out what they did to cause their childrens' disorder. When they can't, they conclude that the problem must be biological. But that doesn't take them off the hook either, since they then feel responsible for the child's biological heritage.

adopting unhealthy habits

Excessive drinking, overeating, substance abuse, and other unhealthy habits are typical ways many people, not just non-BPs, try to cope with stress. Initially, the habits soothe anxiety and stress. As these coping strategies become more habitual and ingrained, they only compound the situation.

isolation

The unpredictable behavior and moodiness of people with BPD can make friendships difficult. That's because:

- Making excuses or covering up the borderline's behavior can be so emotionally exhausting that some people find it's not worth the effort to sustain friendships.

- Many non-BPs say that friends often suggest solutions that are simplistic or unacceptable, which leaves the non-BPs feeling misunderstood.

- Some say they lose friendships because their friends don't believe them or grow tired of hearing about their struggles.

Frequently, non-BPs become isolated because the BPs in their lives insist that they cut off ties with others. Too often, the non-BPs comply. Once a non-BP becomes more isolated, several things can happen:

- They may become more emotionally dependent on the BP.

- Because they are out of touch with the real world, the outrageousness of BPD behavior may seem normal once there is nothing to compare it to.

- Friends can no longer observe the relationship and talk to the non-BP about unhealthy components of the relationship.

With things bottled up inside, non-BPs are left to deal with their problems with BPs on their own.

hypervigilance and physical illnesses

It is very stressful to be around someone who may berate you at any moment with no visible provocation. In an attempt to gain some control over what appear to be unpredictable BP behaviors, non-BPs often find themselves "on alert." Being on alert requires a heightened sense of arousal both physically and psychologically that, over time, can wear down the body's natural defenses against stress, leading to headaches, ulcers, high blood pressure, and other illnesses.

Being on alert requires a heightened sense of arousal both physically and psychologically that, over time, can wear down the body's natural defenses against stress.

adoption of BPD-like thoughts and feelings

Non-BPs often begin to see things in black and white and see all-or-nothing solutions to problems. Moodiness is also extremely common in non-BPs—they're often in a good mood when the BP is up and a bad mood when the BP is down.

> In a way, the person with BPD takes the non-BP with them on a roller-coaster ride. As distressing as this is, it's an opportunity to glimpse what it's like to have BPD.

codependence

The non-BP often performs valiant and heroic acts of kindness, no matter what the price to themselves. In an effort to help the person they love, they:

- swallow their anger

- ignore their own needs

- accept behavior that most people would find intolerable

- forgive the same transgressions again and again

This is a common trap for non-BPs—especially if the borderline had an unhappy childhood and the non-BP is trying to make up for it.

Many non-BPs assume that by subordinating their own needs for the sake of the BP (or to avoid a fight), they are helping. While the non-BP's motives are commendable, this actually enables, or reinforces, inappropriate behavior. Borderlines learn that their actions will have few negative consequences; therefore, they have little motivation to change.

Continuing to put up with BPD behavior rarely makes the BP happy.

Continuing to put up with BPD behavior rarely makes the BP happy. And even if the non-BP endures this behavior, the BP may become isolated because other people won't stand for it. How long will the non-BP be able to keep this up? One family member who smoothed things over for years in order to make up for his borderline wife's terrible childhood said, "I was concentrating on not doning her, no matter what she did. One day, I realized that, instead, I had abandoned myself."

Dean (non-BP)

I felt like such a failure in this relationship. I thought that if I could just persuade my wife to get the help she needed, everything would be all right. Despite the abuse, I felt like I couldn't leave. How could I abandon someone who'd already suffered so many misfortunes? I thought that if I just tried harder, I could make up for all the abuse she suffered when she was a kid.

This was confirmed to me once when I did try to leave. I'll never forget the look on her face as she told me with big sad eyes that she was happy I came back. "Why are you glad?" I asked. She responded, "Because who else is going to make my life better?" I decided to see a counselor. One day he said to me, "Aren't you being a bit pompous? Who do you think you are, God? You're not God. You are not responsible. And you can't fix this person. Your job is to accept that fact. Live with it. And make the decisions you have to make to live your life."

> "You're not God. You are not responsible. And you can't fix this person. Your job is to accept that fact."

effects on the relationship

Borderline behaviors such as verbal abuse, perceived manipulation, and defense mechanisms can shatter trust and intimacy. They make the relationship unsafe for the non-BP, who can no longer feel confident his or her deep feelings and innermost thoughts will be treated with love, concern, and care.

Susan Forward and Donna Frazier, in *Emotional Blackmail* (1997), explain that targets of emotional blackmail may become guarded about certain subjects and stop sharing major parts of their lives, such as embarrassing things they've done, frightening or insecure feelings, hopes for the future, and anything that shows they're changing and evolving.

> Targets of emotional blackmail may become very guarded about certain subjects and stop sharing major parts of their lives.

What's left when we must consistently walk on eggshells with someone is superficial small talk, strained silences, and lots of tension. When safety and intimacy are gone from a relationship, we get used to acting. We pretend that we're happy when we're not. We say that everything is fine when it isn't. What used to be a graceful dance of caring and closeness becomes a masked ball in which the people involved are hiding more and more of their true selves.

is this normal?

It can be very hard to determine what kind of behavior is normal and what isn't. The following questions may help. The more "yes" answers you give, the more we recommend that you take a hard look at how the behavior of the BP in your life might be affecting you.

___ Do people in healthy, happy relationships tell you that they don't understand why you are still putting up with the BP's behavior?

___ Do you try to avoid contact with these people?

___ Do you feel the need to cover up some of the BP's behavior?

___ Have you betrayed other people or told lies to protect the BP or your relationship with them?

___ Are you becoming isolated?

___ Does the thought of spending time with the BP give you unpleasant physical sensations?

___ Do you have other possibly stress-related ailments?

___ Has the BP ever expressed their anger at you by attempting to cause you legal, social, or financial difficulties?

___ Has this happened more than once?

___ Are you becoming clinically depressed? Signs of depression include:

- becoming less interested in normal activities

- taking less pleasure in life

- gaining or losing weight

- having sleep difficulties

- having feelings of worthlessness

- feeling tired all the time

- having trouble concentrating

___ Have you considered suicide? Do you think that friends and loved ones would be better off without you? (If yes, seek help immediately.)

___ Have you acted in ways that go against your fundamental values and beliefs as a result of your relationship with the borderline in your life? Are you no longer able to take a stand for what you believe in?

___ Are you concerned about the effects of this person's behavior on children?

___ Have you ever interceded to prevent abuse from occurring?

___ Have you or the BP ever put each other in physical danger or in a situation where physical danger was possible or likely?

___ Are you making decisions out of fear, obligation, and guilt?

___ Does your relationship with the BP seem to be more about power and control than kindness and caring?

In part 2 we will give you some steps for getting off the emotional roller coaster and taking charge of your life.

PART 2

taking back
control of your life

Now that you understand more about the disorder and how it affects you, the next step is to learn specific strategies to successfully manage your life and avoid getting swept up in the chaos all around you. While you can't change the disorder itself or make your family member seek therapy, you do have the power to fundamentally change the relationship.

In the first edition of this book, we described a variety of techniques for effecting change in no particular order. In this second edition, we will take you to the next level by using the framework laid out in coauthor Randi Kreger's 2008 book *The Essential Family Guide to Borderline Personality Disorder: New Tools and Techniques to Stop Walking on Eggshells*.

While there is some overlap in the tools themselves, *The Essential Family Guide* prioritizes them to create a step-by-step system that will enable you to organize your thinking, learn specific skills, and focus on what you need to do instead of becoming overwhelmed.

The tools are:

Tool 1: Take good care of yourself: obtaining support and finding community, detaching with love, getting a handle on your emotions, improving self-esteem, mindfulness, laughter, and wellness.

Tool 2: Uncover what keeps you feeling stuck: owning your choices; helping others without rescuing; and handling fear, obligation, and guilt.

Tool 3: Communicate to be heard: putting safety first, handling rage, active listening, nonverbal communication, defusing anger and criticism, validation and empathetic acknowledging.

Tool 4: Set limits with love: boundary issues, "sponging" and "mirroring," preparing for discussions, persisting for change, and the DEAR (Describe, Express, Assert, and Reinforce) technique.

Tool 5: Reinforce the right behaviors: the effects of intermittent reinforcement.

Keep in mind that the following is not a comprehensive look at the system, which is outlined in the second half of *The Essential Family Guide to Borderline Personality Disorder*. This is just a look at those elements in the second edition of this book. But it's a great start to get you on track to successfully manage your life and the relationship.

Keep in mind that BPD is a complex disorder and those with it are predictably unpredictable. Customize these strategies for your particular situation. Ideally, find a therapist who can help you personalize and integrate these techniques so they become part of your life.

CHAPTER 5

making changes within yourself

No one can make you feel inferior without your consent.

—Eleanor Roosevelt

you can't make the BP seek treatment

Here is the good news: You have a right to all of your opinions, thoughts, and feelings. Good or bad, right or wrong, they make you who you are. And here is the bad news: Everyone else has a right to their opinions, thoughts, and feelings, too. You may not agree with everyone else, and they may not agree with you. But that is okay. It is not your job to convince everyone to see things your way.

It can be frustrating and heartbreaking to watch people you love act in ways that hurt themselves and others. But no matter what you do, you can't control others' behavior. Moreover, it's not your job—unless, of course, the person with BPD in your life is your minor child. Even then, you can only influence the child's behavior—not control it. Your job is:

- to know who you are

- to act according to your own values and beliefs

- to communicate what you need and want to the people in your life

You can always encourage people to do what you want through subtle or blatant rewards and punishments. But it is still their decision how to act.

reasons for a BP's denial

It may be obvious to you that the person in your life with BPD needs help. But it may not be obvious to him or her. For people with BPD, admitting that anything about them is less than perfect, let alone acknowledging that they may have a personality disorder, can send them into a spiral of shame and self-doubt.

> Imagine feeling empty, virtually without a self. Now think about admitting that what little self you can recognize has something wrong with it. To many people with BPD, this is like ceasing to exist—a terrifying feeling for anyone.

To avoid this, people with BPD may employ a powerful and common defense mechanism: denial. They may maintain that nothing is wrong with them, despite clear evidence to the contrary. They would rather lose things very important to them—jobs, friends, and family—than lose themselves. (Once you understand this, you will truly appreciate the courage of people with BPD who do seek help.)

> Think about something you accomplished that seemed insurmountable. Getting a college degree, perhaps, or losing thirty pounds. Try to remember how your intense desire to achieve this goal made it possible. Now, imagine that your intense need was to avoid this goal. How likely is it that someone else can make you get that degree or lose that weight?

People with BPD may seek to avoid confronting problems other people want them to face. They may ask for help or try to alter their behavior—but not on your schedule. If they change, it will be in their own time and in their own way. In fact, it could be detrimental to force others to admit to having problems before they are ready.

Linda (BP)

Denying our problems is a coping mechanism that helps us borderlines keep the pain and fear under control. The larger the fear, the larger the denial. Please don't try to rip away the denial from borderlines who aren't ready to face the blackness inside. It may be all that's keeping them alive.

So the BP has destroyed a relationship? She moves on to the next one and the next one after that and so on and so forth. A BP loses a job over his behavior? He blames the boss and moves on to the next one and then the next. She loses custody of her children? It's the damned court system. The fear of change and the fear of the unknown are quite compelling. Thus, denial can be extremely powerful. And in the case of the borderline, the fears are so vast, so encompassing, and so overwhelming that denial can be absolute.

when will the BP seek help?

What motivates people with BPD to seek help? In general, people alter their behavior when they believe that the benefits of doing so outweigh the obstacles to change.

The specific catalysts for change, however, vary greatly. For some people, the unbearable emotional turmoil of living with BPD is worse than the fear of change. For others, it is realizing how their behavior is affecting their children. Some face their demons after losing someone important to them because of their behavior.

> People alter their behavior when they believe that the benefits of doing so outweigh the obstacles to change.

Rachel Reiland (author of *Get Me Out of Here*, a memoir about her recovery from BPD).

As a former borderline, I believe there does have to be some kind of shock or jolt that serves as a catalyst for change. At various times in my life, I was forced into therapy. I didn't have a sincere desire to change; I didn't want to lose something. And that just isn't enough.

My own shock was the look in my four-year-old son's eyes when I lost it and began smacking him until his thighs and face were red. He hadn't done anything wrong. I was beating him for being a kid when I didn't feel like being a mother. And when he initially started bawling, it made me angrier. I hit him harder.

Ultimately, he stopped crying. And in his eyes, opened wide in terror, I saw the reflections of my own eyes from years ago—reflections I had spent a lifetime running away from.

I couldn't blame what I had done on a husband who wasn't making enough money. I couldn't blame it on a power-hungry boss, bitchy neighbors, or any of the scores of people I was convinced had it in for me. Looking in my son's helpless and horrified eyes, I could see it was me. And I knew that I could no longer live with the person I had become.

You Can't Make Your Family Member Seek Help

According to *The Essential Family Guide to Borderline Personality Disorder: New Tools and Techniques to Stop Walking on Eggshells*, by coauthor Randi Kreger, techniques like crying, pointing out the person's flaws, logic, reasoning, and begging and pleading are counterproductive to motivating BP family members to seek therapy. Most of the time, all that results is fault finding and counteraccusations (*You're* the one who needs help, not me!).

Even ultimatums are unhelpful. Apprehensive that their loved one might actually carry out their threat, the BP may agree to see a therapist, perhaps with the partner or other family members. Therapy, however, goes nowhere. That's because even the best BPD clinicians can't help a patient who doesn't want to be helped.

Once the immediate threat dissipates, the BP finds some reason to drop out of therapy. This is especially likely if the therapist is a good one, skilled at bringing the focus to the BP's core issues instead of reinforcing the BP's feelings of victimhood. However, if the therapist takes everything the BP says at face value without probing further—and this is not uncommon—the therapist may inadvertently reinforce the BP's twisted thinking, making things worse.

What You Can Do

There is nothing wrong with wanting to change the person with BPD in your life. You may be right: he might be a lot happier and your relationship might improve if he sought help for BPD. But in order for you to get off the emotional roller coaster, you will have to give up the fantasy that you can or should change someone else. When you let go of this belief, you will be able to claim the power that is truly yours: the power to change yourself.

> For you to get off the emotional roller coaster, you will have to give up the fantasy that you can or should change someone else.

Consider a lighthouse. It stands on the shore with its beckoning light, guiding ships safely into the harbor. The lighthouse can't uproot itself, wade out into the water, grab the ship by the stern, and say, "Listen, you fool! If you stay on this path, you may break up on the rocks!"

No, the ship has some responsibility for its own destiny. It can choose to be guided by the lighthouse. Or it can go its own way. The lighthouse is not responsible for the ship's decisions. All it can do is be the best lighthouse it knows how to be.

stop taking the borderline's actions personally

Borderlines tend to see the world in black and white. And they tend to assume everyone else sees things the same way. In the face of this, people who have a consistent sense of their own self-worth have an easier time maintaining their sense of reality. No matter how the BP feels about them at any given moment, these non-BPs can be happy and secure in the knowledge that they're neither a goddess nor a demon. Most people, however, need some guidance in staying clear and focused when the BP splits.

alternate interpretations

Non-BPs don't usually ask for help when the BPs in their lives sing their praises. But it's important to remember that the up side of splitting (idealization) also has its down side (devaluation). This doesn't mean that you

Sometimes it's not the actual event but the borderline's interpretation of that event that prompts splitting.

should discount the good things the BP is saying—by all means, enjoy them. But be careful about positive overstatements and exaggerations that are hard to live up to.

Also be cautious about declarations of love and commitment that come too soon, for they may be based on the BP's image of you rather than the real you. It's important to keep your interpretation of things in mind, since the BP's may often be too negative or too idealized.

Sometimes it's not the actual event but the borderline's interpretation of that event that prompts splitting. Consider an emergency department physician who treated a child who had been in a bad car accident. He tried to save the child's life, but she was already near death when the paramedics brought her in. Clearly, there is nothing he could have done. The doctor goes to the waiting room and tells the girl's parents that the child has died. The father does not take it well.

"You incompetent fool!" he shouts. "She wasn't badly hurt at all! You should have been able to save her. If our family doctor had been treating her, she would have survived. I'm going to report you to the authorities!"

Most physicians would realize that the trauma and shock of his daughter's death could cause the father to lash out and blame them. They probably wouldn't take his words personally because they have comforted dozens of grieving relatives and they know this type of reaction is not uncommon. In other words, they would not take responsibility for the father's feelings. They would realize that his reaction had everything to do with the situation and little to do with them.

In this example, the incident that caused the father's response is external, obvious, and dramatic. With BPD, the cause of an argument is not necessarily the actual event but the borderline's interpretation of that event. As you probably know, you and the person with BPD may come to very different conclusions about what was said and done. Following are two such examples.

1. Robert (non-BP) says:

I have to work late. I'm really sorry, but I'm going to have to cancel our plans.

Kathryn (BP) hears:

I don't want to go out with you this evening because I don't love you anymore. I never want to see you again.

Kathryn says (in either an angry or tearful tone of voice):

How could you! You never loved me! I hate you!

2. Tom (non-BP) says:

I'm so proud of my daughter! Yesterday she hit a home run and won the game. Let's go to a movie tonight to celebrate.

Roxann (BP) hears:

I love my daughter more than you. She is talented, and you are not. From now on, I'm going to give all my love and attention to her and ignore you.

Roxann thinks:

He realizes that I'm flawed and defective. So now he's going to leave me. But no, I'm not flawed and defective. Nothing is wrong with me. So he's got to be the defective one.

Roxann says:

No, I don't want to go to a movie! Why don't you ask me what I want to do? You never think of me. You are so incredibly selfish and controlling!

We don't know why Roxann and Kathryn interpreted the men's comments in the ways they did. Perhaps they're afraid of being abandoned. Or perhaps BPD behavior like this is caused by faulty brain chemistry. Thus, although we can see what triggered the behavior—Tom and Robert's comments—the cause may be unknown.

triggers versus causes of BPD behavior

Understanding the difference between causes and triggers of borderline behavior is crucial to taking the behavior less personally. You can trigger borderline behavior quite easily as you go about your day. That doesn't mean, however, that you caused the behavior.

Imagine that you're having a bad day.

Your happy-go-lucky officemate walks in with a big grin on his face. "Wow, what a beautiful day it is today!" he exclaims. "Kind of makes you glad to be alive, doesn't it?"

> You can trigger borderline behavior quite easily as you go about your day. That doesn't mean, however, that you caused the behavior.

"Not really," you snarl. "I'm trying to work. Can you keep it down?"

Your officemate triggered your rude retort. But he didn't cause it. If you care about someone with BPD, accept that sometimes he will act in ways that make no sense to you. This is something that people with BPD and the more obviously mentally ill have in common. Christine Adamec, author of *How to Live with a Mentally Ill Person* (1996), says:

> Once you begin to accept that a mentally ill person will sometimes behave irrationally, you alleviate some of your own internal stress and strain... [O]nce you do so you can begin to develop more effective coping mechanisms. No longer burdened by the "what-ifs" and "shoulds" in your mind, you can deal with the way things really are. And you seek out what works.

seek support and validation

You may not know anyone else who cares about someone with BPD or has even heard of BPD. So you may have little or no support and no one to do "reality checks" with. For this reason, in 1995 coauthor Randi Kreger created a support community group at www.BPDCentral.com just for family members of someone with BPD called Welcome to Oz. People in the community share their stories and talk about having someone with BPD in their lives. For most of them, it is the first time they have connected with another person in the same situation.

If you care about someone with BPD, accept that sometimes they will act in ways that make no sense to you.

Many members of the group tell us that the list, more than anything else, has enabled them to depersonalize the behavior of the people with BPD in their lives. The stories are so similar—it really sinks in that the behavior is not about them. Many people find this to be a big relief.

> Joining a local or Internet support group can help you depersonalize the person's behavior. If that isn't possible, perhaps a friend or family member can lend a willing ear and will believe you. It's best to talk with someone who will not feel put in the middle between you and the BP in your life.

don't take BPD behavior personally

A woman who found out that her borderline husband had been having an affair asked us, "How can I not take it personally when my husband says he has been unfaithful and lying about it for the duration of our marriage? Am I supposed to feel good when he tells me he's going to leave me for her?" We explained that there is a big difference between working through your grief and not taking things personally.

Imagine if you were planning to have your wedding reception at the nicest hall in town, but two days before the wedding, lightning struck the hall and it burned to the ground. When you tried to find another site, you found that every other hall was booked. Naturally, you would be very upset and angry.

But you wouldn't feel personally attacked, as if the lightning bolt knew you and was deliberately trying to make your life miserable. You wouldn't blame yourself for things beyond your control. But that is precisely what many people do when faced with the actions of a person with BPD. They spend years assuming they're the source of the lightning when, in fact, they're only the lightning rod.

keep a sense of humor

Many family members find that having a sense of humor helps.

Hank (non-BP)

It was October, and my BP wife and I were going to a Halloween party given by my friend, Buck. I was dressed as Charlie Brown, complete with striped shirt and stuffed beagle. She was Lucy. In one hand she carried a football and in the other a sign that said, "Psychiatric Advice, Five Cents." (Ironic, isn't it?)

Buck opened the door, and a terrible realization came over me: this was not a Halloween party! Everyone else had on sweaters and jeans. The three of us—me, my wife, and her friend—all realized my mistake at exactly the same time.

My wife immediately became very angry and started carrying on about how stupid I was. Ordinarily, I would react to her rages and verbal abuse with fear, anxiety, and confusion. This time I just couldn't stop laughing! While my wife raged, the two of us just cracked up. I thought about the episode the next time my wife lost it, and it made me feel better to realize I had a choice about how I was going to react.

take care of yourself

The person in your life with BPD didn't ask to have the disorder. And you never asked for someone in your life to have BPD. But if you are a typical non-BP, you have taken on a huge chunk of the blame for the other person's problems, and you probably feel that you—and only you—can solve them.

Many non-BPs—especially those who have chosen their relationship with the borderline—go through life trying to fix things for other people and rescue them. This gives them the illusion that they can change someone else. But it is just a fantasy that shifts responsibility away from the only person who has the power to change the borderline's life—the BP. You can:

- Spend twenty-four hours a day feeling your loved one's pain for him or her.

- Put your life on hold, waiting for the BP to come around to your way of thinking.

- Let your entire emotional life be dictated by the mood of the moment.

But none of that will help the person with BPD.

In our interview with Howard I. Weinberg, Ph.D., he said, "People with BPD need their friends and family members to be stable and clear—not to reject them and not to smother them. They need you to let them take care of themselves and to not do things for them that they can do for themselves. The best way to do this and help them is by working on yourself."

Patricia (BP)

For those of you who have decided to stay with your BPD family member, thank you, thank you! We so need your love and support. We need you to believe in us and encourage us in our recovery. But if you stay, seek therapy for yourself if necessary and make sure you don't lose yourself in the process. You can't lose your own identity. You must come first. Because if you lose it, then the borderline doesn't really have a supporter. She just has another person in her life with a lot of problems.

detach with love

Some family members practice detaching with love, a concept promoted by Al-Anon, an organization for people whose lives are affected by someone who abuses alcohol. Al-Anon developed a statement about personal limits that is also appropriate for non-BPs, if you substitute "BPD behavior" for "alcoholism." The original reads, in part:

In Al-Anon we learn individuals are not responsible for another person's disease or recovery from it.

We let go of our obsession with another's behavior and begin to lead happier and more manageable lives, lives with dignity and rights.

In Al-Anon we learn:

- Not to suffer because of the actions or reactions of other people.

- Not to allow ourselves to be used or abused by others in the interest of another's recovery.

- Not do for others what they could do for themselves.

- Not to create a crisis.

- Not to prevent a crisis if it is in the natural course of events.

Detachment is neither kind nor unkind. It does not imply judgment or condemnation of the person or situation from which I am detaching. It is simply a means that allows us to separate ourselves from the adverse effects that another person's alcoholism [substitute "BPD behavior"] has upon our lives.

Detachment helps families look at their situations realistically and objectively, thereby making intelligent decisions possible.

take your life back

Don't delay your own happiness. Grab it right now. There are many things you can do today to take your life back. Take some time off to reflect. It can remind both you and the person with BPD that you are two separate individuals. The BP will learn that he can live through a temporary separation and that you will still care about him when you return. Encouraging retreats actually builds the relationship.

Do not try to be the person's therapist. That is not your role. If the person with BPD wants that kind of help, suggest that she see a mental health professional. If you no longer have contact with the BP, don't spend hours psychoanalyzing. It is not your job anymore—actually, it never was to begin with.

Memorize the three Cs and the three Gs:

- I didn't cause it.
- I can't control it.
- I can't cure it.
- Get off the BP's back.
- Get out of the BP's way.
- Get on with your own life.

Be good to yourself. Here are some ideas:

- Visit an art gallery.
- Buy an outrageously expensive chocolate truffle.
- Get a massage.
- Seek out friends and family.
- Volunteer or become politically involved.
- Realize that—illness or no illness—no one person can fulfill all of your needs.
- If you have let friendships falter, "unfalter" them.
- When you go out, do not spend all your time talking about the person with BPD.
- See a movie.
- Try a new food.
- Relax and enjoy yourself!

Have fun. The world will not stop if you take some time for yourself. In fact, you will be able to come back refreshed and with a broader perspective.

If you are eating or drinking too much or engaging in other unhealthy coping mechanisms, stop. Seek professional help if you need to. Maintain realistic expectations. Borderline behavior takes years to develop; it is ingrained. Don't expect miracles. Celebrate small steps in the right direction and appreciate the things you enjoy about the person with BPD.

Tanya (non-BP)

It helps to remind myself that I can't fix everything. I keep reminding myself that being in a situation where I feel helpless doesn't mean I'm a failure.

My therapist told me not to feel guilty about taking care of myself. It's going to take some time to really feel that that's okay. I know I have to deal with my own feelings. But sometimes I long to have my own life back for a little while.

> Celebrate small steps in the right direction and appreciate the things you enjoy about the person with BPD.

bolster your identity and self-esteem

If the person in your life blames and criticizes you, your self-esteem may be in the gutter. If you had low self-esteem to begin with, the situation may be critical. Some non-BPs we spoke with—especially adult children of borderlines—let others take advantage of them because they felt they didn't deserve better. They stayed in abusive work situations or unknowingly sabotaged themselves as if to confirm the BP's low estimation of their worth.

Many people with BPD are able to be supportive of their children and other people in their life. But some are not. If the relationship with the BP in your life is damaging your self-worth, take immediate steps to repair it. Don't depend on the person with BPD to affirm or validate your worth, because she may not be able to. It's not that she doesn't care about you—it's just that at this time, her own issues and needs may be getting in the way.

Chapter 6 discusses the issues of setting limits and responding to rage, blame, and criticism. Read it carefully and practice the communication techniques with a friend before using them in a real-life situation. You do not have to listen to anyone else tell you that you're an awful, terrible person. You have a choice.

Finally, seek therapy to deal with the stress of living with someone who has BPD. In a survey we conducted of non-BPs, 75 percent of the non-BPs said they had sought therapy themselves.

take responsibility for your own behavior

You may feel like a crumpled newspaper in a tornado, buffeted about at the whim of the person in your life with BPD. But you have more control over the relationship than you probably think you do. You have power over your own actions. And you control your own reactions to troublesome BPD behavior. Once you understand yourself and the decisions you've made in the past, it is easier to make new decisions that may be healthier for you and the relationship in the long run.

In *Emotional Blackmail* (1997), Susan Forward and Donna Frazier discuss how even avoidance is an action taken:

> You do not have to listen to anyone else tell you that you're an awful, terrible person. You have a choice.

Every day, we teach people how to treat us by showing them what we will and won't accept, what we refuse to confront, and what we let slide. We may believe that we can make another person's troublesome behavior disappear if we don't make a fuss. But the message we send is, "It worked. Do it again."

Some non-BPs find this step of owning up to their own responsibility difficult because they hear the critical voice of the BP in their head saying, "See, everything is your fault. I told you that something is wrong with you." To these non-BPs, taking this step almost seems like agreeing with the BP's criticisms. If this describes you, silence those voices right now. We are not suggesting that you provoked or caused the person's behavior—rather, we are proposing that you may have unwittingly given the BP permission to repeat behaviors that have worked in the past.

consider how the relationship meets your needs

In our interview with Howard I. Weinberg, Ph.D., he said, "If you care about someone with BPD, remember that you did not choose the borderline because you are sick. You chose this person because they were important to you."

You wouldn't be reading this book if the relationship was completely negative. You would just walk away. So something about the relationship is probably meeting your needs. These reasons may vary depending upon whether you are in a chosen relationship (friend, lover) or unchosen relationship (relative) with someone with BPD.

Many people stay in relationships with borderlines because the person with BPD is incredibly interesting, engaging, bright, charming, funny, witty, and alluring. One woman said that when she met her borderline boyfriend, she felt like she was meeting a member of her own species for the first time.

Diane (BP)

I can understand why non-BPs engage in discussion about the pathologies, the rages, and the rotten things borderlines can do. A BP has the capacity to destroy themselves and anyone close to them. It's healthy to vent this pain.

> Non-BPs aren't masochists; they're optimists.

But sometimes, in the course of the books and the discussion and the clinical terminology, these reasons why you began the relationship become lost. You didn't fall in love with a borderline because you had some hankering to be destroyed. You did it because there were good qualities about the person. And they are just as characteristic of the person as the bad ones.

When the destructive bad qualities began to manifest themselves, you got through it by telling yourself that in the end, these good qualities supersede the bad ones. Well, maybe they will or maybe they won't. Non-BPs aren't masochists; they're optimists—which may or may not turn out to be warranted. It is hard to give up on that optimism and let go of a relationship that's so good otherwise.

stop making excuses and denying the severity of the situation

Remaining hopeful is essential. And it's true that everyone has good and bad qualities. But hope must be tempered with a realistic view of the situation and an assessment of the likelihood of change.

Kevin's girlfriend Judy was bright, talented, and very attractive. Best of all, she loved him. So Kevin overlooked behavior that would have been a wake-up call for others. For example, one day Judy showed up at his workplace and began screaming at him in front of his boss and coworkers. Several days later, he still couldn't figure out why she had been angry.

Judy also impulsively bought luxury items like crystal vases and designer clothing, even though she was on public assistance and lived with Kevin and her nine-year-old son in a roach-infested apartment. She would leave her son alone at home to go shopping.

Denial of problems only enables and reinforces the negative behaviors.

Each time Judy and Kevin had a disagreement, she would throw him out of the apartment and destroy some of his possessions. This became so routine that he began leaving his treasured belongings with his parents. When Kevin's friends tried to convince him that Judy's behavior wasn't normal, Kevin would shrug his shoulders and say, "Oh well, nobody's perfect. Every relationship has problems."

Kevin is using denial as a way of keeping the relationship going and coping with painful feelings of his own. At this point, Kevin is likely to do anything to avoid conflict in the relationship. However, his denial of problems only enables and reinforces the negative behaviors of Judy. Kevin will need the support and perspective of his friends to begin to address these problems and address why he allows Judy to treat him so poorly. Kevin will also need to address why his relationship with Judy is so important that he allows her to treat him badly.

understand the effects of intermittent reinforcement

Let's say that you have a rat in a box with a lever. You teach the rat to press the lever. Every fifth time he presses the lever, he is rewarded with some food. The rat quickly learns to press the lever five times so he can claim his reward. But if you stop giving the rat food, he will quickly abandon the exercise.

Now let's say that you intermittently reinforce the rat with food; that is, you vary the reward schedule. Sometimes you reward the rat after two lever presses. Sometimes you wait until the fifteenth press. You alternate the reinforcement so he never knows when to expect the food. Then, once more, you take away all the food pellets. But the rat keeps pressing the lever. He presses it twenty times; no food. He presses some more. He thinks, "Perhaps the human is waiting for the ninety-ninth press this time."

When a behavior is intermittently reinforced, extinguishing the behavior takes a lot longer once the reward has been removed. Intermittent reinforcement can work both ways. You are intermittently reinforced when the BP is in a good mood. You can't predict when it will occur next—but you know it could be soon. The BP can also be intermittently reinforced when you occasionally cave in to his or her demands.

Molly says, "I am caught right now in Sondra's charming behavior. I am thinking, 'Ah! This is the person I used to know.' My logic tells me not to reconnect with her. But my emotions are telling me another thing."

> If you feel "addicted" to the BP despite his or her harsh treatment of you, consider whether intermittent reinforcement is playing a part in the relationship.

recognize the exhilaration of the roller-coaster ride

Many people say that when things are good, they're really good. The flattery, attention, and obsessiveness are exhilarating to the ego. To feel so important to someone can be exciting and empowering. The exhilaration can be recognized immediately, especially if the non-BP has not been in this position of being an "idol" before.

The non-BP may also begin to look for the exhilaration—to anticipate the flattery and attention. And, after a while, when the flattery begins to gradually fade, the non-BP will miss it and make attempts to get the BP to idolize him or her again. The law of intermittent reinforcement applies here again, since the BP may intermittently engage in the obsessiveness and flattery throughout the relationship. This in turn reinforces the non-BP's commitment to the relationship.

Jim (non-BP)

I found my wife's initial obsessiveness with me very flattering. I mean, I never thought I was worth that kind of attention. Other women didn't pay much attention to me. But she worshipped me. It's easier to feel good about myself when I'm around someone who idolizes me.

> When a behavior is intermittently reinforced, extinguishing the behavior takes a lot longer once the reward has been removed.

But our relationship was like an addiction. I kept going back for more, in spite of myself, filled with self-contempt and even a sort of subtle shame: "I hate myself for loving you."

So began our roller-coaster relationship; living vicariously through the sublime, dizzying heights, I was shaken by the sudden, despairing drops, the switchbacks, the topsy-turvy illogical loops, the stunning stops, and later, the absence, the silence, the flatness at the end.

How To Get Unstuck

Do you feel unable to move because danger lies in every choice, but at the same time feel compelled to do something? Does your satisfaction with this relationship depend on your BP making significant changes—even though it sure hasn't happened yet?

The Essential Family Guide to Borderline Personality Disorder: New Tools and Techniques to Stop Walking on Eggshells, by coauthor Randi Kreger, lists the six most common reasons why non-BPs feel stuck and what to do about them:

Unhealthy bonds forged by emotional abuse: Controlling, intimidating, punishing, and isolating behaviors can lead to a lack of motivation, confusion, and difficulty making decisions—all of which can keep people stuck.

Feelings of fear. These can range from the practical (will the BP be able to make it alone?) to fear of conflict and the unknown.

Obligation, roles, and duty. "How can I not visit my mother on her birthday?"

Guilt. This can drive family members (especially parents) to lose their sense of judgment and go to ridiculous lengths to "absolve" themselves.

Low self-esteem. People with low self-esteem often try to relieve their shame by being good. "Goodness" comes from sacrificing themselves and what they want out of life to make up for their perceived inadequacies.

The need to rescue. Rescuers start out with the best of intentions—they want to help. They will often do anything to keep the peace and avoid conflict, including taking the blame for things that are not their fault. Ultimately, they feel manipulated, angry, and frustrated.

To get unstuck, you must take a different approach. Stop focusing so much on your family member and take a close look at yourself. Work on becoming more of your own person.

Kreger writes, "Own your choices. Recognize that you decide how to respond to the people, actions, and events in your life. You have choices—not necessarily fun ones, but choices nonetheless. Banish phrases like, 'He made me...' or 'She forced me to...' from your vocabulary unless they refer to a legal document. Rather than say, 'I have to,' say, 'Right now, I choose to.' Then, open yourself up to new ideas. If what you've been doing hasn't worked, do something else."

Suggestions from *The Essential Family Guide* include:

- Become more authentic. Act in accordance with your own attitudes and beliefs.

- Learn from the past. Are these feelings familiar? Have you been in a similar situation?

- Help others without rescuing. Express confidence in your family member's ability to start finding solutions to his or her own problems. That helps build confidence.

- Allow people to be who they are instead of what you want them to be. Send healthy support messages like, "I'm here if you need me, but your choices—and the consequences—belong to you."

make decisions for yourself

Acknowledging that you have the authority to make your own decisions is the first step toward making new choices and changing your life for the better.

Some non-BPs think they are helpless in their relationship when, in actuality, they are feeling scared. Fear and anxiety are not the same as being helpless. Non-BPs are typically fearful that their efforts toward limit setting and change will be met with rage and anger. Therefore, in an effort to avoid negative reactions of BPs, non-BPs will describe themselves as "helpless." Moreover, believing you are helpless may also serve the purpose of ridding yourself of any responsibility for making changes or for creating a better life for yourself. You may think that if you're "helpless" that means you're a "victim"—a person that others can't blame for their situation.

> Fear and anxiety are not the same as being helpless.

You must understand that you do have the power to change your relationships and your life, but it is likely going to be frightening at first. The alternative is to live a fairly unhappy and unsatisfying life in which fear dictates your choices and their relationships.

believe you don't deserve to be treated badly

Do you sometimes think that being in an emotionally abusive relationship is better than being in no relationship at all? It sometimes feels easier to be hurt than to be alone, but in the long run, abusive relationships can cause you to lose yourself, which is the ultimate loneliness. People with self-esteem problems are very vulnerable to blame and criticisms. They come to believe they deserve this treatment. They think that if they leave, no one else will want them. Even emotionally healthy people can begin to question their own self-worth.

Alex (non-BP)

I had to examine why I would spend years in abusive relationships. I had to overcome my fears and learn that I am worthy of being in relationships with people who are good to me—without putting me on a pedestal or tossing me into the gutter.

John (non-BP)

I realized that one of the major reasons I stayed in this relationship was that I unconsciously thought I deserved that pain and anguish. Now I'm working on this so I won't be attracted to women like that in the future.

All people, not just non-BPs, have the right to healthy relationships. However, after months or years of enduring excessive criticism, blame, and border-line rage, most non-BPs may begin to question whether they deserve to have a healthy relationship. Do you believe that you have the following rights?

> Abusive relationships can cause you to lose yourself, which is the ultimate loneliness.

- to feel respected as a person
- to get your physical and emotional needs met
- to be appreciated and not taken for granted
- to communicate effectively with your partner
- to have your privacy respected
- to not constantly fight for control
- to feel good about yourself and your relationship
- to trust, validate, and support each other
- to grow within and outside of the relationship
- to have your own opinions and thoughts
- to either stay in or leave the relationship

As you may know, rights are neither respected nor acknowledged unless someone stands up for them. Are you ready to stand up for your rights?

face your own issues about being needed

Codependence expert Melody Beattie, in *Codependent No More* (1987), developed a list of questions for people who feel like they must rescue others. Paraphrased, they include:

- Do you feel responsible for other people's thoughts, actions, and feelings?
- When someone tells you about a problem she has, do you feel it is your duty to solve it?
- Do you swallow your anger in order to avoid conflict?

- Do you find getting more difficult than giving?

- Do you somehow seem to enjoy life more during interpersonal crises? Have you avoided choosing partners whose lives seem to go too smoothly because you become bored?

- Do people tell you that you are a saint for putting up with something or someone? Does part of you enjoy this?

- Is it more tempting to concentrate on the problems of others than to solve difficulties in your own life ?

focus on your own issues

Some people find that trying to change someone else is easier than changing themselves and that focusing on the problems of others helps them avoid their own problems. You may want to ask yourself:

- Do you have a firm sense of who you are apart from the person with BPD?

- Are you where you want to be at this point in your life?

- Is there anything in your life that you are avoiding that you might have to take a look at if you were not concentrating on your relationship with the BP?

- How much time do you spend worrying about this relationship?

- What would you do with that time if life with this person was perfect?

Nina (non-BP)

Because my boyfriends were so obviously out of line, I overlooked my own behavior. So I learned that my responsibility was to admit when I screwed up immediately, to be honest and open—even in the face of BPD rages and blame. I realized that the problems I faced with BPD partners were magnified versions of the problems I had with myself.

I kept thinking it was just those crazy men in my life and that if only they would change, everything would be fine. It was a painful realization to wake up one day and notice that there were no medals handed out to willing sufferers like me!

where to go from here

Ask yourself:

- How did I end up in this position?

- What have I learned about myself?

- What choices have I made in the past, and are they the best ones for me right now?

- What is keeping me from standing up for myself? What can I do about it?

- What am I responsible for in this relationship? What can I do about it?

Note that we are not blaming you for what has happened to you in the past or for the choices you've made. But only you—not the BP, your therapist, or your friends—can resolve these issues. It's up to you. Many introspective non-BPs found that what they discovered about themselves was invaluable.

Alex (non-BP)

This was the greatest gift of being around people with BPD. I got to see myself and how I interact with others. As painful as these relationships were, I needed them to become the person that I am today.

Marilyn (non-BP)

I have been able to move from being a person who lived her life unconsciously to a person who lives a conscious life. Someone said that the unexamined life is not worth living. I am happy to say that my life is very much worth living!

Russell (non-BP)

It helps to view situations as opportunities for growth and personal education. Rather than see every conflict and tribulation as a crisis of unresolvable proportions, I recognize that I am the one with the problem—I detest this person's behavior—and I'm open to learn more about myself. It becomes more about my choices than about my helplessness. And I can learn a lot from my choices.

In this chapter, we've explored ways to better cope with BPD behavior, simply by making changes within yourself: accepting that you can't make the BP seek treatment, not taking the BP's actions personally, taking care of yourself, and taking responsibility for your own behavior.

Next, we'll look at beginning to change the way you interact with the BP in your life.

CHAPTER 6

understanding your situation: setting boundaries and honing skills

identify triggers to intense emotional reactions

When you or the BP have an intense reaction to something, chances are good that one of your triggers or "hot buttons" has been pushed. Hot buttons or triggers are stored-up resentments, regrets, insecurities, anger, and fears that hurt when touched and cause automatic emotional responses. By identifying specific actions, words, or events that seem to trigger emotional reactions—either in you or in the BP in your life—these reactions may be easier to antici-pate and manage.

keeping track

Many family members find that keeping a daily log of their loved one's patterns of behavior helps them understand and depersonalize the person's actions. Parents of borderline children, especially, find records useful in helping obtain proper diagnosis and treatment for their child.

Whether you simply observe the BP or jot down notes about his or her moods and behaviors, your intent is not to make judgments, but to stop reacting to the behavior emotionally and start learning from it. If there appears to be little relationship between your actions and those of the person with BPD, you will see more clearly that the person's behavior is not about you.

If it looks like an external factor triggers the behavior, try to determine what factors might be involved, such as:

- the person's general mood
- the person's stress level and/or responsibilities
- the time of day
- the presence or absence of alcohol
- physical factors such as being hungry or tired
- the immediate environment

If you can find patterns in the person's behavior, it may become more predictable

Portia (non-BP)

Sandy and I are parents of a possibly borderline child. We used a spreadsheet to graph our son's moods and behaviors. The scale varied from –10, for extreme despair, to +10, for extreme optimism. A zero indicated a neutral mood. Our son's therapist was blown away by our documentation, and it helped the therapist determine if our son had BPD or bipolar disorder.

Henry (non-BP)

I never kept a journal, but over a ten-year period, I realized that Barbara's moods occurred in six-week cycles. It went like this:

1. *Explosive, violent raging that lasted from ten minutes to several hours*

2. *Silence that lasted for two to five days*

3. *Friendly, cheerful, affectionate behavior that would last three or four days. (When things were going well, Barbara would apologize and even ask me to find out what might be causing her "crazy behavior.")*

4. *A long deterioration that lasted four to ten weeks. Barbara became increasingly more critical, condemning, and short-tempered. She would deny her earlier apologetic remarks. Finally, there would be an angry explosion and the cycle would repeat anew.*

Once I recognized the patterns, I knew what to expect. This made things feel more manageable for me.

non-BP triggers

Many non-BPs told us that the people with BPD in their lives seemed to be aware of the non-BP's triggers. When the BPs felt threatened, they consciously or unconsciously protected themselves from painful feelings in ways that pushed these buttons.

For example, one non-BP had very poor self-esteem. She had never dated much, and she and her borderline husband had gotten married during high school. The marriage was very difficult because her husband was emotionally abusive. Whenever she spoke of leaving, however, he would tell her that no one else would have her and she would never be able to support herself because she was not smart or talented enough to get a good-paying job.

Some of the things that the BP in your life says or does may sting badly. Others may not bother you. Rather than just reacting, observe and examine your own responses. Is the criticism true, or does it have a grain of truth? Remember, you don't have to accept or reject the statement in its entirety. Look for splitting (black-and-white thinking), overgeneralizations ("you always" or "you never"), and illogical connections ("You didn't take me to the party because you hate me").

Certain hot buttons get pushed so many times that even the slightest touch becomes painful. Hot buttons for non-BPs may include:

- being unfairly accused by the BP

- having needs, feelings, and reactions discounted or denied by the BP

> Rather than just reacting, observe and examine your own responses.

- being overly admired or adored by the BP (because it may be a set-up for later devaluation and criticism)

- other situations and conditions that usually precede rages or acting-out behaviors (e.g., one woman started trembling whenever the phone rang because she was afraid it was her borderline mother)

FOG—Fear, Obligation, Guilt

In *Emotional Blackmail*, Susan Forward and Donna Frazier (1997) write that traits that make people vulnerable to emotional blackmail include fear, obligation, and guilt—FOG for short. FOG obscures your choices and limits your options to those the blackmailer picks for you:

- **Fear:** You may fear losing something: love, money, approval, access to your children, or the relationship itself. You may be afraid of your own anger or of losing control of your emotions.

- **Obligation:** Says Forward, "Memory, as employed by the blackmailer, becomes the Obligation Channel, with nonstop replays of the blackmailer's generous behavior toward us. When our sense of obligation is stronger than our sense of self-respect and caring, people quickly learn how to take advantage."

- **Guilt:** When your normal activities trigger the BP, the person plays the "Tag, You're It" game discussed in chapter 3 and shifts responsibility for her upset feelings onto you. The BP may accuse you not only of devious behavior but of acting in this way to deliberately hurt her. Instead of questioning her assumptions, you may respond by feeling guilty.

coping strategies

Just becoming aware of your triggers can make coping with borderline behavior easier. Other strategies include:

- **Working on yourself:** For example, the woman with poor self-esteem might see a therapist and explore why she thinks so poorly of herself. Or she might take some classes at the local college to improve her professional skills or train for a higher-paying position. This way, she will be in a better position to depersonalize and deflect the BP's criticism—or leave the emotionally abusive relationship.

- **Performing reality checks with others:** If the BP in your life accuses you of being ungrateful or inept, or of having other negative qualities, ask friends if they believe there's any truth to what the BP is saying.

- **Minimizing your exposure to situations that trigger you:** You have the right to take care of yourself.

- **Minimizing any visible reaction:** If the BP knows the button-pushing is having the desired effect—whether consciously or unconsciously—chances are that the behavior will be repeated.

- **Realizing you can't control what people choose to think:** You can't make everyone happy—least of all someone who is projecting their own unhappiness onto you. Stop taking responsibility for the BP's inner world and start taking responsibility for your own.

determine your personal limits

Personal limits, or boundaries, tell you where you end and where others begin. Limits define who you are, what you believe, how you treat other people, and how you let them treat you. Like the shell of an egg, limits give you form and protect you. Like the rules of a game, they bring order to your life and help you make decisions that benefit you.

Healthy limits are somewhat flexible, like a soft piece of plastic. You can bend them, and they don't break. When your limits are overly flexible, however, violations and intrusions can occur. You may take on the feelings and responsibilities of others and lose sight of your own.

You have the right to take care of yourself.

On the other hand, when your limits are too inflexible, people may view you as cold or distant. That's because inflexible limits can act as a defense—not only against others, but also from your own feelings. You may have a hard time feeling sadness, anger, or other negative emotions. Happiness and other positive emotions may also at times be beyond your grasp. You may feel disconnected from others and even from your own experiences.

In *Codependent No More* (1987), Melody Beattie says that setting limits is not an isolated process. She writes:

> Setting boundaries is about learning to take care of ourselves, no matter what happens, where we go, or who we're with. Boundaries are rooted in our beliefs about what we deserve and don't deserve.
>
> Boundaries originate from a deeper sense of our personal rights—especially the right we have to be ourselves. Boundaries emerge as we learn to value, trust, and listen to ourselves. Boundaries naturally flow from our conviction that what we want, need, like and dislike is important.

Personal limits are not about controlling or changing other people's behavior. In fact, they're not about other people at all. They're about you, and what you need to do to take care of yourself. For example, you may not be able to stop nosy in-laws from asking you again and again when you plan on starting a family. But you can control whether you answer their questions and how much time you spend with them.

Sometimes you may choose to overlook your personal limits. For example, imagine that your elderly father slips on an icy walkway and asks if he can live with you and your family until he recovers from his injuries. Because you love your dad, you say yes—even though you value your privacy. The key here is that you feel you have a choice. It's like the difference between giving someone a gift and being robbed.

Emotional Limits

Emotional limits are the invisible boundaries that separate your feelings from those of others. These boundaries not only mark off where your feelings end and someone else's begin but also help you protect your feelings when you are feeling vulnerable and provide others with access to your feelings when you are feeling intimate and safe with them.

People with healthy emotional limits understand and respect their own thoughts and feelings. In short, they respect themselves and their own uniqueness. Anne Katherine (1993) says, "The right to say 'no' strengthens emotional boundaries. So

Sometimes you may choose to overlook your personal limits... The key is that you feel you have a choice.

does the freedom to say 'yes,' respect for feelings, acceptance of differences, and permission for expression."

Healthy examples

Here are some illustrations of how people act in ways that respect their own thoughts and feelings:

- Dan believes that his father has borderline personality disorder. His younger brother, Randy, disagrees. Dan hasn't seen his father in a year, while Randy has dinner with him once a week. Dan and Randy feel free to discuss their opinions about their father though they have differing viewpoints. And they both enjoy their brotherly relationship, realizing that it's separate from their relationships with their father.

- Roberta's lover Cathy (BP) hates it when Roberta (non-BP) goes out with friends. Cathy is always invited along, but she wants to stay home because she thinks that Roberta's friends are "a complete waste of time."

  "Please don't go," Cathy pleads one evening as Roberta gets dressed to go out. "I'm lonely without you," Cathy says tearfully. Roberta gently reminds Cathy that she told her about her plans a week ago and that Cathy had time to find things to do on her own or with one of her own friends. But Cathy just keeps on weeping. "You must not love me anymore," she says.

  Roberta replies, "It sounds like you feel that I am rejecting or abandoning you. That must be very painful. You can believe that and make yourself feel bad or you can try to work through why you doubt my love for you. Let's talk about it when I get back. I'll see you at around eleven o'clock."

the benefits of personal limits

Limits can be difficult to set and keep, but doing so has some invaluable incentives.

> Limits can help you deal with these behaviors so that you don't feel like a puppet on a string.

Limits Help You Define Who You Are

Limits and the struggle for identity are tightly intertwined. People with weak limits often have poorly developed senses of identity. People with weak or nonexistent limits can have difficulty distinguishing between their own beliefs and feelings and those belonging to others. They also tend to confuse their problems and responsibilities with those of others. Left with an uncertain identity, they often take on someone else's or identify solely with one familiar role (e.g., mother, executive, or even borderline).

People with well-developed limits:

- appropriately distinguish themselves from others

- identify and take responsibility for their own feelings, beliefs, and values

- see feelings, beliefs, and values as important parts of who they are

- have respect for other people's beliefs and feelings—even if they are different from their own

- understand that another person's values and beliefs are equally important in defining who they are

Limits Bring Order to Your Life

If you're always at the whim of someone else's desires, your life can spiral out of control. People with BPD tend to change the rules, act impulsively, and demand attention on their schedule, not that of others. Limits can help you deal with these behaviors so that you don't feel like a puppet on a string.

Limits can also help you clarify your relationships with others, and setting limits ahead of time may help you avoid future problems.

Limits Help You Feel Secure

People who don't have limits are always at the mercy of others. They feel helpless when others act upon them, and they take whatever others dish out. On the other hand, people with limits feel more in control of their lives because they realize they have a choice about the behavior they will tolerate. They take the power that is truly theirs to say no. This provides them with a sense of security and control.

For example, Jane and Ben have been dating for several months. Jane's having a hard time because Ben can't decide how he feels about her. When he loves her, she's elated. When he backs off and "just wants to be friends," she's depressed and confused.

One day he has something to tell her. "I've met someone else," he says. "But I don't know if she's the one. I want to date both of you until I know for sure."

Clear limits will enable Jane to stick up for herself and tell Ben what she wants out of the relationship. Because she has healthy limits, she knows that her needs are just as important as Ben's. Jane can tell Ben how his actions have affected her, and she can evaluate his proposed arrangement based on her own values and beliefs. Jane understands that she has many options. She knows one of them is telling Ben that although she cares for him, she needs to leave the relationship because it's not meeting her needs.

Limits Promote Intimacy, Not Enmeshment

The idea used to be that when two people got married, they became one. Today's brides and grooms are more likely to believe that one and one still make two. Many couples acknowledge this at their wedding by having someone read from Kahlil Gibran's *The Prophet* (1976). In the passage on marriage, Gibran urges couples to have spaces in their togetherness. "Stand together yet not too near together: for the pillars of the temple stand apart, and the oak tree and the cypress grow not in each other's shadow."

Gibran is describing healthy limits. The opposite, enmeshment, is comparable to the oak tree and the cypress growing so close together that their branches and roots become entwined. Soon, there's no room for either tree to grow; parts of each tree die, and neither reaches its full potential.

> Unlike compromise, which is a conscious give and take, enmeshment involves denying who you are or what you need, to please someone else.

In *Boundaries: Where You End and I Begin* (1993), Anne Katherine says:

Enmeshment happens when the individualities of each partner are sacrificed to the relationship. Falling in love is exciting and involving. But the truth is, it's a fairly enmeshed stage of the relationship.

It is validating for someone to have thoughts and feelings identical to our own. It feels wonderful. Eventually, though, perceptions will differ. How this is handled is critical for the relationship.

Sometimes people become enmeshed because one partner intimidates the other into giving up their own opinions, perspectives, and preferences. In other cases a partner takes on someone else's view voluntarily because they're so eager to feel close to someone. Denying part of themselves is preferable to being alone—at least at first. But the problem with sacrificing parts of yourself to please someone else is that it doesn't work in the long run. It might take many years, but eventually you realize that while you may have gained a relationship, you've lost yourself. In order to share yourself, you need enough of a sense of your own individuality to have something to present to the other. Even if you have a good sense of who you are, intimacy takes time, openness, a nonjudgmental attitude, listening, and acceptance.

BP and non-BP boundary issues

Some people are lucky enough to have had parents and other role models who taught them about personal rights and limits and why they are important. Unfortunately, many adults grew up with damaged, trampled, or nonexistent boundaries. In many cases, parents routinely violated their children's boundaries and rights or forced them into inappropriate roles.

Different kinds of boundary violations cause different kinds of problems for children when they become adults:

- If parents or other caregivers encouraged children to be dependent, as adults those grown children may believe that they need someone else to make them whole.

- Children of distant or abandoning parents may have a hard time connecting emotionally to others.

- Controlling parents teach their children that others have no rights.

- Overinvolved parents can make it difficult for their children to develop their own identities.

Some people with BPD have experienced childhood sexual or physical abuse—the most horrific violations of personal limits. The abuse, humiliation, and shame can severely damage personal boundaries. Abused children feel confused about what to let others do to them physically, how to let others treat them emotionally, and how to interact with others in socially appropriate ways.

> Children who experience abuse also learn to deny pain and chaos or accept them as normal and proper.

Adults who were abused as children may protect themselves by building strong walls between themselves and others, or they may withdraw physically or emotionally, rarely sharing their emotions. Others do the opposite, becoming too open. They may involve themselves in sexual relationships with people who don't really care about them.

Children who experience abuse also learn to deny pain and chaos or accept them as normal and proper. They learn that their feelings were wrong or didn't matter. They learn to focus on immediate survival—on not getting abused—and miss out on important developmental stages. As a result, they have problems developing their own identities.

Kamala (BP)

My mother and father physically, sexually, and emotionally abused me. They never loved me or cared about how I felt, so I never had the opportunity to go through the natural process of individuation and separation.

When I became an adult, I walked out into the "real" world looking and sounding fine. But I had no concept of the "other" and no boundaries whatsoever. To my underdeveloped sense of self, people around me were extensions of me. I hated and abused myself, so I hated and abused them.

When I tried to have normal relationships, other people's boundaries were my worst enemy. People with boundaries could say "no." "No" was a certain death; I could feel it in the pit of my stomach. People saw me as demanding, unendingly chaotic, grabbing, controlling, manipulating others. But it was really the cry of an insatiable, terrorized, wounded little girl, still struggling to grow up and survive.

When people don't have healthy limits, they need defenses, which damage intimacy. These defenses can include:

- control

- withdrawal

- blaming

- rationalizing

- intellectualizing

- name calling

- perfectionism

- black-and-white thinking

- threats

- fighting about false issues

- excessive concern for the other

"These are all handy ways to avoid feelings and avoid communication," says Anne Katherine in an interview. "The healthy alternative is to state your true feelings."

Non-BPs can have weak limits, too, of course. However, they may be expressed in a different way. Whereas the person with BPD may refuse to take responsibility for his or her own actions and feelings, non-BPs tend to take too much responsibility for what others say and do. This tendency may come from childhood experiences. As children, some non-BPs were expected to act as emotional or physical caretakers for their parents or others. Frequently, they learned to deny their own needs and take on responsibility for other people's feelings, thoughts, and problems.

"The healthy alternative is to state your true feelings."

John (non-BP)

I was eleven years old when my brother was born. A year later, my twin sisters came along. Money, which had always been tight, became a real problem. When I was in junior high, my job was to come home right after school to look after my siblings and get dinner started. One day, though, I watched the cross-country track team warming up. I wanted to be there, running with them.

But when I asked my parents if I could join, my mother cried and said, "We need you here to look after the kids, John. If I quit my job to watch them, we'll have to move to a cheaper apartment." My father got angry. "You're selfish! Can't you think of anyone else for a change?"

John's parents discouraged him from seeing his needs as separate from theirs. In order to maintain his parents' love, he had to deny his true feelings. And as an adult, he continued to deny his feelings because it felt familiar and safer. John also grew up learning that his feelings didn't count. So when he got into a relationship with a BP as an adult, he had difficulty keeping his limits, which he was not practiced in doing.

Scripts From the Past

Some people with BPD frequently won't accept responsibility, and some non-borderlines accept too much. Unaware that they're replaying painful scripts from the past, the BP tries to persuade the non-BP to become the focus of their pain and rage. Often, non-BPs all-too-willingly oblige.

The "bargain" that the BP and non-BP strike may be rooted in deep, largely unconscious beliefs about what it takes to survive in this world. For the person with BPD, feeling separated from someone else can be frightening. It makes the BP feel rejected, abandoned, and alone. So, consciously or unconsciously, the BP may discourage independence or independent thinking in people close to him or her.

Kamala (BP)

Before I got better, if people didn't have any protection in place for themselves I would aim right at them. Who doesn't want a target that they can sink? But what I was doing, and what a lot of borderlines do, is not a game or a way to get kicks. It's about survival. People who had healthy boundaries in place left me feeling too defective, too out of control, and too vulnerable.

In response, many non-BPs avoid doing anything to provoke a negative reaction from the person with BPD—at least at first. They may worry that if they assert themselves, they'll lose the relationship and be unloved and alone. And the person with BPD, who is taking care of his own pain in the only way he knows how, can be skillful at convincing the non-BP that she is being selfish, irresponsible, or uncaring. Over time, the non-BP may eventually lose sight of just how far she has gone to accommodate the BP's skewed sense of reality.

Pushing the Envelope

Without limits, BPD behavior can get drastically out of control. Some non-BPs interviewed for this book have: willingly not answered their own

> When you set and observe personal limits, you are also benefiting the person in your life with BPD.

work phones because their BP wives were afraid of other women calling; tolerated the BP's multiple affairs, including extramarital liaisons that led to pregnancies and sexually transmitted diseases; or not expressed any needs at all, because to do so would lead to accusations of being "needy and controlling."

Other non-BPs have given up rewarding activities and friendships because of criticism from BPs; lied to friends and family members about the behaviors of those with BPD; tolerated regular physical abuse; gone without sex for more than a decade; not left the house for long periods of time because those with BPD refused to be alone; or allowed those with BPD to be abusive to their children.

You may have let someone violate your personal limits in the past. But that doesn't give the person permission to do it again—not unless you hand it to him or her. First, though, you have to decide what your limits are.

How Limits Help the BP

Setting limits can be frightening at first. So it's crucial to remember that you're not setting them just for your own good. When you set and observe personal limits, you are also benefiting the person in your life with BPD. In fact, when you let the BP violate your boundaries, or do not set any for him or her, you may be making the situation worse. Some non-BPs believe that setting aside all their needs will eventually "fix" the BPs they love. This is not true.

> By setting and observing limits, you are acting as a role model for the person with BPD and others in your home.

George (non-BP)

I really don't care about how Kim treats me. Yes, she's done things that have caused me a lot of pain. But thanks to all I've learned about BPD, I know her suffering is so much greater than mine. I like knowing that I'm making a difference in her life. Isn't that what life's about—helping other people?

George's motivation is commendable. But giving up his own needs will not benefit his wife—or himself—in the long run. If George accepts responsibility for Kim's feelings and behavior, then she won't have to. If she's not held accountable for what she does, she won't have to look at how her behavior affects herself and those around her. And until she is held accountable by others and by herself and decides to change, she won't get better. In fact, she could get worse.

How long will George be able to remain in this relationship with Kim? What is he willing to give up in the long term (friends? security? self-esteem?) to have a relationship with someone who causes him a great deal of pain? Is this the example he wants to set for their children?

If you set and observe reasonable limits, and if you learn how to take care of your own needs and live your own life, chances are much greater that you will be able to stay in a long-term relationship with the BP—and the possibility increases that your relationship will ultimately be happy and successful. By setting and observing limits, you are acting as a role model for the person with BPD and others in your home. Firm, consistent limits on your part will help the person with BPD eventually create limits for himself or herself.

the right to set limits

Often, non-BPs look outside themselves for confirmation that it is okay to set limits in a certain area. They wonder if they have a right to get angry when one of their limits is not observed.

Many people—not just non-BPs—seem to divide their feelings into two groups: justified and unjustified. Let's say that your friend Sue is thirty minutes late for your lunch date. If Sue finally arrives without an explanation and doesn't even apologize, you might call your anger at her justified. But if Sue doesn't show up at all and you find out the next day that this was because she was in a car accident, you might decide that your earlier response was unjustified.

People also spend a great deal of time arguing about who is "right" in how they feel and what they want. When they argue, they endlessly debate whose desires are more "normal." Harriet Goldhor Lerner, in *The Dance of Anger* (1985), explains the fallacy of such thinking:

> Most of us secretly believe that we have the corner on the "truth," and that this would be a much better world if every one else believed and reacted exactly as we do. Married couples and family members are especially prone to behave as if there is one "reality"

that should be agreed upon by all.

But it is our job to state our thoughts and feelings clearly and to make responsible decisions that are congruent with our values and beliefs. It is not our job to make another person think and feel the way we do or the way we want them to. We have to give up the fantasy that we can change or control another person. It is only then that we can reclaim the power that is truly ours—the power to change our own selves and take a new and different action on our own behalf.

Let's go back to the example with Sue. You're angry that she was late and didn't phone or apologize. Her position is that you should have gone ahead and eaten without her, and that if you didn't, then you can only blame yourself for being angry.

It's useless to debate whether you "should" feel angry, because the fact is that you do. It's your job to tell Sue how you feel. It's Sue's job to tell you how she feels. You don't have to—nor should you—feel it necessary to convince Sue that your way of thinking is best. Instead, you simply need to protect yourself in the future now that you know Sue's attitude about tardiness.

"Am I selfish?"

Believing that your own needs are selfish is another common trap that people fall into. Barb, a thirty-two-year-old woman, says, "I'm not sure I can continue trying to please my mother. My every minute is consumed with thoughts of helping her, but every now and then I think, 'Forget it, I can't do any more.' Is this selfish of me?"

Setting and enforcing boundaries is not selfish. It is normal and necessary. Some non-BPs label their behavior "selfish" when they are simply watching out for themselves.

Terrell (non-BP)

When I was a kid, "selfish" was an insult in my home. It was something only "bad" people indulged in. But I learned that it was only when I started taking care of myself that I was really able to care for others.

guidelines for setting limits

In the *Essential Family Guide to Borderline Personality Disorder*, author Randi Kreger (2008) discusses the "Five C's" planning method in the chapter "Set Limits with Love." Following is a brief summary.

Clarify Your Limits

Patricia Evans, in *The Verbally Abusive Relationship: How to Recognize It and How To Respond* (1996), suggests that certain rights are fundamental to relationships, including:

- the right to emotional support, encouragement, and goodwill from the other

- the right to be heard by the other and to be responded to with courtesy and respect

- the right to have your own view even if the other has a different view

- the right to have your feelings and experiences acknowledged as real

- the right to a life free from excessive accusations, blame, criticism, and judgments

- the right to live free from emotional and physical abuse

Asking yourself questions can help you better understand your personal limits:

- What hurts?

- What feels good?

- What are you willing to give up for the relationship?

- What are the things that others do that leave you feeling angry and taken advantage of?

- Are you able to say no to requests without feeling guilty?

- How physically close can you allow others to get?

- At what distance do you begin to feel anxious or uncomfortable?

- Does the BP in your life respect your physical limits?

Don't expect to be able to sit down and answer these questions in one night—or even one month. Setting limits is a lifelong process.

Calculate the Costs

How does *not* having the boundary affect you? Kreger writes, "We are so busy living our day-to-day lives that we don't keep very good track of the things that gnaw at us... [W]e ignore [them] and hope [they] will go away" (Kreger 2008).

> Setting limits is a lifelong process.

Come Up With Consequences

Keeping in mind what not having limits is costing you, think about what you will do when (not if!) your family member plows right through your limits. Make the consequences proportional to the limit.

Create a Consensus

Ideally, the whole family should act in a consistent manner.

Consider Possible Outcomes

Things will get worse before they get better as your family member makes countermoves and tests you to see if you're serious. So prepare for this. If things could become unsafe for either you or your family member, you may need help from a professional.

defuse anger and criticism

Steve (non-BP)

I read a story about a Zen seeker who goes to the master and sits across the table at tea time. The Zen master holds a stick in his hand, and he says, "If you drink your tea, I will hit you with this stick. If you don't drink your tea, I will hit you with this stick." So what do you do? Well, I think I figured it out. Take away the stick.

The depersonalization and detachment techniques outlined in chapter 5 are ways of "taking away the stick." The defusing techniques in this chapter can have the same effect. Practice the skills in this chapter in everyday situations—at first, preferably, with a person who does not have BPD.

Don't worry if you get angry or flustered or if you forget these tools in the heat of a real situation. That's expected. Remember that you're accomplishing something that even trained professionals have difficulty with. Reward yourself for every small step forward.

use a noncombative communication style

The first step of good communicating is to become a good listener. When it is your turn to listen, really listen. Don't think about what you are going to say. Do not become defensive and tune the person out, even if he or she is accusing you of things you never did or said. You'll have the chance to address this later.

Pay attention to the person's words, body language, expressions, and tone of voice. This will help you validate the person's feelings. People with BPD are not always in touch with their own emotions, and by listening closely you may be able to hear beyond the words and detect the feelings that lie beneath the surface.

In *When Words Hurt: How to Keep Criticism from Undermining Your Self-Esteem* (1990), Mary Lynne Heldmann says:

> Listening takes concentration and mindfulness. You must focus only on the speaker and forget about what you want to say. Whether or not you ultimately decide that you agree with your critic's perceptions, listening gives you the opportunity to learn.

Heldmann believes that things that get in the way of listening include preoccupation with your own point, distracting thoughts, deciding that you already know what the other person is going to say, and twisting the speaker's message to fit your expectations. (For more information about mindfulness, see Appendix B.)

Ways to show you are listening include being silent, pausing before speaking, making eye contact (unless this is threatening), physically turning toward the person, uncrossing your arms, and nodding when appropriate.

Paraphrasing and Reflexive Listening

Make "I" Statements. When responding to the BP, make "I" statements, not "you" statements. You can't read anyone else's mind. You may be wrong about the person's intentions and feelings. But you are an expert on yourself. You're on safe ground when you describe your own emotions and motivations and let others do the same.

Let's say that you and your coworker Shelby must both pitch in to answer the phones at work. But it seems like you're carrying more of the load. Shelby takes long lunches. Shelby leaves the office for hours at a time. And when he is there, Shelby asks you to take messages for him because "he's busy."

So you decide to have a little talk with Shelby. Following are examples of "you" statements, which all make assumptions about Shelby's state of mind:

- "You are selfish for pushing this off on me."

- "You take long lunches so you won't have to answer the phone."

- "You must think that you're the only one who's busy around here."

No one likes to be told what their intentions are—least of all someone with BPD. Plus, these kinds of statements invite criticism. What if you're wrong about why Shelby is taking long lunches? Even if you're right, what are the chances that Shelby will agree with your statements about his selfishness and overinflated ego? Remember that feeling invalidated is a key trigger for people with BPD. "I" statements will help avoid this trigger.

Following are sample "I" statements you could use with Shelby. Use a confident voice and physical manner. Do not stammer or act apologetic for having feelings and opinions.

- "I feel like I am answering the phone more often, and this is causing problems for me because I can't get all my work done. Can we sit down and talk about this?"

- "I am having a hard time getting all my work done because I'm answering the phone so often. My understanding is that this is a task we are supposed to split evenly. I'd like to set up a time to talk to you about this."

Generally, "I" statements make people less defensive and more open to exploring a solution to the problem. However, it's possible that the person with BPD will hear a "you" statement even when you're really making an "I" statement. But don't give up. Over time, the person with BPD may begin to hear what you're really saying.

Restate Key Points. It is also helpful when communicating with a BP to restate his or her feelings and main points to show that you are actively hearing the person. This does not mean that you have to agree with what the person is saying. People who work in customer service jobs are often taught that one of the best ways to defuse a customer's anger is to acknowledge that person's feelings. This doesn't mean that the company is admitting fault. It does mean, however, that the company cares that the customer is having a difficult time.

Heldmann suggests paraphrasing, or repeating, the key points of the speaker's statements to show that you want to understand what the person is saying. Develop your own style of doing this so it comes across naturally.

Hold the Interpretation. Be careful not to interpret what the other person is saying. That may only make the other person angry and defensive. Here's the difference between paraphrasing and interpreting:

BP:

"You never call me anymore. I always have to call you. I am really beginning to wonder if you still want to be my friend or if you're going to reject me like everyone else. I'm really hurting bad right now. You're acting just like my ex-boyfriend Rick did when he decided he couldn't cope with a girlfriend who has BPD. You both make me sick. I didn't ask to have this disorder, you know. I hope you both rot in hell."

Non-BP (paraphrasing):

"It sounds like you're really upset because you feel like I haven't called you lately. From what you're saying, it seems like you're worried that I don't want to be friends anymore and that I'm behaving just like Rick did a few weeks ago."

Non-BP (interpreting):

"It sounds like you're mixing me up with Rick and assuming that because he left you, I will too. You must still be hurt over that and taking things out on me [notice interpreting and "you" statement]."

Make Neutral Observations. Reflective listening is another helpful style of communicating where you give the speaker your impression of what he or she is feeling to show you are listening and that you care. Says Heldmann:

> We all have feelings, and there is no point in challenging someone else's feelings or telling the other person not to feel that way. Making a neutral observation about the other person's feelings is, however, a good way to invite someone to open up, to give him or her room. It isn't necessary to be "right" in your statement of what the other person is feeling. Merely making your honest observation is often enough to open the door (Heldmann 1990).

If the other person's feelings are obvious, you may phrase your observation as a statement, such as, "I can see that you're very angry" or "You seem very sad right now." If the feelings are subtle and unstated, it may be better to ask a question, "Are you feeling scared right now that I might want to back out of our marriage?" Avoid excessive probing, though—your goal is to help the other person express his or her feelings, not analyze them.

Heldmann says, "Reflective listening can be difficult if the speaker is criticizing you. But if you can stay calm and in control, the speaker will have let off some steam and will probably feel better. And by allowing him free expression of his feelings, you have communicated your openness" (Heldmann 1990).

BPD-Specific Communication Skills

Some of the following suggestions are adapted from Marsha Linehan's workbook, *Skills Training Manual for Treating Borderline Personality Disorder* (1993b).

- Stay focused on your message.
  While you are talking, the other person may attack or threaten you or try to change the subject. This could be happening for many reasons. For example, the person may be trying to divert you because you are touching on a sensitive area. Ignore the attempts to distract you. Just calmly continue making your point and come back to the other subject later if it is appropriate.

- Simplify.

  When you are communicating about a sensitive issue, or if the person with BPD seems upset, simplify your communication. You and the BP may be feeling such strong emotions that there is little energy left for either of you to do much high-level thinking. Make each sentence short, simple, clear, and direct. Leave no room for misinterpretation.

- Give positive feedback, appropriate to the person and your relationship.

  One BP says, "I try to focus on what is right about me, but most of the time the people in my life keep reminding me 'You're mentally ill; you're borderline.' I am working hard to see the possibilities and a future in which I can be happy and productive. This is not made easier by those who label me and refuse to recognize my individuality and potential to grow."

- Ask questions.

  Turn the problem over to the other person. Ask for alternative solutions. For example, try "What do you think we should do here?" or "I'm not able to say yes, and you seem to really want me to. How can we solve this problem?"

- Be aware of your own voice inflection and nonverbal communication.

  These may communicate as much as, or more than, the words you use. Speak calmly, clearly, and confidently.

> When stating what you want or need, don't let your voice rise at the end as if you were asking a question. This is called "uptalk," and it undermines what you are saying.

Responding to Attacks and Manipulation

Sometimes the responses discussed in the previous section are not appropriate because the BP is "snipping" at you rather than initiating an honest conversation about something you said or did that bothered them. In these types of instances, you may feel attacked, manipulated, or undermined. Examples include:

- "Your sister was always prettier than you."

- "I'd be a better kid if you were a better parent."

- "I see you're going out with your friends again" (said in a disapproving way).

- "That's what you think."

Heldmann (1990) writes that most people respond to criticism with behavior they learned in childhood. She calls this behavior "The Four Don'ts": defend, deny, counterattack, and withdraw. You want to avoid these types of responses.

- Don't defend.
  Trying to prove to others that you really haven't done anything wrong can make you feel foolish, childish, and guilty, even when you haven't made a mistake.

- Don't deny.
  You may use denial because you truly haven't been responsible for whatever it is that you're being accused of. But repeated denial can also make you feel like a child again ("Did not!" "Did too!").

- Don't counterattack.
  You may strike back at the person with BPD to try to win the argument or vent your feelings. But when you do this, you'll fall into the projection and projective identification trap that the BP has unconsciously set for you (see chapter 3).

- Don't withdraw.
  When non-BPs realize that defend, deny, and counterattack don't work, they often withdraw. Some non-BPs clam up completely. Some leave physically. Some learn to dissociate. There is nothing wrong with leaving if you feel attacked. In fact, there are times when it's a good thing to do (see chapter 8). The damage comes from remaining passive and silent, absorbing the other person's criticism while your sense of personal power and self-esteem deteriorate.

defusing techniques

Following are some of Heldmann's better choices for responding. These disarm your critics and enhance and empower you. If you use these suggestions, speak sincerely, naturally, and neutrally. Avoid being flippant or counterattacking. Also, use them cautiously, since you never know how the other person will respond. The same technique, used on two different days, may spark different reactions.

Agree with Part of the Statement

CRITICISM: "I see you're going out with your friends again" (said in a disapproving way).

RESPONSE: "Yes, I am going out."

CRITICISM: "When I was your age, I never would have gone on a date looking like that."

RESPONSE: "No, you probably wouldn't have" (said in an agreeable way).

CRITICISM: "I can't believe you won't let me go out with my friends just because you found some pot in my room. If you weren't my mother, my life would be so much better."

> Speak sincerely, naturally, and neutrally; avoid being flippant or counterattacking.

RESPONSE: "True, I'm not going to let you go out with your friends because you've been smoking pot."

Agree with the Possibility That Your Critic Could Be Right

CRITICISM: "I had an affair. Big deal!"

RESPONSE: "Some people might not think it was a big deal if their husband had a affair. But I'm not one of them."

CRITICISM: "How can you even suggest not inviting Mom to the party? So she acts a little strange, sometimes. She's still your mother!"

RESPONSE: "Yes, she is still my mother. And some people would invite all their relatives, no matter how they act. But I believe that Mom has a choice about how she wants to behave. If she's going to choose to say outrageous things that hurt people's feelings, I don't feel comfortable inviting her."

Recognize That the Critic Has an Opinion

CRITICISM: "Children belong with their mother, not their father. And I know the judge will see it that way too."

RESPONSE: "I can see you have strong opinions about custody. The judge may see it the way you do. Or she may not."

CRITICISM: "If anyone has BPD, it's you, not me."

RESPONSE: "I can see that you disagree with the therapist's opinion that you have BPD."

Use Gentle Humor When Appropriate

CRITICISM: "I can't believe you forgot to buy charcoal. How are we going to grill the fish?"

RESPONSE: "Well, we've always been meaning to try sushi" (said without sarcasm).

Practice defusing responses in less threatening situations first. And no matter what happens, congratulate yourself for your efforts.

In this chapter, we've given you the foundation you'll need to make important changes in your relationship with the BP. In the next chapter, we'll show you how to actually discuss this with the BP in your life. Make sure that you understand the information presented in this chapter thoroughly before you go on.

You should have a clear understanding of the following:

- the factors that can trigger BPD behavior, along with the concept that while you may trigger the behavior, you are not to blame for it

- how the BP in your life may trigger you with fear, obligation, and guilt

- how personal limits (boundaries) help relationships

- the personal limits that you would like the BP to observe

- the futility of discussing your "rights" to set limits—the question is not about "rights" but about your personal feelings about how you want to be treated

- guidelines for good communication

In the next chapter, we will go over how you can begin to effectively assert your needs with the BP in your life.

CHAPTER 7

asserting your needs with confidence and clarity

I told my borderline wife over and over again how much I loved her, that I would never leave her, that she was a beautiful and intelligent person. But it was never enough. If a female salesclerk's fingers brushed mine as she was giving me change, my wife would accuse me of flirting. Trying to fill the emotional black hole inside a BP is like trying to fill the Grand Canyon with a water pistol—except the Grand Canyon has a bottom.

—From the Welcome to Oz
Internet support community

You can respond to someone with BPD in two primary ways: like a sponge or like a mirror. It is common for the same person to react both ways—sometimes absorbing, sometimes reflecting.

stop "sponging" and start "reflecting"

Some non-BPs absorb their BP's projections and soak up their pain and rage (sponging). These non-BPs may be under the illusion that they are helping the BP. But in fact, by not reflecting the BP's painful feelings back to their rightful owner (mirroring), they are rewarding the BP for using these defense mechanisms. This may make it more likely the BP will continue to use them in the future.

> The emptiness belongs to the person with BPD, and the only person who can fill it is the BP.

People who act like sponges say they feel like they are trying to fill a black hole of emptiness inside the BP. But no matter how much love, caring, and devotion they provide, it is never enough. So they blame themselves and work even more frantically. At the same time, the BP feels the terrifying pain of the aching cavity and urges the non-BP to work even harder and faster at filling the hole. If the BP is the acting-out type, she may castigate the non-BP for being lazy or indifferent to her anguish. If the BP acts in, she may tearfully beg the non-BP to help end the suffering.

But it's all a diversion to keep the BP and non-BP from addressing the real issue: the emptiness belongs to the person with BPD, and the only person who can fill it is the BP.

stay focused and observe your limits

Don't get caught up in the borderline's accusations, blaming, impossible demands, and criticism. Instead of soaking up the other person's pain, try to:

- Maintain your own sense of reality despite what the other person says.

- Reflect the pain back to its proper owner—the person with BPD.

- Express confidence that the BP can learn to cope with his or her own feelings.

- Offer your support.

- Make it clear that the BP is the only person who can control his or her feelings and reactions.

- Show by your actions that there are limits to the type of behavior that you will and will not accept.

- Communicate these limits clearly and act on them consistently.

You may also need to take steps to protect yourself or your children—not because you are judging or labeling anyone else's behavior, but because you value yourself and your feelings. These steps might include:

- Remove yourself or your children from an abusive situation.

- Let the BP take responsibility for his or her own actions.

- Assert your own feelings and wishes.

- Disregard name calling or provocative behavior.

- Refuse to speak to an enraged person.

- Decline to let anyone else's public behavior embarrass you.

- Simply say no.

what is your bottom line?

You must know your own bottom line for different types of situations. It may be helpful to think through what you would do if anyone else besides the BP were to act toward you in the same way. For example, what would you do if a stranger in the grocery store began talking to you in the same way the BP in your life does? If you would take steps to stop a stranger from treating you in this way, why not take steps to stop the BP from doing the same? If you're concerned about the BP's behavior toward a child, what would you do if your child's teacher behaved toward your child like the BP does? Which do you believe is more potentially harmful: abuse from a teacher or abuse from a caretaker? Another way to think about these tough issues is to consider what advice you would give to a friend or loved one in your situation. Then ask yourself: is any of this advice applicable to you as well?

Avoid the words "all" or "never." Instead of thinking everything is "this way or that way," come up with three more alternatives.

If you find that you feel helpless in these situations, you may wish to work with a therapist to explore and set personal limits. This should help you in all your relationships—not just the one with the BP.

strategies to help you reflect or "mirror" BPD behavior

There are some specific strategies that you can use while talking to an upset BP that can help you reflect BPD behavior instead of absorbing its affects:

1. **Breathe deeply.** When stressed, people have a tendency to take shorter and shallower breaths. The fight-or-flight reaction kicks in, and it becomes hard to think logically. This can happen to the person with BPD as well. Taking slow, deep breaths can help you settle down and think logically instead of simply reacting emotionally.

2. **Keep seeing shades of gray.** Often, non-BPs pick up the borderline defense mechanism of splitting, or seeing things in black and white. Keep in mind the subtleties inherent in all situations. Don't get drawn into the other person's extreme reactions; trust your instincts and form your own judgments.

3. **Separate your feelings from those of the person with BPD.** In chapter 3, we explained that BPs often use projection to try to get others to feel their feelings for them. You may need to keep checking yourself to determine whose feelings are whose. If you start to feel helpless or angry, is it because the other person is projecting his or her own helplessness or anger onto you?

4. **Validate your own opinions and keep an open mind.** The BP may state "facts" you know to be untrue or may assert opinions that you strongly disagree with. Yet people with BPD can be perceptive. So objectively consider what the BP is saying. If, after reflecting, you still disagree, then remind yourself that your version of reality is equally as valid as anyone else's. Your feelings need to be validated just as much as those of the person with BPD.

5. **Be aware of timing.** There are good and bad times to bring up certain subjects. If, for any reason, the BP is feeling rejected, abandoned, or invalidated by other life events, he or she may react strongly to what

you have to say. So you may want to postpone the conversation for a calmer time.

6. **Be aware of your own moods.** If you are feeling vulnerable, lonely, or sad—or even tired or hungry—you may wish to wait until you are feeling stronger.

Don't get drawn into the other person's extreme reactions; trust your instincts and form your own judgments.

7. **Remember that you have a choice about your feelings.** The choice of how someone feels is largely up to him or her. If the BP says, "You're the worst mother in the world," you can choose to believe it and feel guilty or you can depersonalize these words because you know they're not true.

acknowledge before disputing

People with BPD may unconsciously revise their version of the facts to fit their feelings about a certain situation. While it may be tempting to argue about the facts with a BP, doing so neglects the real root of the issue: the BP's feelings. Consider the following example of how to address the BP's feelings without agreeing with or arguing over his or her version of the facts.

Fact: Cynthia, the mother of a borderline teenager, Jessie, occasionally has a glass of wine at night when a friend comes over for a visit.

Feelings: When Cynthia has friends over, Jessie feels ignored, depressed, and angry.

Jessie's "Facts": Because of shame and splitting, Jessie doesn't take responsibility for her own negative feelings. Instead, she accuses her mom of causing them, actually convincing herself that Cynthia has a drinking problem. To Jessie (and other BPs), if an explanation *feels* right, it *is* right. Facts that don't fit the BP's theories may be denied or ignored.

If Jessie accuses her mom of being an alcoholic and Cynthia immediately begins defending herself (a natural response), Jessie will interpret this to mean, "You are wrong and bad for feeling this way." She will then become even angrier at having her feelings invalidated. Furthermore, the real issue—Jessie's feelings of abandonment—would not be addressed. So nothing would be resolved.

By addressing Jessie's feelings before disagreeing with her facts, Cynthia will be able to share her version of reality at a time when Jessie is more open to hearing it. In the example that follows, notice how Cynthia allows Jessie to fully express her feelings before she presents the facts as she sees them. Cynthia doesn't begin by addressing whether she is or is not an alcoholic, because that would be dealing with facts. In Jessie's borderline world, feelings are all that are important right now.

Jessie: (*angrily*) You've been drinking out here on the porch with your friends for hours. You're just a drunk!

Cynthia: You seem angry and upset.

Jessie: You bet I am! How would you feel if your mother was an alcoholic?

Cynthia: (*sincerely*) I wouldn't like it at all. It would make me feel scared and worried that she wouldn't be able to take care of me. Is that how you feel?

Jessie: I'm just mad! I am calling the child-abuse hotline tomorrow. I'm telling them that my mom lies around the house drunk all day!

Cynthia: No one would want a mom who lies around the house drunk all day. It sounds like that's what you think I do. You have a right to your own feelings and opinions. I see things differently, though, and I also have a right to my feelings and opinions. The way I see things, I am quite busy all day, and I drink pretty infrequently. And when I do, I don't do it to a state of drunkenness. I don't feel drunk right now, and I don't believe I'm acting drunk either.

Jessie: You've had too much to drink. You're acting just like Grandpa when he is drunk. Why do you need to sit around the house with your friends? I hate your friends. They're just a bunch of stuck-up bitches.

Cynthia: I know you don't like my friends. You have a right to your opinions about them. We don't always have to like the same people.

Jessie: I don't see why they have to come over all the time.

Cynthia: I know that it seems to you like they're here all the time. Actually, I haven't seen Ronnie and Marta for several weeks. I have a good time with them, and I also have a good time with you when we go shopping and do stuff together, like yesterday when we went to pick up your dress for the prom and stopped for hamburgers and milk shakes. We had a good time, remember?

Jessie: (*calmer*) Yeah. But I just wish you didn't have to drink with them.

Cynthia: (*understandingly*) Yes, I know you don't like it.

Notice that Cynthia reflects Jessie's feelings without agreeing that drinking is the same as being drunk. Of course it's frustrating to be the subject of wild accusations that don't make any sense. It's not fair. Cynthia may go upstairs and grit her teeth with a knot inside her stomach. She may wish that Jessie lived somewhere else. But she has succeeded in talking with her daughter about the real issue that's upsetting her. In addition, Cynthia has expressed her own opinions and observations without invalidating Jessie's. That's quite an accomplishment.

In these kinds of situations, it's helpful to remember the developmental levels that you learned in chapter 3. Jessie looks like a young adult. She sounds like a young adult. But emotionally, Jessie is a small, vulnerable child, feeling forsaken by a mother whom she believes doesn't know or care she exists. But instead of crying for her mommy the way a toddler would, Jessie shouts and threatens. Her childlike feelings bring about very real adult consequences. Such is the nature of BPD. You may make things harder for yourself if you expect adultlike behavior from someone who is currently incapable of it or if you censor your negative feelings and scold yourself for having them.

Expect the unexpected. Accept your feelings for what they are and know that they're normal for people in your situation. See through the BP's exterior and realize that right now, they may not be capable of what most people would consider "normal" behavior.

---

prepare for the discussion

Talking with the BP about your personal limits is something you can and should prepare for. Following are some tips for communicating about your limits:

- Be specific.
  "I would like you to respect me more" is ambiguous. What exactly is respect, and how do you know when you're getting it? "I would like you to stop blaming me for your physical illnesses," is specific and measurable.

- Communicate one limit at a time.
  The BP may be treating you in a variety of ways you find intolerable. But asking him or her to stop blaming you for all problems, to stop raising his or her voice, and to stop calling you names may be too much for the BP to process all at once. Choose one to start with.

- Begin with the easy stuff.
  Telling someone to stop calling you names may be simpler than asking him or her to stop blaming. You can increase your chances of success—and build your confidence—by starting with something easier.

- Practice with a good friend.
  Role-play the situation with a friend. Do this a couple of times, changing the BP's responses each time. Don't feel you have to rush; take as much time as you like to think and respond, both during the role play and the real event. Things will come together, and it will get easier. It just takes time.

- Think about the rewards.
  Maintaining your personal integrity leads to feelings of strength, self-respect, confidence, hopefulness, and pride.

determine your reality and stick with it

Often, the truth is not so clear cut. Many non-BPs we interviewed told us they had trouble trusting their own perceptions of reality because the BPs in their lives were so convincing in their insistence that they were right and the non-BPs were wrong.

Let's look at Sara, a non-BP, and her borderline mother, Maria. Sara tells Maria that she will no longer stay on the phone when Maria blames and criticizes her. Sara also puts limits on the number of times per week that her mother may call her.

"I would never do that to my mother!" Maria snaps. "How can you refuse to talk to your own mother on the phone? How can you hurt my feelings like this? How could I raise such an ungrateful, selfish daughter?"

Sara's father, George, agrees. He takes Sara aside and says, "That's just how your mother acts, Sara. She can't help it. Be a good daughter and make things right with your mother."

Sara feels confused. Is she being bad and selfish? Does she owe it to her mother to stay on the phone, even if she feels a horrible tightness in her chest when her mother berates her?

When the BP or other people around them make countermoves, you will need to return to the belief that you have a right to all of your opinions, thoughts, and feelings. Good or bad, right or wrong, they are part of you. You also need to keep in mind the personal limits you've set for yourself.

asserting your reality statement

If Sara decides to debate proper phone etiquette with her parents, she will be avoiding the real issue: as an adult, she is responsible for making her own choices about how she wants to be treated.

Sara says, "Dad, I appreciate the fact that you have different beliefs about me asking Mom to observe phone limits. I understand that the two of you might do things differently. But I am not you—I am me. And to respect myself and my own feelings, I need to limit phone calls to once a week and not stay on the phone and listen to criticism and blaming that makes me feel bad."

> When the BP or other people around them make countermoves, you will need to return to the belief that you have a right to all of your opinions, thoughts, and feelings.

Reality statements help you and the BP find the grays in between the black and white of your "truth" and theirs. The two of you may negotiate. For example, Sara and her mother may ultimately agree on phone calls twice a week instead of once a week.

Shift Responsibility Back

Once you've asserted your reality statement, you must shift responsibility for the BP's feelings and actions back to the BP. You can let the BP know that you support him or her, but the BP is ultimately the only person who can make himself or herself feel better.

Even if the BP acknowledges he or she has borderline personality disorder, it is usually unwise to make this shift by bringing up the diagnosis. This may be viewed as dismissive and disrespectful.

> You must shift responsibility for the BP's feelings and actions back to the BP.

Here is a more positive way of shifting, using the example of Sara and her mother: "I understand, Mom, that you disagree with my phone limits. I can see it's upsetting to you that I have feelings about the negative things you say to me when we talk on the phone. Hopefully you will realize that I still want to talk with you, but not if you're criticizing and blaming me. I care about you and I want to hear from you—I just want to be treated with respect."

share the responsibility

Let's say that your borderline daughter is upset with you because you forgot to pick up a book from the library for her as you promised. But her reaction is out of proportion. She insists that you "always" forget these kinds of things, that you must have forgotten because you don't care about her, and that you wish she was dead.

In this instance, you might want to share the responsibility rather than just shift it. As you read this, remember that you've already gone through the process of paying attention, understanding fully, and so on.

Here's what you might say: "I know you feel very hurt and angry that I forgot to pick up the book. And you've said you feel that I 'do this all the time' and that 'this means I don't love you.' I can try to make up for forgetting the book by saying I'm sorry and offering to pick it up tomorrow—which I've done. And I can point out the times I have remembered to do you favors. And I can tell you that I do love you—which I do, very much. That's all I can do. I can't change the past. I can't make you believe that I love you. I know it hurts and you're mad. You can choose to keep thinking these things, or you can choose to try to calm down, accept my apology, and see where we can go from here."

> If you've made a mistake and the BP is upset, you should share the responsibility.

build communication skills

When the BP is not agitated, you can pursue the issues even further than Cynthia was able to do with Jessie and attempt to clarify and even resolve issues. When engaging in this type of discussion with the BP, it is essential that when it is your turn to listen, you really listen. Here are some tips:

- Don't think about what you are going to say.

- Do not become defensive and tune the person out, even if the BP is accusing you of things you never did or said. You'll have the chance to address this later.

- Pay attention to the person's words, body language, expressions, and tone of voice. This will help you validate his or her feelings. People with BPD are not always in touch with their own emotions, and by listening closely, you may be able to hear beyond the words and detect the feelings that lie beneath the surface.

It is also important that you understand fully what the BP is upset about. Sometimes the person with BPD will say something or accuse you of something that makes no sense to you. It's easy to get frustrated and angry, which simply escalates the situation if the BP feels invalidated and misunderstood.

> Remember that you and the BP may be speaking two different languages. Try to stay calm and gently ask the person to clarify what he or she means.

Following is an example of how to go about better understanding the BP, in a conversation between Tara (BP) and Cory (non-BP). No matter how angry or upset Tara gets, Cory remains calm and composed.

Tara: I know you're having an affair.

Cory: (*surprised*) What makes you think that?

Tara:	Because you don't love me anymore, you never loved me, and you want to leave me.
Cory:	Whoa, let's take those one at a time. Why do you doubt my love for you?
Tara:	You don't spend enough time with me, for one thing.
Cory:	You said I don't spend enough time with you. Can you tell me what you mean?
Tara:	You know what I mean!
Cory:	No, I'm not sure I do. But I want to understand. Can you help me?
Tara:	Last Saturday, you went out with your friends to a movie without me.

In this situation, asking Tara to elaborate gave Cory some much-needed information. If he had immediately responded by denying the affair, they probably would have fought at length without uncovering the real issue—Tara's fear of abandonment, sparked by Cory going out with friends.

validate the BP's emotions

If you want the conversation to facilitate change, you must validate the BP's emotions. This combines the paraphrasing and reflective listening skills you learned in chapter 6.

Lynn (BP)

When I finally got counseling, it was like a miracle to be given permission to feel my feelings and to be told those were healthy, intelligent reactions to have, given the situation I had been in. My family had been telling me I shouldn't feel the way I did, which just made me angrier and more upset.

The feelings of the person with BPD may not make sense to you, but they do make sense to the BP. Here are some guidelines for how to address them:

- Don't judge the person's feelings, deny them, trivialize them, or discuss whether or not you think they are "justified."

- Restate the BP's feelings; dig a bit beneath the surface for feelings that may not be as obvious.

- Ask the other person if your perceptions are correct.

- Show the BP you are hearing what he or she is saying.

- Avoid sounding patronizing or condescending, or the BP may get enraged because you don't sound like you are taking his or her concerns seriously.

> If you want the conversation to facilitate change, you must validate the BP's emotions.

This conversation demonstrating validation is a continuation of the one between Tara and Cory:

Tara: Last Saturday, you went out with your friends to a movie without me.

Cory: You sound really upset and angry—both about me going out to the movie and about thinking that I don't love you. I can see that from the tone of your voice and the expression on your face. Tara, I can understand if you thought I didn't love you, that would be upsetting. If that were true, it would be more than upsetting—it would be devastating. Are you feeling hurt and sad right now?

Tara: Yes!

express your reality statements

After you have validated the BP's feelings, assert yourself with "my reality" statements. In this example, Cory's reality is straightforward: He knows that he asked Tara if she wanted to go to the movie, and she refused. And he knows that indeed, he does love her. In this case, he could say, "Tara, it's true that I did go out with friends. You didn't want to go, so I went by myself. I had a good time—I enjoy being with my friends. But that doesn't mean I don't love you—I do, in fact very much."

Some reality statements will be factual (e.g., "When I said that I smelled something burning, I wasn't commenting on your cooking. I was just noticing a burning odor"). Other reality statements will reflect your opinions (e.g., "I don't believe that wanting to see a movie with friends is selfish. I think that even when two people are married, it's good for them both to have other friends and pursue their own interests").

> Resist the temptation to justify, overexplain, or debate. Simply stay focused on your message.

Express your reality statement clearly. The BP may try to argue with you about who is "right" or who is to "blame." Some of these arguments may be illogical; for example, one BP insisted that she was justified in punching and kicking her husband because he had called her "violent." Resist the temptation to justify, overexplain, or debate. Simply stay focused on your message, for example, an appropriate response to an accusation would be: "I understand that you feel this way, but I see it differently." Repeat it as often as is necessary.

ask for change

Once you know what your personal limits are, it's time to communicate these to the BP. But before you do, be clear on what you can reasonably ask for—and what you can't.

It is reasonable to ask the BP to change his behavior. Chances are the BP acts differently with you than he does in front of friends, when out in public, or when at work. If the BP can control his behavior under some circumstances, it's likely he can control it in others.

Of course, people with BPD may need help in order to change their actions. If the BP in your life seeks help, he or she may have a much easier time observing your limits. But as you know, this is a decision people with BPD must make for themselves.

But while it's reasonable to ask someone to change his or her behavior, it isn't reasonable for you to tell someone how he or she should feel. In other words, you can ask the BP not to yell at you, but you can't tell him or her not to be angry. You can request that the BP not call you more than twice a day, but you can't tell him or her not to feel alone and panicky when you're not around. If people with BPD could change their feelings through sheer willpower, they would have done so already!

> While it's reasonable to ask someone to change his or her behavior, it isn't reasonable for you to tell someone how he or she should feel.

In *The Dance of Anger* (1985), Harriet Goldhor Lerner writes:

Most of us want the impossible. We want to control not only our own decisions and choices but also the other person's reactions to them. We not only want to make a change; we want the other person to like the change that we make. We want to move on to a higher level of assertiveness and clarity and then receive praise and reinforcement from those very people who have chosen us for our old familiar ways.

communicate your limits

Pick a good time to talk—a time when both you and the BP are feeling grounded and in good spirits. Many times, when things are going well, non-BPs don't bring up difficult issues because they do not want to spoil the mood. You will need to overcome the urge to leave well enough alone.

BPD researcher Marsha M. Linehan (1993b) has developed a communicating style known as DEAR, which stands for describe, express, assert, and reinforce. Following are each of the steps and how you can use them to explain your personal limits.

> Describe the situation as you see it without exaggerating, making judgments, or explaining how you feel about it.

Describe

Describe the situation as you see it without exaggerating, making judgments, or explaining how you feel about it. Be as objective and as specific as you can. It may help to pretend you are a video camera capturing the action exactly as it happens. Do not use judgmental or loaded words or phrases. Do not claim that you are privy to the person's inner motivations or feelings, although you can say that it "appears as if" the person was upset, angry, and so on.

For example, you can say, "Yesterday, we were driving home from our vacation. Around lunchtime, we began talking about when we were going to stop to eat when you began speaking to me in angry tones that got louder and louder. You seemed to be very upset about something that had happened the day before. After about ten minutes, I asked if we could continue the conversation at another time. Then you continued to yell at me. After several more minutes, I asked again if we could talk about this after we got home. You refused and swore at me and called me names."

Express

Express your feelings or opinions about the situation clearly. Take responsibility for your own feelings; do not say, "You made me feel this way." Instead say, "I felt this way." You may need to do some thinking beforehand to determine your exact emotions.

For example, you can say, "When you were shouting at me, I felt very bad. I was afraid because I didn't know what you might do or say next. I felt helpless because there was no place for me to go because we were in the car. I felt sad because you were angry at me. And when I asked you to stop and you didn't stop, I became mad because you were not responding to me. I also felt concerned because our son was in the back seat, and I was worried about how the argument was affecting him."

> It's very difficult for people with BPD to understand that you can be angry or upset with them and still love them. You may wish to remind the BP that even though something is bothering you, you still care about him or her deeply.

Assert

Assert your limits, making them simple. Again, explain that you've decided on this limit not because it is right, expected, normal, or how the other person "should" act. Instead, you want this because it is your personal preference, it is how you would like to be treated, and it is behavior that makes you comfortable.

For example, you can say, "I do care about your feelings, and I do want to resolve our difficulties. When things get intense and we start yelling at each other, I may need to stop the conversation and return to it later when we have both calmed down. This is something I need to do to make myself feel better."

Again, the BP may try to engage you in a debate about what is right or wrong or who is at fault. Once more, resist the temptation to justify, over-explain, or debate. Listen carefully, then repeat your message: "I hear what you're saying and understand that you think it's all my fault. However, I see things differently. My firm position is that this kind of behavior toward me is unacceptable, and I want it to stop."

Reinforce

Reinforce the benefits of your limits, if appropriate. Explain the positive effects of getting what you need. If appropriate, help the person with BPD see the negative effects of the status quo, too.

> Explain that you set a limit because it is your personal preference; it is how you would like to be treated; and it is behavior that makes you comfortable.

For example, you can say, "When we resume the conversation, I can be in a better position to hear your concerns because I feel calm and more centered. And we will not get bogged down in angry conversations that do not seem to resolve anything and leave us both upset."

Don't threaten your loved one in an attempt to control their behavior. For example, let's say that you and the BP are attending your grandma's eighty-fifth birthday party. The BP sees that everyone else is dressed very nicely and gets mad at you because you dressed informally in shorts and a faded T-shirt. The BP screams at you, calling you a slob in front of everyone. A natural—but unhelpful—response would be to say in an angry tone of voice, "If you don't stop it right now, I'm walking out the door!"

Instead, make it clear that you are not acting against the other person, you are acting for yourself. For example: "I am extremely uncomfortable when you yell at me—especially when other people can hear. It makes me feel angry and helpless. I am asking you to stop this right now, so we can keep on having a good time at the party." You may need to assert your wishes and reinforce the positive consequences (e.g., "we can keep on having a good time") more than once.

Don't threaten your loved one in an attempt to control their behavior. Instead, make it clear that you are not acting against the other person; you are acting for yourself. You may need to assert your wishes and reinforce the positive consequences more than once.

You may also wish to bring up the negative consequences: "If you don't stop this, I am going to have to go somewhere else and take a break." Then do it if the BP still doesn't respond.

Be Prepared for Countermoves

When one person gives up ineffective fighting and makes clear statements about their own needs, desires, and beliefs, the other person usually shifts their behavior in response. This happens in all relationships. But when one of the people has BPD, it is crucial to anticipate the ways in which he or she might react to the changes you are making.

People with BPD try to manage their pain through their interactions with other people. As we have explained, projections, rages, criticism, blaming, and other defense mechanisms may be attempts to get you to feel their pain for them. When you assertively redirect the pain back to the BP so he or she can begin to deal with it, you are breaking a contract that you didn't know you signed. Naturally, the person with BPD will find this distressing. The BP will probably make a countermove. This is an action designed to restore things to the way they were. Countermoves also help people justify their actions, both to themselves and to you. This element is crucial because it seems to make the blackmail acceptable—even noble. Your ability to withstand these countermoves will determine the future course of your relationship.

According to Harriet Lerner (1985), people react to limit setting in three predictable and successive steps: mild disagreement, intense disagreement, and threats. (Be aware that someone with BPD, however, may skip right to threats.) In our discussion of these steps, we will focus on mild and intense disagreement. In chapter 8, we'll discuss unsafe threats.

How to Respond to Mild Disagreement

Following are some countermove tactics discussed by Susan Forward and Donna Frazier in *Emotional Blackmail* (1997):

- **The spin:** The blackmailer tells you that his or her motivations are pure and honorable, while yours are underhanded, unscrupulous, and self-serving. (It's common for non-BPs who set limits to be split into the "bad" person.)

- **Labeling:** The blackmailer calls you names that reinforce his or her "spun" viewpoint and undermine your sense of reality. Many of these are actually projections.

- **Pathologizing:** The blackmailer tries to convince you that you are not just acting bad—you are bad (or sick, messed up, damaged, etc.). The higher the stakes, the more likely it is that this will happen. Many non-BPs told us that the BPs in their lives accused them of having BPD.

- **Enlisting allies:** The blackmailer asks other people to pressure you. This seems to be most common when the BP is a parent. In one case, a borderline mother showed up at her daughter's door with four relatives to back her up.

> People react to limit setting in three predictable and successive steps: mild disagreement, intense disagreement, and threats.

When responding, it's important to stay away from arguments about whether your limits are right or wrong. Here are some sample responses to some typical statements:

BP: You're a bad (selfish, etc.) person for making this request.

Non-BP: I understand you think that I'm a bad person, but I feel good about myself and I'm proud that I respect myself enough to set this limit.

BP: You must hate me.

Non-BP: No, I don't. In fact, I care about you so much that I want to work together to make our relationship better. I also care for and respect myself, which is why I'm bringing this up.

BP: You're manipulative and controlling.

Non-BP: I understand that you think I'm manipulative and controlling. I feel it's your job to make choices and decide how you want to act. And it's my job to think about the things I'm comfortable with and the things I'm not. I've thought about this a great deal, and this is very important to me and my own self-respect.

BP: You shouldn't feel that way.

Non-BP: Perhaps if you were in my position, you wouldn't feel this way. We're two different people and we each have our own beliefs, feelings, and opinions. I am asking you to respect my feelings, even if you don't share them.

BP: You're the child. I'm the parent.

Non-BP: I am your child. And I'm not a little girl (boy) anymore. I'm an adult, and it's time for me to make my own decisions based on my own feelings and beliefs. You may not agree with me, and that's your right. It's my right to act in ways that respect myself.

> Countermoves are not a sign that what you did was wrong or did not work. It means that you have asked the BP to do something difficult.

Other nonargumentative responses include:

- That's your choice.

- I would like to talk about this later when things have calmed down.

- I need to think about this more.

- There are no villains here. We just see things differently.

- I'm not willing to take more than 50 percent of the responsibility.

- I know you don't like this, but it's not negotiable.

- I know you want an answer right now, but I need time to think.

- I won't be put in the middle. You need to work that out with them.

How to Respond to Intense Disagreement

When the BP increases the intensity of his or her responses, the implicit message is: "You are taking away my method of coping, and I cannot stand these feelings—so change back!" If the BP shouted before, he may now rage out of control. If he previously accused you of being selfish, now he will call you the most self-centered, egotistical, and controlling person in the world. If she coped by using violence—either against herself or others—the violence may become more severe. Chapter 8 will address how to protect yourself from violence.

remember countermoves are normal

It is important to remember that countermoves are not a sign that what you did was wrong or did not work. It means that you have asked the BP to do something difficult. Nobody likes doing things that make them uncomfortable.

It is possible that over time, your limit setting will lead to the BP taking a hard look at themselves and deciding to seek help. Or the BP could devalue you, accuse you of abandoning him, and claim that he never wants to see you again. Or he could do both.

Whatever happens, it is possible that it would have happened eventually anyway. Your actions may just have accelerated the pace of things.

persisting

if your limits aren't observed

If you want the BP to change, you have to be willing to make some changes yourself if the person does not observe your limits. Think about the things you can do, not the things you feel you can't do. Be creative. Here are some examples:

- You can change the subject or refuse to discuss the matter.

- You can leave the room or hang up the phone.

- You can change your phone number, get Caller ID, or change the door locks.

- You can go in your room and shut the door.

- You can be with the person only when a third party is present.

- You can refuse to read the person's mail or e-mail. You can change your e-mail address.

- You can stop the car or refuse to drive with the person.

- You can say no firmly without changing your mind.

- You can ask for help from therapists or friends, even if the BP doesn't want you to do so.

- You can call a crisis line or shelter.

- You can call the police and get a restraining order.

- You can stop seeing the person for a while or break off the relationship altogether.

- You can find alternative places for a child to stay (e.g., a group home, with a distant relative, etc.).

- You can take steps to protect children from abusive situations (e.g., taking the kids out when the BP is raging, reporting child abuse, and seeking sole custody).

Naturally, all of these things will be perceived as abandonment by the person with BPD. That's why you may need to gently point out that you are not acting against the person; you are acting for yourself. Explain that your limits are essential to the health of the relationship and that you are asking the BP to observe them so you can be with him or her for a very long time.

consistency is the key

Within reason, we suggest you observe your limits in a gentle way every time—even when you're tired or when you'd rather avoid a fight. You may not always be able to take immediate action, but you can't let unacceptable behavior go unnoticed or you may actually reinforce it. Again, preparation is key. Think through the "what ifs" and decide ahead of time, if you can, what steps you will take in each case.

use caution and seek help

BPD is a serious personality disorder. It is crucial that you seek outside help from a competent mental health professional if you have any reason to believe that the countermoves may be more severe than you can handle alone. Here are some specifics on getting help:

- **Consult a qualified professional.** If children are involved, we strongly suggest that you consult with a qualified mental health professional about how to best protect children under difficult circumstances. It is essential that this person be knowledgeable about both BPD and issues involving children. If this person's recommendations go against your gut instincts, you may wish to get a second opinion. Remember, each person with BPD is different, and each child is different.

- **Seek legal counsel if needed.** If you are a parent who is worried about visitation, custody, or false accusations, we strongly rec-

ommend talking with an attorney who is familiar with personality disorders before you
make any sudden moves. It is crucial that
anyone you consult with is familiar with
these types of situations and has dealt
with them successfully.

> Observe your limits every time—even when you're tired or when you'd rather avoid a fight.

- **Prepare emotionally.** If the BP in your
life is your parent and you were physically or
emotionally abused as a child, we suggest that you
work with a mental health professional to make sure that you are
emotionally ready to ask your parent to observe your limits and
that you are prepared for any response he or she might have.

Whatever your circumstances, you may need a great deal of love, support, and validation as you stand up for yourself. Some of the important people in your life may be able to support you; ask for their help. Other people may disagree with your actions because they feel it threatens their own relationship with the BP, or because it contradicts their own firmly held beliefs about how things should be. This is normal. Acknowledge their right to have their own opinions and express your desire to keep your relationship with them separate from your relationship with the BP.

measure your success by the things you can control

The person with BPD in your life may or may not respond as you would like during any one particular conversation. This is beyond your control. So measure your success by the factors you *can* control. Ask yourself:

- Did you respond as an adult, not as a child?

- Did you act in a way that demonstrates your self-respect?

- Were you clear about your position?

- Did you remain focused, even if the BP tried to draw you off track?

- Did you remain calm and composed?

- Did you refuse to be baited and drawn into a losing argument?

- Were you considerate of the other person's feelings, even if he or she did not give you the same consideration?

- Did you maintain a firm grip on your own reality while maintaining an open mind toward the BP's concerns?

If you can answer yes to any of these questions, pat yourself on the back.

We've covered a great deal in this chapter. Don't try to absorb it all at once. It may seem overwhelming now—but you can change the way you interact with the BP in your life. Just remember these key points:

- You're asserting your limits for the long-term health of the relationship—not just for yourself.

- Be a mirror, not a sponge.

- Stay on track. Don't let the BP distract you from your communication goals.

- Feel good about the steps you've taken. You've come a long way.

In the next chapter, we'll discuss what to do when the BP's behavior becomes unsafe.

CHAPTER 8

creating a safety plan

Yeah, make your arm bleed, bang your forehead on the headboard, harder, harder! Scream at those you love until they slink off terrified of you, the traitors! Burn your fingers on the stove, prick your hand with a pin over and over and over and over. Take those pills. Buy more, stock up. This might just be the big eclipse.

—Melissa Ford Thornton, *Eclipses: Behind the Borderline Personality Disorder*

Rages, physical abuse, self-mutilation, and suicide threats are the most isolating, frightening kinds of behaviors non-BPs must contend with from the BPs in their lives. Sometimes non-BPs also rage, become abusive, or consider suicide. The keys to managing these difficult situations are planning and obtaining outside help. Hopefully your behavior will encourage the BP to get the professional assistance he or she desperately needs.

out-of-control rages

Borderline rages can be terrifying. The BP may be completely out of control, acting on impulse, and heedless of the consequences of his or her behavior.

Karen Ann (BP)

When I am angry, I can't think rationally. I'm possessed by emotions that cause me to act out viciously. The feelings overpower me, and I have to lash out to let them escape. It's an attempt to protect myself, knowing that what I am doing will drive a person further away.

> When someone with BPD is highly emotionally aroused, do not expect them to act in a logical way.

Dick (BP)

When I rage at people, they are no longer real people with real feelings. They become the object of my hatred and the cause of my distress. They are the enemy. I get paranoid and believe they want to hurt me, and I am determined to strike out to prove control over them.

Laura (BP)

I think that borderlines are concerned about only one thing: losing love. When I am cornered, I get very scared, and I show that by getting angry. Anger is easier than fear and makes me feel less vulnerable. I strike before being struck.

rage and logic don't mix

In our interview with clinician Jane Dresser, RN, she said, "When someone with BPD is highly emotionally aroused, do not expect them to act in a logical way. It isn't going to happen, not because they're not willing to, but because they cannot."

Dresser notes that when people who have experienced trauma are emotionally aroused, the logic centers of their brains do not seem to function as well. This finding is not a surprise to most non-BPs, who find reasoning with an enraged BP pointless and frustrating. The time for rational discussion is later, when both you and the BP have calmed down.

Dresser also points out that because some people with BPD do not have the capacity to regulate their emotions, all anger has the same intensity. A mild irritation seems indistinguishable from an impassioned fury. Dresser suggests, "Sometimes it's important to ask the person with BPD, 'On a scale of 1 to 10, how mad are you?'"

what to do

During a rage, the best thing to do is temporarily remove yourself and any children from the situation. In our interview with Margaret Pofahl, ACSW, she suggested that non-BPs say calmly, "I will not discuss this further with you if you continue to yell and scream at me. I am willing to be supportive if you can calmly tell me what it is that you want or need." Note that you've given the BP a choice and made it clear that his or her actions will be responsible for your temporary withdrawal. If the raging continues, immediately retreat to safer ground. Here are some ways to do this:

- Retire to a room that is off limits to everyone else.

- Call a friend and go to his or her house.

- Call a relative and have him or her come to your house.

- Take the kids and go to a movie.

- Put on some headphones and listen to music.

- Take a taxi home.

- Turn on the answering machine or disconnect the phone and take a hot bath.

- Refuse to read the BP's letters or e-mail.

If the BP in your life routinely loses control, think through your options now and make concrete plans for the next time he or she flies into a rage. Make arrangements to leave quickly if you need to: for example, know the location of your purse or wallet, or have the phone number of a friend written near the phone.

Sometimes it can be helpful to ask the person with BPD, "On a scale of 1 to 10, how mad are you?"

what not to do

It's important that you don't continue to ignore or accept rages. Realize that extreme rage directed at you or your children is verbal and emotional abuse. Even if you think you can handle it, over time it can erode your self-esteem and poison the relationship. Seek support immediately.

It is in your own best interest not to respond to borderline anger with rage of your own. Cory F. Newman, Ph.D., who treats many BPs and non-BPs, said during our interview, "This will escalate the pattern of hostility and coercive control. When you fight fire with fire, the problem gets worse and nothing is resolved." Remember that the BP may be trying to provoke you into anger, consciously or unconsciously. If you find yourself losing control, stop and leave the scene. If you do get angry, however, don't be too hard on yourself. It's human nature to want to fight back. Just tell yourself that you'll try to be calmer next time.

"When you fight fire with fire, the problem gets worse and nothing is resolved."

You probably know how to fight back and say things hurtful to the BP, and retaliation can be tempting in the face of a rage. However, try not to push the BP's shame or invalidation buttons if you can help it. Comments like, "You have no right to be angry" can make things worse. You can't control the BP's actions, but with the knowledge that you handled his or her rage well, you can feel good about yourself.

Don't take out your frustration on other people. This is another reason why enduring abusive behavior is a bad idea. When you try to swallow your feelings, they usually ending up surfacing elsewhere in a way you didn't expect. This can leave you even more isolated in the long run.

---

set personal limits around rages

What you learned in the last chapter about setting limits applies when it comes to rages, too. If possible, try the following:

- Discuss your limits with the BP beforehand so the two of you have a shared understanding of what steps you're going to take the next time this happens.

- Set this limit when things are on an even keel, using the communication tools described in the last chapter.

- Assure the BP that if you leave, you will be back.

- Explain that the BP has some control in the matter: If he or she chooses to calm down, you will stay. If the BP chooses to rage at you, you may leave and return when things are calmer. The decision is the BP's.

> If the BP won't seek help or keeps repeating the behavior, you may need to decide what you will and will not accept in the relationship. It's up to you.

Before you implement the plan, review the information in chapter 7 about responding to counter-moves. You must be prepared for any escalation. And remember the importance of consistency. In our interview with therapist Margaret Pofahl she said, "If you say today that you are not going to take angry blaming, then tomorrow you cannot take it, either." Otherwise, you may intermittently reinforce the behavior.

The BP may apologize sincerely—and then repeat the behavior the next time he gets angry. This may be because the BP doesn't have the tools he needs to calm down and choose another course of action. If the BP won't seek help or keeps repeating the behavior, you may need to decide what you will and will not accept in the relationship. It's up to you.

suggestions from people with BPD

Many BPs have given us suggestions to pass on to non-BPs who must bear the brunt of borderline rages. Evaluate these recommendations in light of your own unique circumstances. Because each person and situation is different, these suggestions may or may not work for you. You may wish to discuss them with a therapist.

Chris (BP)

When people try to calm me down, it only makes me feel more angry and invalidated—like they are telling me that I shouldn't feel the way I do. I feel this way even if I intellectually understand that they did not mean things the way I've interpreted them.

Laura (BP)

The only thing that helps me get less angry is when my husband says to me, "I know you are scared, not angry" and gives me a hug. At that moment, my anger melts away and I can feel my fear again. Reacting in anger only makes it worse.

Jean (BP)

If a borderline is being dangerous, others better stay away until things are safe. Let the borderline know that anger is okay and normal but that he or she needs to express it in ways that do not attack another person's self-esteem.

Annie (BP)

When I am angry, the best thing someone can do to make me feel better is to listen to me. A lot of current literature on BPD encourages others to ignore what the borderline is saying because supposedly they do not know what the truth is or they are "manipulative." My anger is caused by others not listening to me or believing me. It makes me feel as if I don't exist.

physical abuse

In our interview with Don Dutton, a psychologist and researcher at the University of British Columbia, he estimated that about 30 percent of men who batter their partners or children have BPD. The percentage of physically abusive women who have BPD is probably much higher.

Take all forms and instances of physical violence very seriously—even if it never happened before and you doubt that it will happen again. The potential is there for the violence to escalate. Children who witness violence experience many of the same ill effects as those who are directly abused. You must be prepared.

Space limitations prevent us from listing all the steps that victims of domestic violence should take to protect themselves and their children. But the information is widely available from shelters, crisis intervention programs, and online. Search under "domestic abuse" or "crisis intervention" in the yellow pages of the phone book or using a search engine. Plan what you will do if the situation arises again. Find out your legal options.

male victims

Family violence is a recognized serious problem for women. The subject of battered men, however, often remains quiet or is viewed as a joke: a cartoon image of a heavyset woman in curlers and a robe wielding a rolling pin while a tiny, undignified man covers his head with his hands and runs away.

But non-BP men have reported being slapped, scratched, punched, clawed, and stabbed with small objects by the BPs in their lives. One man was tripped and fell down a flight of stairs.

Mike (non-BP)

Sometimes when my ex-wife was in a rage, she would claw me, smash me across the side of the head, and punch me in the chest. I'm six feet three inches tall and weigh 215. Yet she could knock the wind out of me. My father taught me not to hit a woman. So what was I supposed to do?

Men who are physically attacked by women may not see themselves as having a problem. More often, they see the woman as the one with the problem. Many men also believe they should suffer in silence to "protect" the abuser or avoid being embarrassed.

When men do realize they need help, they are often unable to find it in a society that does not believe or understand their complaint as credible. This hurts the non-BPs and denies the violent women the opportunity to get help of their own.

If you are a man who is being battered, we have some suggestions for how you can address and cope with the situation:

1. Do not, under any circumstances, hurt the other person. This goes double if you are bigger or stronger than the BP. Maintain control of yourself and remain calm at all times—especially when talking to authorities.

2. Organizations involved with domestic violence vary tremendously as to their attitudes about the physical abuse of men by women. However, reports of battered men are not as uncommon as you might think. (Some come from men battered by other men, usually a gay partner or male relative.) If you're being battered, don't wait for an emergency to discover the attitudes of the police, justice system, and social service agencies in your town. Talk to someone now.

3. Consult with legal resources about documenting the abuse and protecting yourself and your children. Know your legal rights and responsibilities. Don't make assumptions or go on advice from a friend of a friend. Find out the facts and be assertive about using your resources to protect yourself.

self-mutilation

Non-BPs may feel frightened, angry, frustrated, disgusted, and helpless in the face of borderlines who mutilate themselves. Responding to such behavior requires a balancing act: you should be concerned and supportive without unintentionally rewarding the behavior or making the person feel even more ashamed.

what not to do

- Don't take responsibility for someone else's actions. You did not cause this to happen. If an event that involved you preceded the episode, recall the difference between causes and triggers (chapter 5).

- While you can do your best to provide a safe environment, realize that you can't remove every potentially sharp object in the house or watch the BP twenty-four hours a day. As the mother of a borderline teen says, "If my daughter is determined to hurt herself, she will."

- Don't try to be the person's therapist. Leave that to the professionals.

- Don't keep weapons such as guns in the house.

- Don't define the person with BPD in terms of the self-mutilation. It is something the BP does, not something the BP is.

- Don't dwell on the details of self-injury when discussing it with the person. Self-harm can be addictive; you don't want to trigger the behavior. In our interview with Cory F. Newman, Ph.D., he said, "Addictive behaviors can be cued, such as when a cigarette smoker craves a smoke when he hears someone else talking about lighting up. However, this doesn't mean that it's your fault if the person with BPD engages in self-mutilating behavior after you confront them about it. I am merely stating that you have to handle dynamite with great care."

- Don't moralize, preach, or act disgusted. One woman who hurts herself says, "My friends lecture me about self-injury—as if I didn't know it was wrong. What if I were overweight? Would they follow me around and slap my hand every time I reached for a candy bar?"

- Don't say things designed to evoke shame or guilt, such as "How could you!" The BP already feels ashamed.

- Don't make threats in an angry or controlling way ("If you do this again I'm leaving you!"). This may come across as punishing. Even if you choose to set this limit, it should come across as something you are doing for yourself, not something against the other person. For example, during times when you're both calm, you could explain which actions you cannot tolerate and which of these will force you to leave the relationship.

what to do

- If the BP threatens harm to themselves (or others), notify the person's therapist (if they have one) at the earliest possible time. You, the BP, and the therapist may all want to meet to discuss how you will handle self-harm in the future. If this is not possible, seek professional help on your own to discuss how to handle the situation. If you believe that the BP may be a danger to himself or herself or others, the BP may need to be evaluated for hospitalization.

- Remain calm and speak in a calm and matter-of-fact way. In *Lost in the Mirror* (1996), Richard Moskovitz says, "Since self-mutilation usually occurs when the borderline feels out of control; it is important that those around them do not add to the inner chaos with their own panic" (Moskovitz 1996). Moskovitz points out that although the behavior may be shocking and new to you, it may have been going on for a long time.

- Seek appropriate medical treatment for the BP if warranted. You may wish to call medical professionals to obtain their advice. In our interview with Elyce M. Benham, MS, she said, "This also needs to be handled in a supportive, yet composed and factual manner. What I usually say is, 'Let's take care of this' or 'I'm going to take you to the doctor and have them check this out.'"

- Help the BP put together a support team so you don't feel over-burdened and exhausted. The first person should be the BP's therapist, who can work with the BP to reduce self-harm.

- Empathize with and listen to the BP. Show that you are trying to understand how she feels. Ask questions in a concerned way, such as, "How are you feeling?" and "Is there anything I can do?" Don't underestimate the BP's fear, anguish, and inner turmoil. Imagine the worst you have ever felt, and then triple it.

- Emphasize messages of love and acceptance for the person, while making it clear that you wish she would find another way of handling problems. One BP suggests saying, "I feel helpless and angry when you hurt yourself. I want to understand this, even though I don't fully. But I know I don't want you to do this anymore, and if you feel those urges again please talk to me or call your therapist."

- Stress the positive and offer encouragement (e.g., "Before you did this, you went fourteen days without cutting yourself, and I know you can get back on track.").

- Suggest alternatives to self-harm such as squeezing ice, plunging his or her hands into very cold water, heavy exercise, biting into something strongly flavored (hot peppers or unpeeled lemon, lime, or grapefruit), or other activities that produce an intense sensation that is not harmful. However, realize that using these alternatives—or not—is up to the BP.

- Refuse to be put in no-win situations—for example, promising not to seek outside help because the BP is embarrassed and ashamed. This is unfair to you both. If the BP insists that you keep the self-mutilation a secret from people who could help, point out that you are not qualified to handle this on your own.

(See the upcoming section in chapter 8 for no-win situations involving suicide threats.)

> If you start to feel consumed by the BP's behaviors, step back. You may be exaggerating the influence you have on the person's self-mutilating behaviors. The best way to be there to support the BP in the long run is to make sure that, in the short run, you're taking care of yourself.

set personal limits around self-harm

As with rages, planning and setting limits beforehand is the key to reclaiming your own life when someone you care about hurts himself or herself. Make sure that you can follow through with the consequences that you set.

Penny (BP)

My therapist taught me to tell my friends that if I contacted them before doing anything self-destructive, they could talk to me and reassure me if they wanted to do so. But if I contacted them during or after doing something like drinking or cutting, they were to simply say, "Penny, I love you, but I'm absolutely not going to deal with you when you're like this." Then they were to hang up and refuse to accept any contact with me while I was in that condition.

They wouldn't feel pressured to be my caretakers, and so our friendship would have a better chance of surviving because of less stress placed upon it. It also kept my self-destructive behavior from being reinforced, because drinking and cutting would no longer be rewarded with solicitude from my friends. A phone call before the fact has so far been sufficient to prevent relapses. I dread the dial tone and what it represents enough to find other ways of coping. Plus, my friends have said that this contingency plan relieved them considerably because they knew they wouldn't have to feel guilty about abandoning me.

Compared to people with depression or schizophrenia, borderlines are more likely to make nonlethal suicide attempts, constantly think of suicide, and make repeated suicide threats.

Karen (non-BP)

My husband Eric's self-harm used to hurt me more than it hurt him. He sensed this and when nothing else worked and he felt awful and couldn't get what he wanted, he would self-harm. The guilt trips were powerful and controlling my life. But I refused to keep being put in this position. I told him clearly when he was calm that I was not taking responsibility for his actions. If I saw blood, I was calling an ambulance and leaving. If I stayed and soothed him, I would be enabling him. He knows that if he doesn't want to be alone, he has to maintain that boundary. Eric's therapist and I each made separate contracts with him not to self-harm. He values his honor and honesty, so this works.

suicide threats

According to the *DSM-IV-TR* (2004), 8–10 percent of all people with BPD commit suicide. Of the six million people in North America who have the disorder, 180,000 to 600,000 will die by their own hands. This number is equivalent to a Titanic sinking every day for between four months and a year.

According to Beth Brodsky and John Mann (1997), when compared to people with depression or schizophrenia, borderlines are more likely to make nonlethal suicide attempts, constantly think of suicide, and make repeated suicide threats. The presence of other illnesses such as major depression, substance abuse, and eating disorders seems to magnify the likelihood of actual suicide.

> If the BP in your life really wants to die, you need assistance beyond what we can provide in this book. Please seek immediate professional help. You may also wish to call a local crisis line or hospital emergency department and ask for guidance. Then, keep the phone numbers of these people and places right by the phone.

feeling manipulated by suicide threats

When the suicide threats appear to be an attempt to scare you or make you do something you don't want to do, your sympathy and concern may begin to dissolve into anger and resentment. For example, many non-BPs said that when their relationships with the BPs were over, the BPs implied that they would kill themselves if the non-BPs did not return. Non-BPs on the receiving end of these threats feel extremely guilty, confused, and worried.

In their book *Choosing to Live,* Thomas Ellis and Cory Newman (1996) explain:

> The sense of collaboration and togetherness you once had with the suicidal person diminishes, while the uncomfortable power struggle increases. Comments like, "If you really cared whether I lived or died, you would come back to me" and "You make me want to die" have something in common: they make someone else's decision whether to live or die conditional on your response. This is unfair to both parties.

Sometimes the BP will try to make you believe that you are responsible for his or her misery and that you will be to blame if he kills himself. Remind yourself that you are not threatening the other person with homicide—the other person is threatening suicide. You're dealing with someone who needs immediate professional attention much more than he or she needs your capitulation.

what not to do

Newman and Ellis suggest avoiding the following actions with someone threatening suicide:

- Don't fight.
  Don't get into an argument with the BP about whether he or she is serious about wanting to die—even if you're angry and feel like venting. The person may attempt suicide simply to prove you wrong.

- Don't accuse.
  Don't confront the BP and accuse him or her of manipulating you. Again, this may turn into a power struggle. If the BP is asking you to do something that is against your better judgment, follow your instincts. However, if the two of you are in a session with a mental health professional, it can be helpful to talk about how this behavior is making you feel.

- Don't give in to threats.
  Be extremely cautious about relenting just to prove that you really care. Contrary to what an angry, distraught BP may be telling

you, you don't have to prove anything. Say Ellis and Newman, "When you give in to the threats, you will still be angry, the BP will still be at risk for self-harm at any time, and the underlying issues will not have been addressed. Plus, it is likely that the same scenario will repeat itself again and again" (1996).

Express your support and concern for the BP while firmly maintaining your personal limits.

• Seek help for yourself.

If you have a history of complying with demands because you believed that suicide was imminent, we suggest obtaining professional help for one or the both of you before the next crisis occurs.

what to do

Suicide threats that feel manipulative are the ultimate in no-win situations. Whether you comply with the BP's wishes or not, the risks are unacceptable. So, Ellis and Newman say, the best thing to do is to simply refuse to be put in this position, despite the BP's attempts to make you feel responsible for his or her life and death. Just say no, following the guidelines below.

Express your support and concern for the BP while firmly maintaining your personal limits. You can do both, even if the BP thinks otherwise. You can accomplish this with mirroring responses that put the choice of life or death back where it belongs—with the BP—while stating as strongly as possible that you care about the BP and you want them to choose life and seek help.

Ellis and Newman give these sample responses, which we have paraphrased:

In response to, "I'll kill myself if you leave me":

"I'm not breaking up with you to be cruel. I'm very, very sorry that this hurts you. I want what's best for you in the future, but I just can't be part of it. And even if I were to stay with you, that wouldn't solve our problems. For one thing, your life's worth should be based on much more than just being in a relationship with me. Secondly, I know that you know deep inside that our relationship shouldn't be based on me staying because I'm afraid of you dying and you staying because you think you can't live without me. That's not healthy. I care about you. And because I care about you, I want you to live. And I want you to find your own happiness, and your own life's worth, without me."

In response to, "If you really cared whether I lived or died, you would come home every weekend":

"The fact that I love you and am concerned about you is already beyond doubt. I feel like I have proven my love time and time again, and I suspect that even if I did come home every weekend, that wouldn't be enough for you. I want to see you, and I do plan on coming up once a month or so. The fact is that I can't visit every weekend because I have my own family now and my own life to attend to. Perhaps the answer is that you need more things to do on your own, or more friends you can get together with on Saturday and Sunday. You used to talk about a lady you played cards with from your church; have you seen her lately?"

These statements should be accompanied by statements that show that you are taking the threats of suicide very seriously. Show warmth and concern in your voice and actions. For example, you might say, "We have to get you to the hospital. This is a matter of life and death." Show that a serious threat warrants a serious response. In this way, you give appropriate attention to the BP's cry for help while making it clear that you aren't qualified to give the professional help that is necessary in such extreme situations.

In certain circumstances, you may wish to enlist the support of other people in the BP's life: parents, relatives, friends, teachers, and so on. Don't keep this kind of behavior a secret; find other people who are willing to support you and the BP.

---

when the BP is your child

When a child or teenager becomes a danger to themselves or others, parents are often at a loss as to where to turn for help. Believing the child's behavior is always their responsibility, they may tolerate behaviors they would never accept in anyone else. If your child is violent to him- or herself or others, it's

> You have been doing the best you can with the resources available to you.

all right to ask for help from therapists and other outside authorities, family and friends, crisis hotlines, treatment centers, and support groups.

admission to a treatment facility

Admission into a treatment facility is usually voluntary; the child must agree to treatment. However, if professionals believe that the child is a danger to him- or herself or others, they and the police can authorize a legal commitment that can last from twenty-four to seventy-two hours.

Sharon, who manages an Internet support group for parents of children with BPD, says that some parents in her group are concerned that a child may be discharged before the parents feel the situation is really safe. In one instance, a prematurely discharged child took an overdose of pills and ended up back in the hospital. As a last resort, Sharon advises simply refusing to take the child home—even if the hospital protests. This, she feels, gives parents additional time to make other arrangements such as residential care. However, the laws about this vary from state to state, and even from county to county. In some areas, you might be charged with neglect. So seek legal advice from a qualified professional as soon as possible.

police intervention

You can call the police to intervene if the child is becoming violent or threatening. As with most police and 911 calls, response time is based on the perception of immediate risk. If you explain that the threat of harm is clear and present, the response may be quicker.

Sharon suggests telling the police as soon as possible—beforehand, if possible—that the child has a mental disorder. "Otherwise they will assume this is just another rebellious teen getting out of hand," she says.

Christine Adamec, in *How to Live With a Mentally Ill Person: A Handbook of Day-To-Day Strategies* (1996), suggests that you immediately give police a "crisis information" form you have prepared ahead of time and kept in a safe place. You can find a copy of the form in her book. This form consists of:

- a brief medical history

- the diagnosis and its definition

174

- the names of the child's doctors

- names of the medications the child is taking

When the police arrive, they will first contain the situation and then discuss alternatives. If the crisis has passed, no further intervention may be made. If parents choose to press charges, the police will explain the procedure.

According to Sharon, parents in her group who were concerned that the child would become violent after the police departed insisted that the authorities take the child to a safer environment.

If the child's behavior continues to escalate and the child is not agreeable to treatment, he or she may be placed in juvenile detention overnight or be treated as "allegedly mentally ill" and placed under emergency psychiatric detention at the nearest county-operated hospital.

Unsafe behavior is probably the most difficult aspect of caring about someone with BPD. But by planning for it and asking for outside help, you can defuse its power and make it a lot less frightening.

CHAPTER 9

protecting children from BPD behavior

My narcissistic father never spoke to me about my mother's borderline behavior. He emotionally abandoned me when I was still in grade school. I wish he could have shown me unconditional love. I wish he had not left us alone with her and her moods.

I am glad I was born. But sometimes I wish I wasn't. I am still on an emotional roller coaster; I am still that child looking for the unconditional love I never got. It is too late for me, but it is not too late for the other kids of BPs out there.

—Joan (BP)

Many people with BPD never act out in front of their children. Others feel the urge but consciously make an effort to shield their children from their BPD behavior. Indeed, borderlines who are aware of their issues and work to overcome them can be excellent parents—better parents, even, than those who don't have the disorder but aren't as introspective.

However, some people with BPD are unable or unwilling to adjust their behavior around their children. Perhaps they raise their voices more than they should. Or they may experience states of depression that leave them unable to focus on their children as much as they would like to. At the other end of the spectrum, BPD can cause parents to be extremely abusive or neglectful.

As you read this chapter, keep in mind that not all people with BPD act out toward their children. In addition, borderline behaviors directed toward children can vary greatly in their intensity depending on the situation and the person involved.

typical problems with BP parents

As we said in chapter 3, in some ways people with BPD are emotionally and developmentally similar to children. Like children, they:

- may find it difficult to set aside their own needs to focus on those of others.

- may not be able to adequately consider the children's needs, feelings, and wishes.

- may be so preoccupied with their own emotional difficulties that they overlook their children's emotional needs.

- may also resent that the children's needs and feelings are different from their own and may therefore ridicule, invalidate, or dismiss them. If the child is happy when the parent is sad, this may be taken as a sign of disloyalty and insensitivity.

> Borderline behaviors directed toward children can vary greatly in their intensity depending on the situation and the person involved.

problem: difficulty separating relationships with children from problems with others

Some BPs find it difficult to separate their relationships with their children from their problems with others. For example, they may have a hard time acknowledging that their children can have their own positive relationships with people the BP may not like. They may also try to get back at others through their children. Some BPs try to force children to choose between a relationship with them and being true to themselves; for example, they may tell a child he or she is selfish for wanting to spend time with friends.

problem: inconsistent parenting

Other BP parents are inconsistent with their parenting. They may vacillate between over-involvement and neglect, depending upon their moods and emotional needs at the moment. They may only pay attention to the children when the kids are doing something to meet the borderline parents' needs. Some BPs try to cope with their own feelings of inadequacy by demanding that their children be perfect. Children may then feel worthless when something goes wrong. They may also try to get their emotional needs met through the children in ways that are inappropriate (e.g., having a ten-year-old sleep in the same bed or miss a classmate's birthday party because the BP doesn't want to be alone).

> "Many adult children have trouble recalling times when they just felt like fun-loving, silly kids."

problem: unpredictable love

Some BPs alternate between taking too little and too much responsibility. For example, the BP may ignore the negative effects of his or her actions on the children but then feel guilty or depressed when a child gets a bad grade.

Other BPs may treat their children as if they are all good or all bad. This can hurt children's self-esteem and make it difficult for them to develop a consistent sense of self. BP parents may turn their love off and on; their children thus learn not to trust them—and, sometimes, not to trust anyone else either. The BP's behavior may be so unpredictable that the child's focus becomes stabilizing the parent and trying to anticipate the parent's moods and actions—to the detriment of the child's normal development.

Children of parents with BPD are often "parentified," according to Kimberlee Roth and Freda B. Friedman, Ph.D., coauthors of *Surviving A Borderline Parent: How to Heal Childhood Wounds and Build Trust, Boundaries and Self-Esteem:* "[T]hat is, they learn to act as caretaker, perhaps for their siblings or for their parent(s). Many adult children have trouble recalling times when they just felt like fun-loving, silly kids."

problem: feeling threatened by a child's normal behavior

BP parents may feel threatened by children's normal behavior. As children grow and become more independent, the BP may feel abandoned and subsequently become depressed and may rage at the children. The BP may also unconsciously try to increase a child's dependence. Children thus may have a hard time separating from the parent or feeling competent at handling their own lives. When children become angry themselves, the BP may act in invalidating ways or rage back, thereby escalating the situation.

problem: inability to love unconditionally

Some BPs may have a hard time loving their children unconditionally. They may need the children to be perfect to make up for their own feelings of inadequacy. When children disobey, the BP may feel unloved, become angry or depressed, and withdraw his or her own love. Children learn that their parent's love is conditional. BPs may need to believe that their children are stupid, failures, or unattractive so they don't have to be alone with similar feelings about themselves. Also, this conditional love allows the BP to feel more competent than someone else in his or her life.

problem: feeling threatened by child's feelings and opinions

BPs may need their children to be just like them and may feel threatened when children have different feelings and opinions. This parenting trait is common in people with another personality disorder: narcissistic personality disorder. In *Trapped in the Mirror: Adult Children of Narcissists* (1992), Elan Golomb writes:

> The pressure to conform to expectations is like the water in which a fish swims, so relentless and uniform that the child is hardly aware of it. [These children] feel as if they do not have the right to exist. Their selves have been twisted out of their natural shape since any movement toward independence is treated as a betrayal that can cause the parent irreparable harm.

Though Golomb writes about another disorder, the effect on children is similar. Some BPs may be physically or emotionally abusive or neglectful. Their impulsive behavior may threaten the safety or well-being of their children, or they may hit or slap the children. The BP may also call the children damaging names or tell them outright that they are bad and unworthy. This sabotages the child's self-concept, self-esteem, and self-worth. In a less directly abusive but equally damaging way, the BP may be unable or unwilling to protect children from the abuse of others, either because he or she feels that doing so might threaten the BP's relationship with a partner or because the BP is too consumed by his or her own problems. Children often interpret this as a reflection of their own lack of self-worth.

potential consequences of uncontrolled BPD behavior

In our interview with Andrew T. Pickens, MD, he said, "Parents who verbally abuse their children will cause emotional damage. How much damage depends on many factors, such as the inherited temperament of the child, the amount of love and empathy given to the child by other adults, the age of the child (the younger the child, the more vulnerable they are), the intensity of the abuse, and other factors."

Janet R. Johnston, Ph.D., the executive director of the Judith Wallerstein Center for the Family in Transition, said in an interview that the impact of BPD behavior on children varies according to the behavior of the BP parent and the temperament of the child. For example, if a BP parent who primarily acts in is matched with a child who has a "caregiver" personality, the child may feel responsible for keeping the parent alive and happy.

Sela (BP)

My three-year-old, Bess, watched when the ambulance took me away after I had taken too many pills. She plays quietly with her toys when I lie in bed, so depressed that I can barely get up to feed her. When I even pretend to cry, her eyes well up with tears. Her first full sentence was, "Is Mommy okay?" When I am happy and beginning to pull out of the black pit, she grows and changes at lightning speed, as if to make up for the time she has lost trying to cope within my shadow. I am determined to get through this horror so I can be a real mommy, not a burden to her.

181

A primarily acting-out parent combined with a more assertive child could create a unique type of chaos. When one BP mother raged, her son would write phrases like "Shut up!" and "I hate you!" on pieces of paper and throw them at his mother.

Many studies have shown that BPD tends to run in families. Whether the tendency is due to genetics or environmental factors, such as learning behaviors from a parent with a mental illness like BPD—or some combination—is still not fully understood. Children who do not develop BPD themselves may still be at risk for developing BPD-related traits such as:

- difficulties regulating their emotions.

- problems with eating disorders, addictions, and substance abuse.

- tendencies to over-idealize or devalue people.

- feelings of shame, emptiness, and inferiority. This tendency may result from biological factors as well as environmental ones.

A study published in the *Journal of Personality Disorders* found that BPD symptoms in a mother are related to interpersonal and family relationship problems and in a fearful attachment style in the BP's adolescent children, and that these children are at risk of psychological and social problems in settings outside the family, too (Herr, Hammen, and Brennan 2008).

According to MaryBelle Fisher, Ph.D., when a parent has BPD, the normal formation of the child's identity may be derailed. In our interview with Fisher she said, "The child's 'self' becomes a mechanism to regulate the borderline parent rather than an internal, cohesive event."

In *Surviving a Borderline Parent* (2003), Roth and Friedman write:

But who *are* you? As the child of a parent with BPD and/or other emotional and cognitive difficulties, it may be surprisingly difficult to answer this question. You likely didn't have much mirroring, or validation, when you were young, which babies need in order to know where they stand in the world, that their feelings and observations and perceptions are healthy and normal. Without that early mirroring, it was difficult to see yourself, to know yourself... As a child, you wanted to please. If Mommy wanted a little ballerina for a daughter, you tried hard to excel in ballet class,

Children who do not develop BPD themselves may still be at risk for developing BPD-related traits.

even though you really wanted to be out playing kickball or at home reading a book. If Dad needed someone to guide him into the house when he was too drunk to find his way from the garage, you probably associated being a good person with downplaying your own feelings and needs.

Elan Golomb (1992) says:

To grow up as a whole person, children in their formative stages need the experience of genuine acceptance; they have to know they are truly seen and yet are perfect in their parent's eyes; they need to stumble and sometimes fall, only to be greeted by a parent's commiserating smile. Through parental acceptance, children learn that their "is-ness," their essential selves, merit love.

Similarly, Roth and Friedman list "six seeds to grow a healthy child" in *Surviving a Borderline Parent* (2003):

1. support

2. respect and acceptance

3. voice

4. unconditional love and affection

5. consistency

6. security

People with BPD "likely didn't receive them or have them modeled by their own parents when they were children, so they didn't have an appropriate, healthy point of reference. And with a fragile sense of self, they may not have been able to ask for help or accept their own shortcomings," the authors write (Roth and Friedman 2003).

Children with BPD parents may also receive a distorted view of how interpersonal relationships work. For example, one of Fisher's patients feels that he can't become emotionally involved with anyone because he's afraid the other person will take over his life. He stays on the edges of all his relationships, and his emotional life is very sterile.

Children whose borderline parents vacillated between extreme love and raging or abandoning behaviors often have particular difficulty developing trusting relationships with others. They may unconsciously set up tests designed to prove the other person's love, or they may feel abandoned because of small or imagined rejections.

Matthew McKay and his coauthors in *When Anger Hurts Your Kids: A Parent's Guide* (McKay et al. 1996) summarize studies showing that children of angry parents grow up to face more severe problems than those raised in less angry homes. In women, effects include:

- depression

- emotional numbness

- painful yearnings for closeness and intimacy

- a sense of powerlessness

- a limit of achievement in school and work

In men, the primary outcome seems to be difficulty sustaining emotional attachments.

practical suggestions for protecting children

Most BPD parents love their children very much and worry about the effects of their borderline behaviors. Many BPs told us that the knowledge that they could be harming their children gave them the courage and determination to recover from BPD. If the BP in your life has a similar attitude, then it will be easier to be supportive, set limits, and help the BP in his or her efforts to improve parenting skills.

However, if the BP refuses to admit that his or her behavior is abusive and damaging to the children, or if he or she is unwilling to change, then you may wish to take a more assertive role. Keep in mind that while borderline behavior can be difficult for adults to cope with, it is much harder for children. They have no sense of perspective, little experience, and little or no intellectual understanding of BPD. Furthermore, they are dependent on their borderline parents to meet their most basic physical and emotional needs.

Children whose borderline parents vacillated between extreme love and raging or abandoning behaviors often have particular difficulty developing trusting relationships with others.

Your ability to shield children from these behaviors will depend on many factors, including your legal and emotional relationship to the child, the nature of your relationship with the BP in your life, the laws in your locality, and your willingness and ability to set limits. In general, however, the closer you are to the BP and the children, the greater an impact you can have—and the greater your responsibility. Following are some suggestions.

> Keep in mind that while borderline behavior can be difficult for adults to cope with, it is much harder for children.

determine your priorities

Some non-BPs don't take action because they fear harming their own relationship with the BP. They're afraid that if they set limits regarding children, the BP will rage at them, belittle them, or cut them out of their life.

Only you can decide what risks you can afford to take. Whatever you decide, you must be able to live with the long-term consequences.

> Be honest with yourself; don't downplay or explain away the negative effects of the BP's behavior toward the children. One non-BP justified his inaction by telling himself that his children would learn a valuable lesson from their stepmother's rages: that the world can be a bad place. These justifications may make things easier on the non-BP, but they do nothing to shield children.

set a good example

Children mostly learn by observation. What you do is more important than what you say. That's why mentors and role models "can play a large role in modeling healthy behavior, providing insight into a parent's emotional challenges or simply removing a child periodically from a dysfunctional home," write Roth and Friedman in *Surviving a Borderline Parent* (2003).

Watching you put the steps discussed in this book into practice is also a powerful way for children to learn the basics of detachment, self-care, limit setting, and so forth. Of course, the opposite is also true: if you model less-healthy coping mechanisms, they may learn those as well.

Sam, for example, was embarrassed when his children witnessed fights between him and his borderline wife. He mistakenly believed that his wife's behaviors reflected negatively on him. So he did everything he could to keep the peace—including allowing her to be verbally abusive. If he protested, his wife would call him names and make angry accusations. When this happened in front of the children, he felt ashamed.

> Children mostly learn by observation. What you do is more important than what you say.

Sam's intent was to be kind and responsible. But his children learned that when their mom acted out, it was their job to absorb it. They began to believe that she must be right about what she was saying, because if she were wrong, they believed their dad would say so.

If Sam had used limit-setting and mirroring techniques and defused the situation, while simultaneously keeping his limits in place, the children could have learned an important lesson: although their mom acted in unhealthy ways sometimes, she was responsible for her own behavior.

We have two additional ideas for demonstrating healthy behavior in front of children:

- First, make sure that you hold to your limits in front of the children. Explain, "Mommies sometimes get mad, and it's okay to be mad. But it wasn't okay for Mommy to scream at Daddy."

- Second, if the BP is often unpredictably moody, don't let his or her moods affect everyone else or spoil the children's plans. Show children that it's all right to be joyful and have fun even when a parent is feeling down. Try not to cancel fun activities with your kids when your BP partner is feeling upset.

enlist the support of the BP

Janet Johnston and Vivienne Roseby, in *In the Name of the Child: A Developmental Approach to Understanding and Helping Children of Conflicted and Violent Divorce* (1997), say that people with BPD want to feel support, caring, and acknowledgment that they try their best. But even if you couch your criticisms and suggestions in a supportive way, whatever you say may be interpreted as devastating criticism.

Johnston has three suggestions for overcoming this:

1. Appeal to the BP's natural inclination to want the very best for their children. In other words, don't imply that the BP's parenting may be poor. Simply point out that certain actions are good for kids and some are potentially damaging.

2. Emphasize that parenting is the toughest job there is and that all parents need some help now and then.

3. If the BP had an unhappy childhood, appeal to the BP's desire to give his or her own children a better experience.

MaryBelle Fisher, Ph.D., advises approaching the BP when he or she is calm and starting out by acknowledging the BP's genuine love for and dedication to their children: "Build an alliance with the person by emphasizing the positives and the areas in which you agree. Appeal to their sense of fairness. Don't blame, shame, or attack, which simply makes people defensive."

Two examples of shaming phrases are, "What's the matter with you?" and "How could you do that?" Instead, you might say something like: "It's so hard to bring up kids these days, and I know you want the best for Tim. But we just can't ignore that you seem to be losing control with him sometimes. I can certainly understand what a handful he is after you've come home from a long day at work. And I know you've been under a lot of stress lately. But the other day it looked like you were about to hit him, and I'm very concerned about that. We need to figure out a strategy that allows you to do something differently when you're losing it—perhaps call someone or go somewhere. A lot of people find it helpful to get some outside advice from a counselor about how to make things work out better."

Assist the person with BPD in obtaining help and building a network of support. Offer positive feedback and constructive comments rather than criticism and blame. Fisher says, "Tactfully work with the BP parent so [he or she doesn't] become alienated. There's a tendency for people to close ranks and think, 'Mom's the problem,' and leave it at that. Instead, say, 'Mom's the problem, but how do we maintain respect for her and the integrity of the family?'"

Ask the BP how and when he or she would like feedback about parenting. Above all, try to enlist the BP's support in helping the children adapt to having a parent who loves them but sometimes can't regulate his or her own emotions.

strengthen your own relationship with the children

Whether you're a parent, family member, or a friend of the family, you can make a big difference simply by increasing the amount of quality time you spend with the children.

Ask the children questions about what's going on in their lives. Be involved. Give them lots of hugs—even the older ones, if they let you. Consistently show them love and affection.

If appropriate, try to subtly counteract the types of behaviors that concern you. For example, twenty-seven-year-old Lisa was concerned that her boyfriend's daughter didn't have enough privacy at home. At the time, the ten-year-old girl, Stephanie, was sleeping in the same bed as her mother, who had custody. Whenever Lisa was with her boyfriend and Stephanie was visiting, Lisa would take special care to respect Stephanie's boundaries and give her as much privacy as possible. She also spent time developing a trusting relationship with the girl. Eventually, Stephanie insisted on having her own space at home.

Listen to the children nonjudgmentally. Help them trust their own perceptions. Encourage them to talk about their feelings, which may range from grief to rage. They may even be angry at you—perhaps because it feels safer than being angry at the BP. Let them know that their feelings are normal. Be as consistent as you can. Keep your promises. Let the children know they can count on you. Encourage them to call you when they need to and let them visit as often as feels comfortable for you.

Encourage other adult relatives to develop relationships with the children as well. Grandparents, aunts, uncles, in-laws, and friends of the family can all make a real difference in children's lives. Everyone involved should make it clear that they are not taking sides, but they are offering their love and support to both parent and child.

---

encourage independent thinking and new experiences

Children who feel dependent on the BP parent can benefit from interaction with other parents and children. Provide experiences without the BP parent and reward children's natural curiosity and sense of adventure. Encourage kids to follow their own interests and dreams.

In our interview with Fisher she said, "Take care not to wrench the child from the BPD parent. If Janey doesn't want to go somewhere without Mommy for several hours, don't force it. But you might take Janey on a short walk and point out that Mommy's going to be there when she gets back."

If you are a non-BP parent, and the BP parent objects to the child's independence, you may need to set some limits: "Hanna really is old enough to go on a sleepover at her friend's house. I know that this upsets you, but I feel very strongly that we need to encourage her normal friendships with other children. I gave her permission, and she is going to go. Maybe the two of us can go out to dinner and a movie that night."

Help children trust their own perceptions.

help children depersonalize the BP's behavior

Most children believe that everything is their fault. So you'll need to help them depersonalize the BP's behavior—especially if the BP outwardly blames the children.

Rachel Reiland is the author of the book *Get Me Out of Here: My Recovery from Borderline Personality Disorder* (2004). Here, she explains how her husband, Tim, helped their children depersonalize the disorder.

He would tell our kids, "Mommy is sick. Not the kind of sick that makes your throat or tummy hurt, but the kind of sick that makes you very, very sad. Mommy was in the hospital because there was a special doctor to work with this kind of sickness, a doctor who would help Mommy get better and not cry so much or get so mad. Mommy didn't get so mad or cry because of anything you've done, kids, but because she is sick. Mommy loves you so much, and you two make her so happy that you are one of the biggest reasons she can smile or laugh at all." He said this over and over again. And it really made a difference—you could see the relief in their eyes.

189

Jennifer (non-BP)

When my BP husband yelled at our children for ten minutes for disturbing him when he was reading the newspaper, I told the kids: "I know that Dad is upset because of what you did. But understand that Dad is really upset about more than that. We can tell by the way he's reacting so strongly. He could have asked you quietly to talk to him later, but instead he got really excited and yelled. That's just way out of proportion to what you did. Even though Daddy is grown up, sometimes he loses control. Remember when you got really upset yesterday when I said you couldn't have candy at the grocery store? You started to cry and you couldn't stop, and Mommy had to calm you down. Daddy's reaction is kind of like that. But how he acts is his responsibility; you aren't to blame.

Older children, of course, may understand this intuitively. However, even if a child realizes intellectually that the BPD parent's behavior is not his or her fault, the child may still feel responsible on some level. Your own close relationship with the child is your best guide to helping him or her understand the BP's behavior and handle his or her own feelings.

set limits with the BP concerning children

Rachel Reiland (BP)

Tim set firm limits with me regarding the children. In the worst of times, there were out-of-control episodes of rage and hysterics. Tim knew my actions scared the hell out of our kids. So he'd pull me aside and let me know, quite firmly, that the kids were listening and scared by it. "You're not going to put the kids through this," he would say. "You're out of control. Why don't you just go upstairs?" I almost always did. And the few times I didn't, he'd find a place to take the kids until things calmed down.

Like most borderlines, I had moments of control and moments of loss of control. My husband's firm reminders were not just limits but reality checks, pulling me out of childish regression long enough to realize that I had adult responsibilities and that my behavior could have an impact on my kids. It might not have been enough to get me to snap to and think rationally, but it was enough to get me to take it elsewhere.

Some parents with BPD, however, will not be as agreeable. When one father came home and discovered that his wife had just hit their son on the head and called him a disparaging and inappropriate name, he soothed his sobbing son and took his wife out to their planned dinner. As they ate and drank, he gently suggested that hitting and name calling were not the best ways for her to express her frustration. The mother agreed, but excused her behavior by saying, "I had a head-ache." The father then felt frustrated that his wife didn't understand the seriousness of the problem and was shrugging off responsibility for her actions.

Children are unable to set limits for themselves; therefore you will need to do it for them.

There are times when making gentle suggestions to the BP is the best course of action. This was not one of them. In this case, the father could have postponed the dinner and addressed the problem on the spot, explaining the damage that her behavior could do to their son, insisting that this never happen again, and working with the mother to help her find other ways to cope with her frustrations.

Take all physical and emotional abuse of children very seriously the first time you see or hear of it. Ignoring it may give the BP permission to do it again. And once you set limits regarding the children, observe them consistently.

seek therapy for the children

Children can benefit tremendously from working with a therapist who is experienced in treating people with BPD and their families. Signs that chil-dren may benefit from therapy include the following:

- **Difficulty coping with painful feelings:** Intense or long-last-ing feelings of sadness or other distressing emotions; recurring thoughts of harming themselves, others, or animals.

- **Self-defeating behaviors:** These include actions that lead to problems at home, at school, or with friendships (e.g., substance abuse, fighting, unusually poor grades, and other unmanageable behavior). In younger children, signs may include frequent, unexplain-able temper tantrums or persistent disobedience or aggression.

Take all physical and emotional abuse of children very seriously the first time you see or hear of it. Ignoring it may give the BP permission to do it again.

- **Unexplained physical problems:** Marked change in sleeping or eating habits; hyperactivity.

To find a child therapist, ask your pediatrician for a referral or call a local helpline or the National Alliance on Mental Illness. Interview clinicians by phone or in person to make sure you feel confident in them.

remove children from abusive situations

You may need to take the children and withdraw when situations become unsafe. Before you retreat, ask the BP to speak with you out of earshot of the children. Like Tim in the preceding example, point out that children should not be exposed to this behavior and offer to discuss the situation later, just the two of you. Or offer to take the kids elsewhere to give your partner some time to calm down.

Remove the Child from the Situation

If the BP remains out of control, take the kids shopping, out for ice cream, over to a relative's house, to a park, to the movies, to a children's museum, to the playground, to the zoo, and so on. If the BP frequently acts out in front of the kids, you may wish to prepare ahead of time by generating a list of things to do and places to go, keeping a few of the children's things packed and ready to go, and/or making arrangements with friends or relatives to be "on call" to help.

Involve Children in Activities

When children are older, help them become involved with rewarding after-school activities. This accomplishes four things:

1. It minimizes the children's exposure to the behaviors.

2. It boosts their confidence and self-esteem.

3. It puts them in contact with other caring adults.

4. It takes some of the pressure off you.

If You Seek a Divorce

If you have decided to seek a divorce from your BPD spouse, you may be worried that you won't be there to run interference if the BP becomes abusive. This fear is much more common among men than women—and justifiably so.

Men who sought custody told us they faced three major obstacles:

1. The court system is often biased in favor of mothers. This is chang-
    ing, albeit slowly.

2. The court system, by and large, is unconcerned with the type of emo-
    tional abuse we've been discussing in this chapter. Judges, lawyers,
    and activists tell us that while physical abuse can be verified and
    measured in court, emotional abuse cannot. Judges know that
    parents battling for custody often make false or exaggerated claims.
    So unless you have expert testimony (which can be expensive) or
    credible witnesses, judges may discount or ignore even what you
    believe to be extreme emotional abuse.

3. Some borderline soon-to-be-ex-wives, frantic at the prospect of
    losing custody and furious at their husbands for abandoning them,
    engage in dishonest tactics to discredit their spouses. Their strategies
    included denying visitation, filing for restraining orders, and making
    false accusations of sexual abuse of the children.

For the sake of your children and yourself, if you are a man seeking
custody, it is absolutely critical that you obtain legal help as soon as possible
from an attorney who has much experience with issues surrounding men and
custody, as well as with dealing with the kind of tactics we've just described.

As an attorney, mediator, and therapist, William A. Eddy has an international reputation as an expert in legal disputes with high-conflict personalities—especially those with borderline and narcissistic personality disorders.
His book *Splitting: Protecting Yourself While Divorcing a Borderline or Narcissist*
(2004) reveals how to find such an attorney—and much more—in sections
on Preparing For Court, the Court Process, and Special Issues. (*Splitting* is
only available from www.BPDCentral.com.)

Eddy says, "Managing high-conflict people usually involves using skills
[that] are the opposite of what one feels like doing. Learning these skills takes
time and practice but can make an amazing difference in resolving, managing,
and containing high-conflict disputes" (2003).

Eddy's main message in the book, as well as an accompanying CD, is
that the divorce process sets the stage for the non-borderline's relationship
with his or her child post-divorce, and the key is what he calls the "assertive
approach": one that is sensitive without being passive and persistent without
being aggressive.

When people go to court, says Eddy, the judicial system can actually encourage splitting. "When people go into court, they enter an adversarial decision-making system that is splitting people into 'all good' or 'all bad'.... This reinforcement of splitting can be extremely threatening to the fragile identity and embedded insecurities of [a BP]. It allows their daily exaggerations and fears to be taken seriously and provides them a forum for putting all of the blame on the 'bad spouse'" (Eddy 2003).

The assertive approach contains five tenets:

1. **Think strategically, not reactively.** Stop and think when you are angry. Don't act impulsively.

2. **Choose your battles.** Talk to your attorney about which issues need a response and which don't. Some provocative letters, for example, often don't need a response.

3. **Don't make yourself a target.** When in court, expect that innocent things you've said and done may be twisted for adversarial purposes. Keep your composure.

4. **Be very honest.** Things that are half-true are harder to deny than statements you can prove to be totally false. You need that credibility to counter emotional blaming.

5. **Gather evidence that shows the true nature of your spouse's behavior patterns.** Some of the most useful evidence may appear during the actual court case.

talking to younger children

Johnston and Roseby (1997) advise fathers of children aged four to six to simply give the children good, positive messages like, "That's not true. Daddy loves you very much no matter what anybody says." She advises, "Don't worry about undoing what their mother is saying; they're too young to understand motivation and they can only hold one set of information in their minds at a time."

talking to older children

When the children are older—aged eight to ten—they have the ability to sort out different perspectives. Your goal is not to put the children in the

middle by telling them "your side of the story," but to give them factual information that will gently guide them to believe the truth. Remind them of all
the loving things you've done together, using concrete examples from the
recent past. Help them explore their feelings and assure them of your love.
Whatever you say, do not denigrate the other parent.

Here is an example of what you might tell a young child. The central
message to a teen will be the same, but the language you use will be
different:

> "You know, divorce is a very hard on moms and dads. When people
> break up, everyone's feelings get hurt. And I think that right now
> Mommy is very mad at Daddy. And when your mom is mad, she
> tends to think very bad things about people. Remember the time
> that I came home late on your birthday? Your mommy told you that
> I was out with my friends, and when I came home, you found out
> that a nail punctured my tire. That night, I gave you a basketball for
> a present and we went to the playground and played and had a lot of
> fun. I loved you back then, and I love you today, and I will always
> love you, no matter what anybody tells you. And if you feel scared,
> call me up right away, and I will give you a big hug over the phone,
> day or night."

Abe (non-BP)

*A few weeks ago I was on vacation with my three kids (without my wife). I told
them that they may have heard bad things about me from their mother. I told
them that they didn't have to believe what she says—that they
can believe what they feel or see is true. I also told them
that I wouldn't force them to see things my wife's way or
my way—that they get to decide on their own what is
true. And if they decide to have an opinion that's different from mine, I will still love them and I won't get mad
at them. I could tell that this really helped my kids a lot.*

Whatever you
say, do not
denigrate the
other parent.

for those considering having children

In this chapter, we've provided a variety of suggestions for protecting children from borderline behavior. We would like to close with this thought: if
you and the BP in your life don't have children but are considering doing so,

we suggest postponing having a family until the BP is well into his or her recovery.

Here's why: having their emotions invalidated is one of the biggest triggers for people with BPD (chapter 6). Yet children constantly invalidate their parents—it's what being a child is all about.

When parents set necessary rules and boundaries, children don't thank their parents for providing guidelines. They cry, scream, and may shout, "You're the worst parent in the world!" When parents feel hassled and ask their children to give them some peace and quiet, children may instead demand that the parent read them a book or take them to the mall.

> If you and the BP in your life don't have children but are considering doing so, we suggest postponing having a family until the BP is well into his or her recovery.

Just when parents want closeness with their children, the children may decide to assert their independence. Parents may teach their children certain values that their children choose to reject. And children usually don't appreciate the sacrifices their parents make for a long time—often not until they're grown and have children of their own.

Parenting is the toughest job in the world. Constant invalidation is part of it. Make sure that you do what's best in the long term for you, the BP, and any children you might bring into the world.

PART 3

resolving
special issues

CHAPTER 10

waiting for the next shoe to drop: your borderline child

sharon and tom's story

Sharon and Tom are the parents of two teenagers, Amy and Kim. Amy was diagnosed with BPD at age fourteen, a year after she had sex with several men at a party and tried to hire gang members to kill her parents. The day Sharon learned of the plot, she had Amy admitted to a psychiatric facility. Says Sharon, "Amy tells us that had we not hospitalized her, three days later we would have been dead."

getting the diagnosis

In the hospital, psychiatrists diagnosed Amy with bipolar disorder. A year later, they changed the diagnosis to BPD when the medication proved ineffective and Amy began mutilating herself with a razor blade. At the time, Amy met each of the nine criteria for BPD.

During the years that followed, Sharon and Tom lived from crisis to crisis. When things seemed to be going well, Amy would do something to shatter the calm. "We were always waiting for the other shoe to drop," says Sharon. "And sometimes, it was a big, heavy boot." Tom's hobby was listening to a police scanner; one evening he heard an ambulance being dispatched to his address. In her room upstairs, Amy had taken a handful of pills, panicked, and called a suicide hotline.

parenting challenges

Aside from running their printing business and trying to pay more attention to their non-BP daughter, Kim, Tom and Sharon's main challenge was helping Amy cope with depression, overeating, and social problems while surviving the fallout from her lies and distortions. Once, Amy spread rumors about a popular girl at school being pregnant; another time she told an African American printing customer that her family didn't like his kind. At one point, authorities were going to remove Amy and Kim from the household for supposed neglect; Kim finally convinced them that Amy's accusations were false.

life today

Amy, now eighteen, is attending college and living on her own, close to her family. She has a part-time job and receives financial assistance from her parents. She believes she has become more stable because of the support of her family, the proper medications, and successes at school and work, which boosted her self-esteem. "I wasn't ready to work at therapy until recently," Amy says. "I finally realized that seeing a therapist was nothing to be ashamed of, since people who don't have BPD see counselors, too."

Today, Sharon and Amy have a very close relationship. When we asked Sharon how she was able to put aside the past, she simply said, "That's why they call it unconditional love." She says, "The pain of this mental illness is the worst pain any of us have ever felt. We live with it twenty-four hours a day, seven days a week. There is no way to explain the hell it was for Kim growing up, or how hard it was for my family to watch Amy hurt me to the core. But our determination to get through this with all the love and support we can muster is what will make it possible for Amy to find her little niche and happiness in the world."

helping other parents of children with BPD

As a result of her experiences, Sharon formed an online support group for parents of borderline children of any age. The group is called NUTS, an acronym for parents Needing Understanding, Tenderness, and Support to help their child with Borderline Personality Disorder (www.parent2parent bpd.org/).

Like Amy, the children of the NUTS parents show unmistakable signs of BPD. Yet most of the parents spent years playing diagnostic eeny meeny miney mo, seeing one specialist after another and getting one diagnosis after another.

can children really have BPD?

At the heart of the problem is this contentious question: can children be diagnosed with BPD? Clinicians who say no believe that an individual's personality fluctuates during childhood and is not formed until late adolescence. Part of the definition of BPD, they point out, is that the behavior is pervasive, persistent, and unlikely to change. Since a child's personality is still developing, these professionals argue that children can't be borderline.

Other clinicians disagree. They believe that the emotional and behavioral problems associated with personality development are clearly present early in life and are often evident for one or two years before help is sought. This, they believe, demonstrates "persistence" and "pervasiveness."

To resolve this debate, the *DSM-IV-TR* (2004) provided new guidelines for diagnosing BPD in people younger than eighteen. It states that children can be diagnosed with BPD as long as:

1. the borderline traits have persisted for at least one year; and

2. the behavior is not better accounted for by either a normal developmental stage, the effects of substance abuse, or a more transient condition, such as depression or an eating disorder.

Many professionals are still reluctant to diagnose a child or adolescent with BPD, because patients with the disorder are often labeled and stigmatized by the mental health system. However, the National Education Alliance for Borderline Personality Disorder recommends that children with borderline behavior get help right away.

For more information about children with BPD, including obtaining a diagnosis and treatment plan for your child, see *The Essential Family Guide to Borderline Personality Disorder* by Randi Kreger, the coauthor of this book.

An inaccurate diagnosis often serves to deprive the child of appropriate therapy and medication.

adoption and the incidence of BPD

About 20 percent of the parents in NUTS adopted their children. Psychiatrist Richard Moskovitz, in *Lost in the Mirror* (1996), has noticed from his own practice that adoptees make up a significant portion of adults with BPD and adolescents with borderline tendencies. He believes this may be so for the reasons listed below. Keep in mind that these represent Dr. Moskovitz's professional opinions—not necessarily the results of research.

early separation and loss

Some states require a delay in the adoption process in order to protect the rights of the child's biological parents. During the waiting period, infants may be placed with foster parents for weeks, or even months, until the adoption is final. The experience of being torn from their very early caretakers could interfere with the infant's capacity to develop basic trust.

identity issues

Regardless of the circumstances that led to their adoption, many adoptees struggle at some point in their lives with concerns about rejection, which are in turn connected with feelings of defectiveness. These may occur despite the best efforts of many adoptive families to help their children feel chosen and cherished.

inherited temperament

While many scenarios may lead to adoption, a common one is accidental pregnancy. Moskovitz says, "We might expect this to occur most frequently among people who tend to be impulsive and take risks. If this were true, adoptees might be genetically predisposed, as a group, to impulsiveness" (1996). Impulsivity is an important criterion of BPD.

temperament mismatch

While children raised within their biological families may not always fit well with their parents' temperaments and values, with adoption, the fit is possibly less likely. This may cause a child's behavior to be met more often with disapproval than praise, which could predispose the child to loss of self-confidence and self-esteem.

experiences of non-BP parents

Sharon (non-BP and creator of NUTS)

Most NUTS parents realize something is wrong when their child is in grade school. The BPD child doesn't get along with other kids, and punishments seem to be ineffective at reducing problem behaviors. In Amy's case, the school psychologist maintained that she was just spoiled and would grow out of it.

Most NUTS parents, like us, finally receive a diagnosis of BPD after a life-threatening event such as violence toward others or a suicide attempt. One NUTS parent who was threatened by his son put a lock on his bedroom door and slept in his clothes with the car keys under his pillow. No one can live like this. I tell parents that if they cannot control the abuse, they should call the authorities. You have the right to say no to abuse—even if it is from your own child.

how parents feel

If you have a child with BPD, expect your feelings to vary widely and change constantly. The unconditional love is always there, but it can be challenged beyond belief. Your heart is broken again and again because it hurts to see someone you love suffer so much.

Destructive acts may cause you to actually feel hate toward your own child. And in between the love and hate come fear, confusion, resentment, wonder, happiness, and guilt.

Every parent wonders whether they did something to cause the BPD or whether they could have done something to prevent it. We fear for our children's future—will they ever be on their own? Will we spend the rest of our lives trying to help our children live normal lives? As much as we love them, we look forward to the empty nest.

sharing with your spouse

It's important to share your feelings with your spouse. Having a BPD child can destroy your marriage. It can also make it stronger. It is crucial that parents approach their child as a team and understand and support each other. Don't let the BP child "split" the two of you, in either sense of the word. It's going to be a long roller-coaster ride, and it is much easier when the two of you are facing in the same direction.

money and family concerns

Money is a big worry. Some parents have given up everything they have to pay for treatment. Residential facilities can be up to $1,500 per day; every trip to a therapist or psychiatrist is well over $50. Other children in the family may need to do without to help their brother or sister.

It would be nice if extended families were always supportive. But mental disorders are not well understood or accepted, and sometimes people deny that someone in their family could have a problem. Family members don't have to agree with the diagnosis. But they should respect that you believe the diagnosis and proceed from there.

On top of all this, people may believe terrible things about you. Sharon says, "My borderline daughter used to tell stories and tried to convince people that she was a prostitute and a drug addict. In this society, whenever a child has problems, everyone figures that the parents are to blame—especially the mother. I kept telling myself that we knew the truth and that what other people thought did not affect who we really were."

trying your best, despite it all

Parents of borderline children try their best despite the void of information. One common mistake is blaming the child for having BPD or expecting the child to change too quickly. Unlike a child with a physical impairment, no physical cues remind you that your child has a disorder. It is important to keep in mind that there is a biological basis for BPD (see Appendix A), and if the child could easily change and put a halt to his or her own suffering, he or she would do so!

Our children need extra care and nurturing, and we give it freely. But if we step in too much, we may teach our children that they cannot survive without us. We must walk a fine line between letting our children learn from their mistakes and protecting them when the disorder limits their capabilities.

effects on siblings

It's common for siblings of troubled children to starve for parental attention until they cry for help with disruptive behavior of their own. Parents should be aware of how the intrusive behavior of one child might threaten the security of another. Just as borderlines have problems defining their own personal boundaries, they are often disrespectful of the boundaries of others. Boundary violations may be subtle, or, at worst, may extend to physically or sexually abusing a sibling. You must be on the alert for this.

> I kept telling myself that we knew the truth and that what other people thought did not affect who we really were.

Sharon, founder of NUTS, recommends trying to find a friend or family member to help out so you can give your other children the time and attention they need. Be very open with siblings. Talk to them about BPD and explain that the borderline child feels they have no control over their behavior. Siblings may be afraid to tell you their negative feelings. So explain that angry and even hateful feelings are normal. Make sure that your other children have a safe place to go that is all their own, a place they can retreat when things become overwhelming.

Kim, Sharon's daughter and Amy's older sister, describes what it's like growing up with a BP sibling.

Kim (non-BP)

I have a lot of guilt about my sister. At times, I wished her next suicide attempt would be successful. When I have cooled down, I feel sickeningly guilty. Sometimes I find it hard to find any love for her at all—even when I'm not mad at her. She can be so socially inappropriate, like the time my friend came over for dinner and Amy asked her if she was still a virgin. I am worried about my future family.

Even though I don't even have a boyfriend, I'm anxious about my wedding. I know I will feel obligated to make her a bridesmaid, even though I don't want her to be one. I am afraid of the temper tantrums she will throw—will it be about the dresses, who is the maid of honor, or something else? What will my future husband think of her? What kind of aunt will she be for my children? Can I trust her to babysit? Will my own children have this horrible disorder?

But right now, I have more immediate worries. My mother is supposed to visit me at college for parents' weekend. Will she have to call home to check on Amy every fifteen minutes? Will Amy throw a fit and ruin everything? Will I always have to fight for our mother's attention?

the role of non-BP parents

Members of NUTS have found they can divide their responsibilities into four major tasks:

1. keeping family members safe

2. taking care of themselves

3. taking charge of their child's medical care

4. providing a structured, consistent, and loving environment that stresses self-responsibility

keep family members safe

It can be very difficult to balance the needs of the borderline child with the needs of the rest of the family. But the safety of each family member is of paramount importance. Use the information in chapter 8 and ask for help when you need it.

take care of yourself

The next time you're on an airplane, read the safety material. When oxygen is running low and the oxygen masks appear, the literature instructs parents to put on their own masks before putting masks on their children. This makes good sense—a parent who isn't breathing is of little help to a child.

In the same way, it's vital that you take care of yourself first. An emotionally exhausted and physically run-down parent can barely nurture an emotionally healthy child—let alone one who has borderline personality disorder.

Think of yourself as a whole person, not just your child's parent. It's common for one parent, often the mother, to take on the lion's share of the burden of caring for a child with BPD, but we urge you to share the work more or less equally so that one parent doesn't become burned out or resentful.

Parents may also try switching roles (e.g., if one tends to provide the emotional nurturing and the other handles more practical matters, try reversing tasks for a while to give each person a break). Most importantly, don't become isolated. Sharon says, "You may lose friends because of this. Some won't be able to handle your child's behavior problems. Some will judge or blame you. Look for people whom you can count on to validate your feelings. They don't need to solve your problems; they only need to listen with a sympathetic ear."

take charge of your child's medical care

Over the years your child may see many different clinicians, receive numerous diagnoses, and encounter several agencies designed to stabilize him or her. Consider yourself the CEO of your child's care, directing the professionals, managing the budget, and making decisions based upon what's best for all concerned. Don't depend on anyone else to do this for you because they won't. Remember, you care the most about your child and are ultimately responsible for him.

Keep Careful Records

One important duty is keeping a record of your child's behaviors, moods, and encounters with the legal and mental health system. Jot down your child's medications, dosages, and clinical appointments; note your conversations with school officials, specialists, and other involved parties. This journal may assist clinicians in making a diagnosis, and it could be vital if you ever need documentation for legal purposes. The journal doesn't have to be elaborate; a few brief words will do. See the following example.

Date	System	Note
11-2-2009	Clinic	Appointment with Dr. Smith. Changed Prozac to 40 mg.
11-5-2009	School	Met with Mrs. Jones (math) who said Mari has missed six assignments, was tardy three times, and is "mouthy" at times.
11-15-2009	Clinic	Family therapy today. Worked on "expectations."
12-4-2009	Clinic	Appointment with Dr. Smith. No med changes.
12-5-2009	Home	Big blowup tonight. Mari threatened suicide but cooled down after an hour. Stated we didn't "trust" her after she missed curfew by two hours.
12-6-2009	Police	Mari picked up for underage drinking. She was with two older boys who she met tonight.
12-7-2009	Home	We found cuts on Mari's left wrist. She had superficial bleeding. Mari cried a lot tonight and said she feels "bad."
12-9-2009	Clinic	Counseling appointment. Mari was very quiet afterward.

Working with Care Providers

Some parents are intimidated by mental health professionals. Keep in mind that they're working for you. Respect their position and expertise but don't assume that they will always know best. Listen to clinicians with an open mind, even if what they say is something you don't want to hear or it seems to be critical of you. But pay attention to your inner voice and assert yourself when you feel it's necessary. The final decisions are always yours.

> If the clinician mistakenly thinks that BPD is always the result of abuse, or if he or she implicitly or explicitly accuses you of mistreating your child despite lack of evidence, consider switching professionals.

Dealing with the System

Many NUTS parents find that dealing with health insurance providers, the schools, the legal system, and other institutions can be almost as challenging as coping with the behavior of their borderline child. Gail, a NUTS parent, says, "Do your best to ensure that your child doesn't fall through the cracks. It may mean making phone calls and personal visits; it may mean telling the powers that be that you won't take 'no' for an answer. When you advocate for your child, you may find you possess an inner strength you never knew you had."

"When you advocate for your child, you may find you possess an inner strength you never knew you had."

provide an appropriate environment

Borderline children and teens require structure and consistency in the same way that roadways require traffic lights and stop signs. Without them, utter confusion reigns, and physical or emotional injuries are more likely to result.

Routines

Structure refers to consistent routines. NUTS parents find that their children do best with firm schedules that tell them when to get up, when to go to school, what to do after school, when to eat, and so forth. Sharon even wrote a morning routine for her daughter to help her remember to brush her teeth and get dressed. "When something unexpected happens—even a good thing like a surprise birthday party—Amy doesn't know what to feel or how to act," Sharon explained. "A rage often results. We found that Amy needed to know in detail what was expected of her and what she could expect from others at all times."

Consequences

As part of creating this structure, try to help your child grasp what will happen if he or she does not meet his or her responsibilities. Be as specific as possible. For example, you might tell your child, "If you are late for school they will mark you tardy. If you are tardy three times without an excuse, you will be suspended. If you are suspended again, we may have to look at alternatives such as boarding school."

It is extremely important that you let your child learn from his or her own mistakes at an appropriate level for his or her age. If you continually rescue your child from the results of his or her own actions, your child may never learn to function at a higher level without you. It may be difficult to watch your child suffer the consequences of impulsive behavior, but in the long run, your child may suffer more if he or she never learns to control himself or herself.

> If you continually rescue your child, he or she may never learn to function at a higher level without you.

Consistency

Consistency means holding your child accountable for his or her actions every time. All parents have to fight the urge to let things slide sometimes. But with a borderline child, inconsistent enforcement of rules can be outright disastrous.

Obtaining a Diagnosis for Your Child

Distinguishing between typical adolescent acting-out behavior and behavior that's indicative of BPD can be difficult. To make a determination, look at the reason for the behavior. Adolescents with BPD often act out by using drugs, or raging to cope with profound misery, emptiness, self-loathing, and abandonment fears.

According to *The Essential Family Guide to Borderline Personality Disorder: New Tips and Tools to Stop Walking on Eggshells,* a comprehensive psychiatric evaluation is mandatory for potentially borderline children. The psychiatrist develops a report that becomes the foundation for the treatment plan. The evaluation may include the following:

- a description of the child's present problems and symptoms
- information about health, illness, and treatment
- parent and family health and psychiatric histories
- information about the child's development, school performance, friends, and family relationships
- if needed, laboratory studies such as blood tests, X-rays, or special assessments (for example, psychological, educational, and speech and language evaluation)

Brannon (non-BP)

I wanted my son, Michael, to be happy. So if he was being punished for a week, by the third day I pretended to "forget" the punishment. But Michael quickly learned not to take any punishment seriously. If I grounded him, he simply walked out the front door. As a teenager, Michael became involved with drugs and began skipping school and threatening violence. I placed him in one residential facility that allowed too much freedom; the drug use simply continued. Eventually, Michael settled into a very strict residential facility that meted out privileges for good behavior. There, he seems to be learning account-ability for his actions.

Borderline children need love and affection as much as other kids. Says Sharon, "The key to loving your child is to remember that their behavior is caused by borderline personality disorder. Love your child; hate the disorder. Having a BPD child can be tough. But there are wonderful moments as well. When your child learns how to cope with certain aspects of his or her illness, there is cause for celebration. When he or she finally makes that most important step of realizing and accepting love for his or her parents, it is so strong, so sweet, and so very precious."

Borderline children need love and affection as much as other kids. "Love your child; hate the disorder."

For more information about raising a borderline child, see the book *Hope for Parents: Helping Your Borderline Son or Daughter Without Sacrificing Your Family or Yourself*, by K. Winkler and R. Kreger (2000), which is listed in appendix C, along with other valuable resources.

Also see the website of the National Education Alliance of the National Education Association for Borderline Personality Disorder (www.NEABPD. org) for information on its Family Connections program.

CHAPTER 11

lies, rumors, and accusations: distortion campaigns

Hell hath no rage like a borderline scorned.

> —From the Welcome to Oz family member support
> community, www.BPDCentral.com.

Some non-BPs told us that they have been falsely accused of harassment and abuse by the BPs in their lives, been the subject of damaging rumors, and even faced legal action brought against them by borderlines without legiti-mate cause. We call these distortion campaigns.

Jerry (non-BP)

My soon-to-be-ex-wife got a protection order and had me evicted from my own home. She cut me off from our daughters and told all the neighbors that I am violent. They won't even look me in the eye. She systematically sought out *the people in social and professional organizations I belong to and attempted to turn them against me. She told my boss that I was impotent—and that I gave her herpes! She told her lawyer that I raped her ten years ago because we had had sex when she didn't want to—and she hadn't even told me she wasn't in the mood! I haven't seen the woman in months, nor have I called her. In the meantime, I am paying $3,500 a month for support. I can't sleep at night thinking of the injustice of it all. I am terrified of what she will allege next week in court.*

Here are other examples of distortion campaigns:

- Valerie's borderline mother, Hannah, told family members that Valerie had stolen money from her and had been violent on several occasions. Family members refused to speak with Valerie. Hannah made the accusation after Valerie told her she couldn't visit her over Christmas.

- Judy was stalked by her former borderline friend, Elizabeth, who sent threatening letters to herself in Judy's name. Elizabeth would then call Judy's answering machine and beg her to "stop threatening her." The matter ended up in court, where Elizabeth broke down under questioning and insisted that Judy had "forced" her to write the threatening letters to herself.

> Many distortion campaigns seem to revolve around either real or perceived abandonment, loss, and rejection—terrifying issues for people with BPD.

- Majel's son, Rick, was engaged to a borderline woman named Jeri. Jeri began telling Rick that Majel had made some highly negative comments about him to her when no one else was around. Although these comments were pure fabrications, Rick felt torn and didn't know whom to believe—his mother or his fiancée.

Not all people with BPD distort the truth. Many borderlines would never do such a thing. We are not invalidating the experiences of people with BPD who have been victimized; we are merely validating the experiences of those non-BPs who have been falsely accused. All types of people, both those with and without mental disorders, may make false claims.

motivations for distortion campaigns

Several theories account for what might motivate someone with BPD to engage in a distortion campaign.

abandonment and anger

We have explained that BPD does not cause fundamentally different behavior but behavior that is very far to one side of the continuum. Or, as one BP put it, "Borderlines are just like everyone else—only more so."

We all experience feelings of loss and rejection when relationships end or are threatened. These emotions are especially intense when the other person decides to leave and we want the relationship to continue. Many distortion campaigns seem to revolve around either real or perceived abandonment, loss, and rejection—terrifying issues for people with BPD.

Divorce—the issue in Jerry's case—is an example. Hannah may have felt rejected when her daughter decided not to come home for Christmas. Elizabeth may have felt humiliated when her friend Judy terminated the friendship. But sometimes the perceived loss is not so apparent. Jeri, for example, may have felt that her own relationship with her fiancée Rick was threatened by his close relationship with his mother, though he had love enough for them both.

Johnston and Roseby in *In the Name of the Child* (1997), explain how grief can manifest itself as anger:

> Loss—whether that of a loved one, the intact family, cherished hopes and dreams, or the threatened loss of one's own children—evokes powerful feelings of anxiety, sadness, and fear of being abandoned and alone. Some people have difficulty acknowledging these feelings. Instead, they seal over their grief with anger and try to prevent the inevitable separation by embroiling their spouse in unending disputes. Fighting and arguing are ways of maintaining contact (albeit of a negative kind). Even throughout the fighting these same individuals harbor reconciliation fantasies. People who have suffered a dramatic loss in the past (e.g., parental death or divorce) may be also reacting to these earlier, unresolved traumas.

identity and aggression

A woman whose husband divorces her loses her identity as wife; a woman whose children are grown may feel as if she's lost her identity as mother. In the face of real or perceived losses, people with BPD may feel:

- empty
- insignificant
- helpless
- unable to survive

Johnston and Roseby believe this may lead people to adopt a false front of being fiercely independent, refusing to negotiate lest they lose part of themselves. (They call this, "I fight, therefore I am.") People may also become overly dependent and clingy—or alternate between aggression and clinginess. BPs who see themselves as victims may thus feel that distortion campaigns help give them an identity.

shame and blame

Divorce and relationship problems can also spark feelings of rejection, which in turn evoke feelings of inadequacy, failure, shame, and humiliation. As you know, people with BPD often feel awash in shame and have low self-esteem. They may then try to cover up with a mask of absolute competency. Johnston and Roseby say that this exaggerated sense of failure may lead people to try to rid themselves of all blame by proving that the other person is totally inadequate or irresponsible.

> BPs who see themselves as victims may feel that distortion campaigns help give them an identity.

The authors write, "The fragile self-esteem of these people depends on keeping all sense of failure outside the self. So they present themselves with a self-righteous air of angry superiority and entitlement and accuse the ex-spouse of being psychologically and morally inferior" (Johnson and Roseby 1997).

When a psychologically vulnerable BP views the spouse's desertion as a total, devastating attack, he or she may develop paranoid ideas of betrayal, exploitation, and conspiracy. Johnston and Roseby write, "As the spouse surveys the rubble of their marriage, they begin to rewrite history and perceive their partner as having intentionally plotted and planned from the outset to exploit and cast them off" (Johnson and Roseby 1997).

At that point, they say, the "betrayed" spouse may respond aggressively with a counterattack that becomes the central obsession in his or her life. The spouse, along with any allies, is viewed as dangerous and aggressive. Having been wronged, these people feel justified in seeking retaliation. Or, more urgently, they believe in launching a preemptive strike. Their motto is "attack before being attacked."

assessing your risk

In analyzing dozens of distortion campaigns, we noticed several similarities:

- BPs who set up distortion campaigns often claimed to have had a history of being victimized by others. Sometimes, they even described how they sought revenge against people who they said had victimized them in the past.

- The borderlines often possessed the ability to appear calm, logical, and persuasive under certain circumstances. However, when under emotional distress or alone with the non-BPs, they appeared to lose contact with reality or become paranoid.

> The "betrayed" spouse may respond aggressively with a counterattack that becomes the central obsession in their lives.

- Non-BPs victimized by distortion campaigns often viewed themselves as protectors and caretakers. As a result, they had great difficulty looking out for their own best interests. Many overlooked warning signs, disregarded admonitions from friends, denied what was happening, and refused to take precautions or defend themselves.

It is hard for most people to accept that someone they love could do something to hurt them. If love for the BP in your life, or happy memories of the good times you shared, are preventing you from protecting yourself, it's essential that you understand that the BP may not feel the same way. Splitting may render the BP unable to remember the good feelings he or she had for you or to see you as a whole person with both good and bad qualities. As a result, the BP may view you as an evil monster who deserves to be punished. The sooner you realize this, the better chance you have of emerging from a distortion campaign with your dignity and rights intact.

Most complaints of distortion campaigns came from men and women who had recently asked for a divorce from a BP partner or who had broken up with a borderline girlfriend or boyfriend. Parents of borderline children were the second most frequent source of complaints, followed by children of borderline parents.

combating distortion campaigns

First, an important disclaimer: Each person's situation is different, and each person with BPD is unique. The right approach for one person could be totally wrong for another—even if the situations seem similar. The following guidelines may help.

> Before you take action, consult with a qualified mental health professional who is familiar with your unique situation. If the allegations involve the law, it's vital that you discuss the situation with a qualified attorney as soon as possible.

Secondly, recognize that BPD is a mental disorder. People who have it deserve to be treated with sensitivity, respect, and dignity. Protect yourself, but don't try to hurt the other person out of spite or revenge. For example, it might be prudent to remove your clothing and personal belongings from the house before asking for a divorce. However, hiring a moving company and taking half of everything the two of you own is probably going too far. In fact, it might understandably trigger a hostile response.

reduce your vulnerability

The best way to handle a distortion campaign is to prevent it from happening. If you can't do this, be proactive and protect yourself as much as you can—legally, financially, and emotionally.

Some distortion campaigns seem to occur for no discernible reason. But others seem to be triggered by actions the BP perceives as hostile. Start with these steps:

> Be proactive and protect yourself as much as you can—legally, financially, and emotionally.

- Consider any major actions you may be taking that involve the BP—anything from setting limits to seeking a divorce. What kind of reaction might you anticipate from the BP?

- Consider yourself: what are your vulnerable areas, and what could you do ahead of time to guard against any actions the BP may take? Hope for the best; prepare for the worst. Non-BPs have found that typical areas of concern include their finances, children, property, job, reputation, and friendships.

- Formulate a plan and implement it before you take any action that could trigger the BP.

Consider the example of Lyndia and Elicia. Lyndia needs to tell her borderline daughter, Elicia, that Elicia can't come home from the residential facility for the upcoming weekend. The last time Elicia came home for a visit, she threatened to burn down the house if Lyndia wouldn't let her spend the night with her drug-abusing boyfriend.

Lyndia knows from experience that after Elicia hears the news, she will immediately go to her counselors, grandparents, and anyone else who will listen and possibly believe Elicia's story, and tell them that Lyndia hates her (and always has) and that her behavior is spotless and that Lyndia is a bad parent.

So before Lyndia tells Elicia the news, she communicates the reasoning for her decision to anyone who might become involved. By the time Elicia speaks with them, they will already know what is going on.

consider not responding

There may be times when responding in any way at all simply prolongs the BP's abusive actions. That is because this entire matter may be an effort on his or her part to keep you engaged in the relationship. Any response—particularly an emotional one—may reward the behavior.

Think through the short-term and long-term ramifications of the other person's actions. If the consequences are insignificant or simply embarrassing—or if you believe the BP is trying to goad you into more contact with him or her—it may be best to simply let the matter go.

answer questions without being defensive

Alison was alternately suicidal and incensed when Luke broke up with her. She called Luke at work several times a day, screaming at him and begging him to take her back. When Luke had his work number changed, Alison retaliated by calling Luke's boss, David, and informing him that Luke often snorted cocaine while at work. "Luke's a crack head," she insisted. "Don't trust him."

Naturally, David confronted Luke with Alison's accusation. Several years earlier, Luke had tried cocaine at work when it was offered to him by one of the stagehands. But it happened just once. Other than that, Luke was a responsible employee and did not drink or use drugs on the job.

Luke owned up to what he had done but emphasized that it had happened just once. Luke also explained what was going on without intruding upon Alison's privacy any more than was necessary. Luckily, David understood and did not fire Luke for violating the company's drug policy.

A BP may also tell family, friends, and acquaintances untrue things about you. Before you decide whether to respond, ask yourself what you hope to achieve. Do you want to clear your name? Or is there something tangible at stake, such as the loss of friendship of people who are important to you?

> When consequences of the BP's actions are relatively minor, it may be best to act in a way that reveals the lie for what it is.

When consequences of the BP's actions are relatively minor, it may be best to act in a way that reveals the lie for what it is. For example, if the BP in your life tells the neighbors that your new wife is a shrew, it may be best to simply let them meet her and make their own decisions. However, if the BP in your life tells the neighbors you've been arrested for battering her and their opinion matters a great deal to you, you may wish to try to set the record straight.

When talking with people about false accusations, keep the following guidelines in mind:

- Act calm, composed, and in control—no matter how upset you feel.

- Validate the other person's concerns before explaining the facts. Say that if the rumors had been true, it would be a very serious matter.

- Do not disparage the BP—no matter how much you think he or she deserves it. Instead, sincerely express your concern for the BP or acknowledge your own confusion about why the BP would say such things. Be cautious about discussing BPD or any other psychological problem—people may misunderstand and think you are trying to belittle the BP.

- Realize that you cannot control what other people think about you. Say what you need to say and then let it go.

Benjamin (non-BP)

Here's what I said to a neighbor who wrongly believed I'd been violent toward my former wife: "I'd like to clear the air about something. It may make you a bit uncomfortable, and I understand that because it makes me uncomfortable too. But it's important, so I'm willing to stick my neck out. I heard that my former wife, Kassidy, told you that I was arrested for battering her. Someone told me that she had some cuts on her arm and she was showing them to people and saying that I attacked her. I wouldn't blame you if you felt horrified and didn't want to talk to me. If I thought that someone I knew had done such a thing, I would probably avoid them too. But it never happened. The divorce hasn't been easy, it's true. But I never did anything remotely like that. And I'm very concerned for Kassidy's sake—both that she would tell this to people and that somehow her arm is being cut.

"I'll understand if you feel confused and wonder about what really happened. But we've known each other for awhile, and I did want to set the record straight with you. I appreciate your listening."

prepare for false accusations of abuse from BP children

Children who falsely accuse parents of abuse is a growing phenomenon. Reasons for doing this include revenge for perceived abuse, retaliation for being treated "unfairly," and an attempt to split their parents' loyalty to one another.

Dealing with False Accusations

As you may suspect, an angry child's phone call to 911 or to the local child protection agency can have devastating effects on the family. Typical investigations can often take more than a month to complete. In the meantime, the accused parent is often ordered by the court to stay away from the child and temporarily live outside the family home. The child is often required to remain with the other parent, who experiences the conflict of trying to be supportive and loyal to both the child and to a spouse or partner. The family's friends, relatives, and employers may be caught in the same trap of feeling they must either demonstrate support for the child or loyalty toward the accused parent.

Being defensive and uncooperative can hurt your case.

In our interview with attorney Charles Jamieson, he advised that the parents of a child who makes false accusations do the following:

- Keep detailed records documenting the child's diagnosis or BPD behaviors. Examples include letters from school authorities, medical records, court papers, and reports that unsubstantiate prior allegations. This will enhance your credibility.

- Keep a diary of your activities, including where you were, who you were with, and what you did. If allegations come weeks or months after the supposed event, this may provide you with an alibi.

- Ask your other children if they would be willing to help explain your innocence to the authorities.

- If necessary, make sure that a third party is present when you are with the child.

- Take all accusations seriously. They may quickly snowball out of control. If you need to, hire an attorney who specializes in false allegations.

Coping with Your Feelings

From an emotional perspective, there are some things to keep in mind that can help you cope with the situation. Usually, false accusations center around abuse or neglect. Therefore, they are followed up with investigations by your county's social service department or child protection unit. While the investigation will seem to be accusatory, remember that the investigation is merely a fact-finding process. Only hard evidence can be used to render charges.

Remember that being defensive and uncooperative can hurt your case. Do not take questions personally; keep telling yourself that the process is necessary to ferret out real cases of abuse. In some cases, parents may be separated from their children while the investigation is going on. Siblings of the borderline child need to know that the separation is temporary and that they may be asked questions during the investigation. Stress your love for them and the need to answer the legal authorities' questions honestly.

Finally, remind yourself that BPD is a mental illness. Anger toward your borderline child is normal; however, remember that the illness is really to blame—not the child.

If the BP is trying to hurt you by mounting a distortion campaign, you might consider the BP to be your enemy. In reality, your enemies are:

The truth has a way of revealing itself, and lies are eventually exposed for what they are.

- **denial:** doing nothing about the problem in hopes that it will go away

- **wishful thinking:** doing nothing because you're sure that a miracle will occur and the BP will have a change of heart

- **emotionality:** reacting emotionally rather than remaining calm and thinking through logical solutions to your problem

- **martyrdom:** doing nothing because you can't bear to hurt the BP's feelings, which you may think are more important than your own

- **isolation:** trying to handle the problem by yourself instead of asking for help

- **legal delays:** not hiring the right attorney before you lose legal rights and the situation becomes critical

Most non-BPs find that if they react quickly and logically and obtain the right legal help when needed, distortion campaigns sputter and fail. The truth has a way of revealing itself, and lies are eventually exposed for what they are. By acting appropriately, you can help that occur sooner rather than later.

CHAPTER 12

what now?
making decisions
about your relationship

People who care about someone with BPD are usually in a great deal of pain. Staying in the relationship as it is seems unbearable. But leaving seems unthinkable or impossible. If you feel this way, you are not alone. Nearly every non-BP we spoke with echoed the same sentiments. But you do have options, even if you can't see them right now. This chapter will help you think through your choices and come to a personal decision that feels right for you.

predictable stages

People who love someone with BPD seem to go through similar stages. The longer the relationship has lasted, the longer each stage seems to take. Although these are listed in the general order in which people go through them, most people move back and forth among different stages.

confusion stage

This generally occurs before a diagnosis of BPD is known. Non-BPs struggle to understand why borderlines sometimes behave in ways that seem to make no sense. They look for solutions that seem elusive, blame themselves, or resign themselves to living in chaos.

You do have options, even if you can't see them right now.

Even after learning about BPD, it can take non-BPs weeks or months to really comprehend on an intellectual level how the BP is personally affected by this complex disorder. It can take even longer to absorb the information on an emotional level.

outer-directed stage

In this stage, non-borderlines:

- turn their attention toward the person with the disorder

- urge the BP to seek professional help, attempting to get him or her to change

- try their best not to trigger problematic behavior

- learn all they can about BPD in an effort to understand and empathize with the person they care about

It can take non-BPs a long time to acknowledge feelings of anger and grief—especially when the BP is a parent or child. Anger is an extremely common reaction, even though most non-BPs understand on an intellectual level that BPD is not the borderline's fault.

Yet because anger seems to be an inappropriate response to a situation that may be beyond the borderline's control, non-BPs often suppress their anger and instead experience depression, hopelessness, and guilt.

The chief tasks for non-BPs in this stage include:

- acknowledging and dealing with their own emotions

- letting BPs take responsibility for their own actions

- giving up the fantasy that BPs will behave as the non-BPs would like them to

inner-directed stage

Eventually, non-BPs look inward and conduct an honest appraisal of themselves. It takes two people to have a relationship, and the goal for non-BPs in this stage is to better understand their role in making the relationship what it now is. The objective here is not self-recrimination but insight and self-discovery.

> Be guided by your own values—not someone else's.

decision-making stage

Armed with knowledge and insight, non-BPs struggle to make decisions about the relationship. This stage can often take months or years. Non-BPs in this stage need to clearly understand their own values, beliefs, expectations, and assumptions. For example, one man with a physically violent borderline wife came from a conservative family that strongly disapproved of divorce. His friends counseled him to separate from her, but he felt unable to do so because of his concern about how his family would react.

You may find that your beliefs and values have served you well throughout your life. Or you may find that you inherited them from your family without determining whether they truly reflect who you are. Either way, it is important to be guided by your own values—not someone else's.

resolution phase

In this final stage, non-BPs implement their decisions and live with them. Depending upon the type of relationship, some non-BPs may, over time, change their minds many times and try different alternatives.

beyond black and white

It is easy to adopt the BP's black-and-white way of thinking and believe you only have two choices—stay or go. But many other options also exist, for example:

- leaving the situation temporarily whenever the BP violates your limits

- taking a temporary break (days, weeks, or months) from the relationship

- learning to depersonalize the BP's actions

- remaining in the relationship but living apart

- making the relationship less close

- spending less time with the BP

- achieving balance by cultivating your own interests, friends, and meaningful activities

- telling the BP that you will remain in the relationship only if he or she is willing to work with a therapist or make specific changes; this means holding the BP to any promise he or she makes, and it may mean leaving if he or she violates such a promise

- putting off making a decision until you feel comfortable making one

- putting off making a decision until you see a therapist and work on some of your own issues

questions to ask yourself

These are questions you should ask yourself about your current relationship with your BP partner. Most of these questions address important needs that should be met in relationships. The answers to these questions can provide you with some direction on how to proceed in the relationship. Generally, the more needs and wants that go unfilled and the more "unbalanced" the attention and energy in the relationship, the more likely it is that the relationship is unhealthy.

- What do I want from this relationship? What do I need from this relationship?

- How open can I be with my feelings with this person?

- Am I putting myself in physical danger by staying in this relationship?

- How will this decision affect any children?

- How does this relationship affect my self-esteem?

- Do I love myself as much as I love the borderline?

- Have I accepted the fact that the BP will change only if and when he or she is ready to do so? Am I able to wait until that happens or live with things the way they are if it never happens?

- What practical considerations do I need to consider, particularly financial ones?

- Do I believe that I have the right to be happy?

- Do I believe that I am only worthwhile when I am sacrificing myself for others?

- When am I currently the most content: when I am with this person, when I am alone, or when I am with others?

- Do I have the energy and fortitude to go against my family or other people who might be upset with my decision?

- Am I truly making my own decision, or am I doing what other people want me to do?

- What are the legal ramifications of my decision?

- If a friend was in my place and told me the story of this relationship, what advice would I give them?

when children are involved

One non-BP says, "I am not one who believes that unhappy people should stay together for the sake of the children. I think they would be far better off living with one happy parent than one miserably unhappy parent and one who is completely delusional."

While many parents worry about the effect of divorce on children, Janet R. Johnston, Ph.D., executive director of the Judith Wallerstein Center for the Family in Transition, said in our interview that studies consistently find that children's exposure to unresolved conflict and verbal and physical abuse is a better predictor of children's adjustment than the marital status of their parents.

According to Johnston, children do the best in a happy, intact marriage with both parents present; next best is a divorce in which the parents protect the children from conflict. Third best is an unhappy, intact marriage in which children are exposed to unresolved conflict and verbal abuse. Worst of all is a conflict-ridden divorce where the children are put in the middle.

chosen relationships

When it comes to chosen relationships, we found that the BP's willingness to admit he or she had a problem and seek help was by far the determining factor as to whether the couple stayed together or not.

Of the hundreds of people we spoke with, when the BPs were truly committed to recovery, non-BPs were almost always willing to stand by them and help them through it. But when BPs refused to take any responsibility for the couple's problems, no matter how hard non-BPs tried to rescue the relationship, the relationship usually ended.

Richard (non-BP)

I stayed with my wife for the same reasons I fell in love with her. She is bright, beautiful, witty, passionate, and fun. When we got married, I didn't know she had borderline personality disorder. In fact, I didn't know what BPD was until it was clinically diagnosed.

I knew early on that there were problems; sometimes they were frustrating; sometimes they made me angry. Sometimes they scared the hell out of me. No matter what, however, she was still the person I loved who just happened to have a mental illness. Even during the worst of it, I never considered leaving. I wasn't about to throw away a relationship so easily, especially one where so much of it was good. She was very sick, but I could always see the good in her.

After her four years of therapy and hospitalizations, our marriage is very close. The reward for loyalty has been great—the same passion, the same beauty, the same wit that attracted me to her in the first place are all there. But the fear and confusion of BPD are gone.

Rhoda (non-BP)

I have broken up with my BPD boyfriend many times. When he is able to see what he is doing, apologize for it, and tell me how he is going to change, I go back.

To me, he is worth it. He is a kind, beautiful, passionate, generous man. I have never met anyone in my life who has made me feel more loved. And he can't destroy me because he does not define me. I do. And I am very fortunate to have a "moderate" BP—he is not prone to rages or violent outbursts, doesn't cheat on me, and makes a sincere effort to modify his behavior.

This relationship suits me because I sometimes have a strong need for privacy and solitude. I take the time to be alone and enjoy other things without him.

I am aware of the risks. But I love him and I plan to enjoy his presence in my life as long as I can.

Marie (non-BP)

My soon-to-be-ex-husband gave me a surprise visit this afternoon. The conversation started out all business and finances, but then the conversation changed. He said I hadn't given him a chance (twenty years of chances are obviously not enough). I guess he forgot he threatened to kill me in no uncertain terms. Silly me—can't I just get over the death threat? I could go on with the twisted logic, the convenient amnesia, and the transparent manipulation. But I will get to the point. Which is: there is no point. He just doesn't get it. It was my job to seek the proper ways to communicate with him. My job to set boundaries. My job to understand the illness. What was his part?

What kind of relationship can you have when one person must do all of the work? What kind of relationship is it when one person must have all of the understanding, have all of the forgiveness, and do all of the giving to the needy other?

He called me a few hours later and began sighing on the phone that he might as well quit his job. He told me he was eyeballing a handgun in the house where he now lives. It took every fiber of me to hang up—but I did hang up. I released him to his own pitiful misery. I didn't even know the power still existed within me. But it does. And it's perfectly okay for me to own my own feelings again.

As I'm writing this, I'm watching my eight-year-old fill a decorative birdcage full of oatmeal cookies. It's his science project. Why is this relevant? Because he's free and safe to be himself, without risk of raging or verbal abuse from someone he should have been able to trust. Because his mother is free and safe to just let him be an eight-year-old. Because all of us non-BPs have this option, and there should be no apologies forthcoming for an illness we did not cause.

Fill the birdcages with cookies, pour milk all over them, eat them with your fingers and make a big mess. Laugh until your sides ache, cry when something is wrong, spend some time doing absolutely nothing, say what you mean, and mean what you say. Invest in your own sanity for once.

unchosen relationships

With unchosen relationships, such as those with BP parents, minor children, or minor siblings, sometimes the choice is not to stay or go as much as it is to set and observe your limits and not let the BP's problems overwhelm your own life. But that doesn't mean you need to feel helpless and hopeless. While you may not be able to end the relationship or "break up," you can set limits on how much contact you have with that person and how much of your energy you invest in maintaining the relationship.

> With unchosen relationships, you need to be the one in charge. Identify your emotional and physical boundaries. Reinforce the limits you set in the relationship with your BP by consistent modeling and consistent responding to the disturbing behavior of the BP. As an adult, when the relationship causes too much pain and your relative is unwilling to change, you have the option to temporarily or permanently step away.

Sylvia (non-BP)

I love my borderline son, John, very much. For many years, I lived or died depending upon how well he was doing. Was he drinking again? Getting involved with self-destructive women? Spending all of his money on things he didn't need? I continually gave him cash and provided him with a place to stay when yet another one of his roommates threw him out. I listened to him as he ranted and raved and blamed me and his father for everything that had ever gone wrong in his entire life.

Things changed after my husband had a heart attack. Paul is doing well now, but for a while, we weren't sure if he was going to pull through. This crisis helped me realize that I was concentrating on my son so much I was losing myself, my husband, and my relationship with my daughter.

I had to back away from my son's chaos. I set some personal limits around bailing him out and listening to his tirades. John wasn't happy about our new limits—he cut us off totally for three years. That was very painful. But eventually, John decided that having a relationship with us with limits was better than no relationship at all. We see him about once a month. There are phone calls, too. It's strained, but I can live with that.

I feel like a human being again, with goals, dreams, and happiness. Everyone benefited from the limits—even John, I think. He learned that he can manage to run his life without us.

I still wish that I could have a closer relationship with my son. I wish that he would take care of himself more and get help. But I've learned to accept that I can't change John. I can only love him and be the best mother I know how to be while still loving myself and caring for the rest of my family.

healing and hope

Whatever you decide, there can be healing and hope: healing when a relationship ends and hope for your loved one's recovery from BPD.

Many people from the Welcome to Oz online support group (www.BPD Central.com) resolved their relationship with the BPs in their lives years ago. But they stay on the list to provide support to others, and to assure them that life does, indeed, get better after a relationship with a borderline.

Marilyn (non-BP)

It has been ten years since my divorce from my borderline ex-husband, and I am still dealing with the aftereffects. I spent so much time trying to hide his behavior from others that it left its mark upon me. Trust in others, faith in the world... these were the things that were destroyed in me.

Yet now, in most ways life couldn't be better! I am a happy and confident person. The experience taught me many things about myself—things that I had avoided or would not admit to myself before that time. Now I use my energy to correct those things that I find negative or unhealthy. I live a more conscious life.

As far as not becoming bitter—I was angry for a long time, until I finally realized that my ex-husband had not deliberately set out to make my life miserable. It would have happened, to one degree or another, no matter whom he had married. Blaming him for who he is is futile and does not help the situation in any way. A few months after the divorce I was having dinner with my parents. My father began to denigrate my ex-husband. I looked at my father and said, "Why would you say such things? Why would you hate someone like him? Don't you understand he has harmed himself more than he has me?" Bitterness and anger are emotions that tie one to the past. Had I held on to negative emotions, I would never have been able to start my life again or ever be happy again.

The last thing my former husband ever said to me was, "I've never been happy, never in my life!" I'll never forget the tears that were streaming down his face. And I will never forget the pain and anguish in his voice. The isolation he felt and most probably still feels—his fear of being alone and isolated in the world—stills any feelings of anger against him. I had been happy in the past. I knew I would be happy again someday. Yet for someone like him, who had never known happiness—what of him? I abandoned him, just as he felt everyone else had done in his life.

I felt a sense of terrible guilt for a long time. But if I was to survive, I had to let go of it. I could not help this man, and I could not destroy myself.

And finally, Rachel Reiland, author of *Get Me Out of Here: My Recovery from Borderline Personality Disorder* (2004), posted this note to Welcome to Oz to show that recovery is indeed possible.

Rachel (BP)

There were plenty of times I felt far worse than when I started it all, and I wondered if I would have been better off never having known about my illness and never having entered therapy. My entire way of thinking had to be disassembled and rebuilt. And for someone inherently struggling with uncertainty about identity, there were dauntingly frightening times when I had disassembled the old ways of thinking but had not yet adopted new ones.

During that time, I looked into a dark hole of nothingness and wondered if I had any identity at all. Luckily, with the help of an excellent psychiatrist and the support of my husband and children, I recovered from BPD. Yet I know enough to realize that what happened to me doesn't always happen in the case of all borderlines. Some BPs are unwilling to take the journey. Other borderlines are outright incapable of it. And thus I would never expect that everyone close to a borderline stay in the relationship. In some cases—perhaps many cases—it is necessary and wise to protect oneself and move on with life. Yet, at other times, if you hang around, you will be rewarded in the end with a relationship that is closer and better than you had dreamed possible.

One of the most profound lessons I learned in my journey was the incredible capacity that people have for goodness, that this world, despite its trials, pains, and injustices, is indeed a miraculous place. It is filled with as much love and kindness as it is with hatred. I have emerged from all of this with a view of life that will never, ever be the same as it was. And that has made all of the pain and struggle eminently worth it.

In this book, you've learned what BPD is, why people with BPD act the way they do, the part that you play in the dynamic, and how to take back control of your life.

But as complex as BPD behavior can be, obtaining knowledge is the easy part. Now comes the wisdom: taking what you've learned and applying it to your own life.

This may happen in many ways, including:

- questioning long-standing beliefs and values

- facing issues that you've been avoiding for years

- revisiting the unspoken "bargain" you've struck with the BP in your life: that their needs and views are always, always more important and more "right" than yours

No one can hold up this kind of bargain very long without seriously compromising their own mental health.

We can't promise that it will be easy. But we can promise that it will be worthwhile. In the process, you will find out what you really value and who you really are. You will discover strengths you didn't know you had. Few things in life are more important than this. As William Shakespeare said four hundred years ago:

This above all, to thine own self be true,
And it must follow as the night the day
Thou canst not then be false to any man.
[*Hamlet,* act I, scene iii, lines 78–80]

We hope that the knowledge and tools you've gained from this book serve you well on the rest of your journey.

causes and treatment of BPD

Much of the information in this appendix has been taken from *The Essential Family Guide to Borderline Personality Disorder* (2008) by Randi Kreger, the coauthor of this book.

risk factors for BPD

There is no single cause of BPD. Instead, there are several risk factors that, when present, increase the chances that a person develops BPD. The risk factors fall into two categories: biological and environmental. A biological vulnerability to BPD combined with a problematic environment can lead to the development of BPD. In some people, biological risk factors may predominate; for others, environmental risk factors will play a larger role.

biological factors

Malfunctions in neurotransmitter levels, as well as other abnormalities in the neurotransmitter system, can lead to problems such as impaired reasoning, impulsivity, and unstable emotions.

The physical brain, too, can be impaired. The amygdala controls the intensity of our emotions and our ability to return to normal after sharp emotions have been aroused. Brain scans show that in people with BPD, the amygdala is more active than those of control subjects.

Robert O. Friedel, MD, suggests that there is not a single, specific gene for borderline personality disorder. He says it appears that the genes that increase risk for the disorder may be passed on by those people who have the disorder itself, or a related disorder, such as bipolar disorder, depression, substance use disorders and post-traumatic stress disorder.

Friedel says it's vital to understand that BPD is the result of instability in specific neural pathways in the brain, and problematic behaviors are not intentional or willful. Research will give us a better understanding of biological risk factors, which will result in more effective treatment.

environmental factors

It's a myth that BPD is a result of some form of childhood abuse. Yes, many people with BPD *have* been the victim of abuse, abandonment, neglect, or other mistreatment—sometimes for years. But we don't really know how many fit that pattern, because of flaws in research.

Studies only reflect BPs within the mental health system and who are suicidal and self-harming. They're not a true random sample of the entire population with BPD because the entire higher functioning population is excluded.

Another issue is that the claims of abuse are self-reported and may lack a standardized definition of abuse.

Environmental factors—abuse, neglect, childhood trauma of many different kinds—do appear to trigger BPD in someone who may be genetically predisposed to the condition.

Friedel calls these "environmental burdens." In addition to abuse, environmental burdens might include:

- ineffective parenting—anything from inadequate parental skills to mental illness or substance abuse

- an unsafe and chaotic home situation

- a clash between the disposition of child and parent

- the sudden loss of a caregiver or the caregiver's attention—even common things such as the birth of a new baby—which the child perceives as abandonment

treatment

The great news is that new forms of treatment are showing success (more about that in a minute). But if you're eager to seek treatment for your loved one, make sure that he or she sincerely wants to make changes for his or her own reasons—not just because you or someone else has given an ultimatum.

medication

Medications help reduce BPD symptoms such as depression, mood swings, dissociation, aggression, and impulsivity. This kind of treatment is very complicated because the details of how brain chemistry provokes BPD symptoms can vary widely from one patient to the next. Doctors using drugs to treat BPD have to be specially trained, and patients need careful monitoring.

Common medications are:

- antipsychotics such as olanzapine (Zyprexa)

- antidepressants such as sertraline (Zoloft) or venlafaxine (Effexor)

- mood stabilizers like divalproex sodium (Depakote) or lamotrigine (Lamictal)

psychotherapy

There are several structured programs just for people with BPD who are motivated to work on their problems. These structured treatments seem to produce better results than treatment as usual. This may be due to factors, though, that are not exclusive to these treatments, including:

- specialized clinician training, which gives them more effective tools

- clinician education, which gives treatment providers a more positive attitude about recovery and working with patients

- treatment twice a week instead of once

- the opportunity to interact with peers who have the same disorder

All of these treatments focus on problematic borderline behaviors. But they vary as to the importance of the healing relationship between the therapist and the patient. Ultimately, for most patients, the decisions about treatment come down to what programs are available, the best fit between therapist and client, health insurance coverage, and other factors.

Dialectical Behavior Therapy

Dialectical behavior therapy (DBT) is probably the best-known structured treatment for BPD. Developed by Marsha Linehan, Ph.D., DBT essentially teaches clients to accept themselves as they are—which then enables them to make changes in their behavior.

People enrolled in DBT programs typically attend weekly group skills training sessions to learn how to tolerate distress, regulate their emotions, become more mindful, and improve their interpersonal skills. They also meet weekly with an individual therapist.

Mindfulness is one of the core concepts of DBT (you can read more about it in Appendix B). Mindfulness is about being in the moment and observing what is happening around you, noticing your emotions without being consumed by them. People who consider entering DBT need to be willing to faithfully attend therapy and fill out daily diary forms. You can find out more about DBT, including finding a DBT therapist, at www.behavioraltech.com.

Mentalization Based Therapy

Mentalization based therapy (MBT) is a specific type of psychotherapy designed to help people with BPD focus on the following:

- making a distinction between their thoughts and those of others

- recognizing how thoughts, feelings, wishes, and desires are linked to behavior—something that is an element is most established therapies, though with MBT, it's the major focus.

The focus of MBT is on the interaction between the patient and the therapist—unlike DBT, which focuses on skills training. The goals of MBT include better relationships with others and improved control over emotions and behaviors. The relationship between client and therapist is considered a vital part of treatment, whereas DBT targets dysfunctional behavior.

Schema Therapy

According to its founders, "schemas" are entrenched, self-defeating life patterns that can occur when vital needs are not met in childhood. They say that our schema modes are triggered by life situations that we are oversensitive to (our "emotional triggers"). These can lead us to overreact to situations, or to act in ways that end up hurting us.

The goals of schema therapy include helping people access their true feelings, turn off the self-defeating schema modes, and get their emotional needs met in relationships.

STEPPS Group Treatment Program

STEPPS stands for systems training for emotional predictability and problem solving. It is popular in the Netherlands and is meant to be used in addition to, not as a replacement for, traditional therapy. Like DBT, STEPPS has a skills-training approach. Family members are an important aspect of this program; they learn how to reinforce and support the patient's new skills.

This program has three stages: awareness of illness, emotion management skills training, and behavior management skills training.

finding a therapist

Unfortunately, these structured treatments are not widely available. They can also be expensive. Since each clinician has his or her own unique "brand" of therapy—even if they come from the same schools of thought—finding the right therapist is a bit like searching for a job.

Therapists who treat BPD should have several qualities:

- They believe recovery is possible.

- They know about the latest research and understand the role of brain disorder in people with BPD

- They can articulate specific goals for therapy that are realistic, especially within the time limits that a health insurance plan might set for the therapy.

- They have support from their colleagues for treating BPD.

- They are confident in their own ability and they are savvy about how BPs can behave. They are compassionate toward the BP but smart enough not to get sucked in emotionally by the BP's dysfunctional ways of relating to others, including therapists.

One way to find a psychiatrist is to develop a list of the best hospitals in your community for psychiatric care. Make sure you include teaching hospitals. Then, call each one and speak to the psychiatric unit nurse manager or the medical staff administrative assistant. Ask for the names of psychiatrists who specialize in treating personality disorders—don't mention BPD specifically at this stage.

Then, check the names you're given against the directory for your insurance plan or HMO. Then call the individual clinician's office and ask the staff about his or her experience in treating personality disorders. Listen for the tone of their response, and choose those clinicians whose employees seem to be enthusiastic about their bosses. Once you find the right psychiatrist, you can ask for referrals to other types of clinicians, such as therapists.

Once you have narrowed the list to a few doctors, make an appointment and ask each doctor the following questions:

- Do you treat people with BPD? If so, how many have you treated?

- How do you define BPD?

- What do you believe causes BPD?

- What is your treatment plan for borderline clients?

- Do you believe people with BPD can get better? Have you personally treated BPs who have improved?

- How much do you know about the stresses of living with someone with the disorder?

Your goal is to pick someone with experience in treating personality disorders, who understands that some BPs are high-functioning and can cause particular problems, and who understand the real causes of BPD. You want to be sure the clinician doesn't wrongly believe that BPD always results from parental abuse, for example.

Finally, you want one who offers a treatment plan that is flexible and has specific, concrete, attainable goals. The chapter Finding Professional Help in *The Essential Family Guide to Borderline Personality Disorder* (Kreger 2008) covers these topics and goes into more detail about finding unstructured therapy, including how to assess the quality of the therapy and the reputation of the therapist.

practicing mindfulness

mindfulness for friends and loved ones of BPs

One essential component of dialectical behavioral therapy (DBT) that has proven very effective for people with BPD is mindfulness. Treatment for BPD often begins with learning mindfulness skills, and the BP repeatedly practices these skills throughout treatment (Linehan 1993a).

These same mindfulness skills can also be beneficial for non-BPs who are coping with the BPD symptoms of loved ones. In fact, for the past decade, the National Educational Alliance for Borderline Personality Disorder (NEA-BPD) has taught mindfulness skills in its Family Connections Program, which offers education, skills training, and support to family members of people with BPD. (To learn more about the program, visit www.neabpd.org /family-connections.)

Mindfulness is awareness without judgment. As mindfulness researcher Jon Kabat-Zinn notes, mindfulness is "the ability to be aware of your thoughts, emotions, physical sensations, and actions—in the present moment—without judging or criticizing yourself or your experience" (2005). Some people call this "being centered"; others call it encountering one's "true self."

People with BPD are often ruled by their emotions. This can lead them to destructive and impulsive actions such as drug use, risky sexual encounters, and self-injury. In DBT, the goal of mindfulness is to get BPs to recognize these patterns of strong emotions and risky behavior so they can act more thoughtfully and less impulsively. In DBT language, the goal of mindfulness is to practice and achieve "wise mind": a balance between "reasonable mind" and "emotional mind" (or, as some clinicians say, "emotion mind"). With a wise mind, we are able to experience life as it comes to us, and appreciate the ambiguity and the shades of gray that we often encounter.

We are in reasonable mind when we approach knowledge from an intellectual and rational point of view. In reasonable mind, our emotions are put away and our responses are planned and controlled. In contrast, we are in emotional mind when our thinking and behavior are controlled by our current emotional state. In emotional mind, rational thinking is difficult and facts may be distorted to match or validate our feelings.

With a wise mind, our emotions and thoughts work together. As a result, we act appropriately and smoothly—even if our life and relationships feel temporarily out of control.

When we are mindful, we are open to life on its own terms, fully aware of each moment as it arises and as it passes away.

In the *Dialectical Behavior Therapy Skills Workbook* (2007), Matthew McKay, Jeffrey Wood, and Jeffrey Brantley remind us that "to be fully aware of your experiences in the present moment, it's necessary that you do so without criticizing yourself, your situation, or other people." The creator of DBT, Marsha Linehan, calls this "radical acceptance" (1993a). (These two words also form the title of a 2004 book by psychologist and meditation teacher Tara Brach.)

Radical acceptance allows us to focus on the here and now and to avoid the mental and emotional traps of focusing on what might lie ahead or what happened in the past. This can be especially helpful when coping with the unpredictable and confusing behaviors associated with BPD.

Mindfulness—and DBT in general—help people with BPD stay off the emotional roller coaster associated with black-and-white thinking. Over time, people who regularly practice mindfulness tend to be better at enduring pain, solving problems, and not creating turmoil and stress in their lives and relationships. Notice, though, that the goal of mindfulness isn't to experience profound happiness or a life without stress or trouble.

We all have the capacity to be mindful. It's a skill anyone can learn. There's nothing mysterious about it. We simply pay attention to the present moment. When mental clutter appears, we let it appear and let it fade away again. Over and over, we return to the here and now.

This isn't usually as easy as it sounds, especially as we're first learning it. But everyone gets better at it with practice. In the process, we also learn a lot about ourselves, others, and our relationships.

Practicing mindfulness can help you achieve a better balance between your rational mind and your emotional mind. This puts you in a better position to respond wisely to distressing situations, in a balanced, healthy manner. You'll also make better decisions, improve your relationships, and optimize your potential for physical and mental relaxation.

The Dialectical Behavior Therapy Skills Workbook (McKay, Wood, and Brantley 2007) offers an excellent introduction to mindfulness as well as many suggestions and opportunities for practice.

mindfulness exercise #1: focus on an object

The purposes of this exercise are to focus your mind on a single object and to be aware of the mental energy needed to stay in the moment.

Find a place where you can be alone and away from TVs, radios, and other distractions and interruptions. Get into a comfortable position—either sitting or standing—that you can maintain for three minutes. Keep your eyes open and breathe normally.

Pick a nearby object that you can see clearly. This should be something you don't have a strong feeling about—a plant, a chair, a book, a cup.

For the next three minutes, focus your attention just on that object. If you like, look at it from multiple angles. Pick it up or run your hands over it. Smell it, if you're so inclined. Take in all the different sensory information about it.

When your mind wanders off—and it will—simply catch yourself and return your attention to the object. This may happen several—or more than several—times. There's no need to get frustrated or critical with yourself. Just keep coming back to the object.

mindfulness exercise #2: watching your thoughts

The purpose of this exercise is to increase your awareness of your own mind and its thoughts. Over time, with practice, it will help you to not get stuck on, distressed about, or overwhelmed by a particular thought.

Again, find a spot where you can be free of distraction or interruption. Get in a comfortable sitting position, with your feet on the floor and your back straight. (This might mean sitting forward on the front part of your chair.) Breathe normally and keep your eyes open.

For five minutes, don't think—or not think—about anything in particular. Just watch your thoughts surface, swirl about, and float away. Don't try to hang onto them, push them away, or judge them. Let them come and let them go.

If your mind wanders or gets stuck on a particular thought, just notice that and return to quietly watching your mind. If you notice yourself getting judgmental ("I'm not very good at this" "Why am I having such awful thoughts?" etc.), just notice your judgment and return once more to watching your mind.

With practice, this skill will help you avoid getting stuck in obsessive thinking or worry. Paradoxically, it will also help you better focus on important tasks, concerns, or activities—doing your taxes, for example—when you need to.

Reading List and Resources

Materials with one or two stars are exceptionally good. Materials with a plus sign speak frankly about the effect of BPD behaviors on family members. They may be triggering for individuals with BPD. Some authors have websites, which are also listed.

Materials About Borderline Personality Disorder

Materials About BPD Not Available in Bookstores

Back from the Edge. 2007. DVD. White Plains, NY: Borderline Personality Disorder Resource Center. www.bpdresourcecenter.org.

Border-Lines. Newsletter subscription available at www.bpdcentral.com.

Eddy, W. A. 2003. *Splitting: Protecting Yourself While Divorcing a Borderline or Narcissist.* Milwaukee, WI: Eggshells Press. www.bpdcentral.com. (888) 357-4355. A companion CD is also available.

Kreger, R., and E. Gunn. 2007. *The ABC's of BPD: The Basics of Borderline Personality Disorder for Beginners*. Milwaukee, WI: Eggshells Press. www .bpdcentral.com. (888) 357-4355.

Kreger, R., and K. A. Williams-Justesen. 2000. *Love and Loathing: Protecting Your Mental Health and Legal Rights When Your Partner Has Borderline Personality Disorder*. Milwaukee, WI: Eggshells Press. www.bpdcentral. com. (888) 357-4355.

Lewis, K., and P. Shirley. 2001. *You're My World: A Non-BP's Guide to Custody*. Milwaukee, WI: Eggshells Press. www.bpdcentral.com. (888) 357-4355.

Rashkin, R. 2006. *An Umbrella for* Alex. Roswell, GA: PDAN Press. www .pdan.org. This is a book for children about a parent with mood swings.

Winkler, K., and R. Kreger. 2000. *Hope for Parents: Helping Your Borderline Son or Daughter Without Sacrificing Your Family or Yourself*. Milwaukee, WI: Eggshells Press. www.bpdcentral.com. (888) 357-4355.

Materials About BPD Available Wherever Books Are Sold

★★Aguirre, B. A. 2007. *Borderline Personality Disorder in Adolescents: A Complete Guide to Understanding and Coping When Your Adolescent Has BPD*. Beverly, MA: Fair Winds Press.

★★Chapman, A. L., and K. L. Gratz. 2007. *The Borderline Personality Disorder Survival Guide: Everything You Need to Know About Living with BPD*. Oakland, CA: New Harbinger Publications.

★★Friedel, R. O. 2004. *Borderline Personality Disorder Demystified: An Essential Guide for Understanding and Living with BPD*. New York: Marlowe & Company. www.bpddemystified.com.

Gunderson, J. G., and P. D. Hoffman, eds. 2005. *Understanding and Treating Borderline Personality Disorder: A Guide for Professionals and Families*. Washington, DC: American Psychiatric Publishing.

★★+Kreger, R., with J. P. Shirley. 2002. *The Stop Walking on Eggshells Workbook: Practical Strategies for Living with Someone Who Has Borderline Personality Disorder*. Oakland, CA: New Harbinger Publications. www.bpdcentral. com.

**Kreger, R. 2008. *The Essential Family Guide to Borderline Personality Disorder: New Tools and Techniques to Stop Walking on Eggshells*. Center City, MN: Hazelden. www.BPDcentral.com

Kreisman, J. J., and H. Straus. 2004. *Sometimes I Act Crazy: Living with Borderline Personality Disorder*. Hoboken, NJ: John Wiley & Sons.

**+Lawson, C. A. 2002. *Understanding the Borderline Mother: Helping Her Children Transcend the Intense, Unpredictable, and Volatile Relationship*. Northvale, NJ: Jason Aronson.

Linehan, M. M. 1993. *Skills Training Manual for Treating Borderline Personality Disorder*. New York: Guilford Press. behavioraltech.org. This manual is written for clinicians who use dialectical behavior therapy (DBT), but it has useful worksheets for those with BPD.

Moskovitz, R. 2001. *Lost in the Mirror: An Inside Look at Borderline Personality Disorder*, 2nd ed. Lanham, MD: Taylor Trade Publishing.

**Reiland, R. 2004. *Get Me Out of Here: My Recovery from Borderline Personality Disorder*. Center City, MN: Hazelden. Warning: This book may be too emotionally intense for some borderline individuals.

+Roth, K., and F. B. Friedman. 2003. *Surviving a Borderline Parent: How to Heal Your Childhood Wounds and Build Trust, Boundaries, and Self-Esteem*. Oakland, CA: New Harbinger Publications. www.survivingaborderlineparent.com.

Other Resources

Anderson, S. 2000. *The Journey from Abandonment to Healing*. New York: Berkley Books. This book is for individuals with BPD.

Beattie, M. 1992. *Codependent No More: How to Stop Controlling Others and Start Caring for Yourself*, 2nd ed. Center City, MN: Hazelden.

**Berg, B. C. 2004. *How to Escape the No-Win Trap*. New York: McGraw-Hill.

**Black, J., and G. Enns. 1997. *Better Boundaries: Owning and Treasuring Your Life*. Oakland, CA: New Harbinger Publications.

Blauner, S. R. 2002. *How I Stayed Alive When My Brain Was Trying to Kill Me: One Person's Guide to Suicide Prevention*. New York: William Morrow.

★★+Brown, E. B. 1999. *Living Successfully with Screwed-Up* People. Grand Rapids, MI: Fleming H. Revell.

Brown, N. W. 2008. *Children of the Self-Absorbed: A Grown-up's Guide to Getting Over Narcissistic Parents,* 2nd ed. Oakland, CA: New Harbinger Publications.

Carter, L. 2005. *Enough About You, Let's Talk About Me: How to Recognize and Manage the Narcissists in Your Life.* San Francisco: Jossey-Bass.

Ellis, T. E., and C. F. Newman. 1996. *Choosing to Live: How to Defeat Suicide Through Cognitive Therapy.* Oakland, CA: New Harbinger Publications.

Engel, B. 1990. *Divorcing a Parent: Free Yourself from the Past and Live the Life You've Always Wanted.* New York: Fawcett Columbine. www.beverly engel.com.

———. 1990. *The Emotionally Abused Woman: Overcoming Destructive Patterns and Reclaiming Yourself.* New York: Fawcett Columbine. www.beverly engel.com.

———. 2002. *The Emotionally Abusive Relationship: How to Stop being Abused and How to Stop Abusing.* Hoboken, NJ: John Wiley & Sons. www.beverly engel.com.

———. 2007. *The Jekyll and Hyde Syndrome: What to Do If Someone in Your Life Has a Dual Personality, or If You Do.* Hoboken, NJ: John Wiley & Sons. www.beverlyengel.com.

———. 2000. *Loving Him Without Losing You: How to Stop Disappearing and Start Being Yourself.* New York: John Wiley & Sons. www.beverlyengel .com. This book is also appropriate for men.

Evans, P. 2002. *Controlling People: How to Recognize, Understand, and Deal With People Who Try to Control You.* Avon, MA: Adams Media Corporation.

Fruzzetti, A. E. 2006. *The High-Conflict Couple: A Dialectical Behavior Therapy Guide to Finding Peace, Intimacy, and Validation.* Oakland, CA: New Harbinger Publications.

★★Forward, S. 1997. *Emotional Blackmail: When the People in Your Life Use Fear, Obligation, and Guilt to Manipulate You.* New York: HarperCollins Publishers.

★★———. 1989. *Toxic Parents: Overcoming Their Hurtful Legacy and Reclaiming Your Life*. New York: Bantam Books.

Greene, R. W. 2005. *The Explosive Child: A New Approach for Understanding and Parenting Easily Frustrated, Chronically Inflexible Children*, revised and updated. New York: Harper.

Jeffers, S. 2007. *Feel the Fear...and Do It Anyway*. New York: Ballantine.

Johnston, J. R., K. Breunig, C. Garrity, and M. Baris. 1997. *Through the Eyes of Children: Healing Stories for Children of* Divorce. New York: Free Press.

★★+Klatte, B., and K. Thompson. 2007. *It's So Hard to Love You: Staying Sane When Your Loved One Is Manipulative, Needy, Dishonest, or Addicted*. Oakland, CA: New Harbinger Publications.

★★Lerner, H. 2005. *The Dance of Anger: A Woman's Guide to Changing the Patterns of Intimate Relationships*. New York: Perennial Currents. This book is also invaluable for men.

McKay, M., and D. Harp. 2005. *Neural Path Therapy: How to Change Your Brain's Response to Anger, Fear, Pain, and Desire*. Oakland, CA: New Harbinger Publications.

McKay, M., K. Paleg, P. Fanning, and D. Landis. 1996. *When Anger Hurts Your Kids: A Parent's Guide*. Oakland, CA: New Harbinger Publications.

McVey-Noble, M. E., S. Khemlani-Patel, and F. Neziroglu. 2006. *When Your Child Is Cutting: A Parent's Guide to Helping Children Overcome Self-Injury*. Oakland, CA: New Harbinger Publications.

Miller, A. 2008. *The Enabler: When Helping Hurts the One You Love*. Tucson, AZ: Wheatmark.

Neuharth, D. 1998. *If You Had Controlling Parents: How to Make Peace with Your Past and Take Your Place in the World*. New York: Cliff Street Books.

Paleg, K., and M. McKay. 2001. *When Anger Hurts Your Relationship: Ten Simple Solutions for Couples Who Fight*. Oakland, CA: New Harbinger Publications.

Rossi, M. 1996. *Courtney Love: Queen of* Noise. New York: Pocket Books.

Rubin, C. 2007. *Don't Let Your Kids Kill You: A Guide for Parents of Drug and Alcohol Addicted Children*, 3rd ed. Petaluma, CA: NewCentury Publishers.

**Savage, E. 1997. *Don't Take It Personally! The Art of Dealing with Rejection*. Oakland, CA: New Harbinger Publications. www.queenofrejection .com.

Smith, S. B. 1999. *Diana in Search of Herself: Portrait of a Troubled Princess*. New York: Times Books.

Stenack, R. J. 2001. *Stop Controlling Me! What to Do When Someone You Love Has Too Much Power Over You*. Oakland, CA: New Harbinger Publications.

Spungen, D. 1996. *And I Don't Want to Live this Life*. New York: Ballantine Books.

Young, J. E., and J. S. Klosko 1993. *Reinventing Your Life: How to Break Free from Negative Life Patterns*. New York: Dutton. www.schematherapy .com.

Wexler, D. B. 2005. *Is He Depressed or What? What to Do When the Man You Love Is Irritable, Moody, and Withdrawn*. Oakland, CA: New Harbinger Publications.

BPD Organization

National Education Alliance for Borderline Personality Disorder (NEA-BPD)

neabpd.org

The NEA-BPD works to raise public awareness, provide education, and promote research about BPD, as well as enhance the quality of life of those affected by BPD. It offers family education programs, annual conferences, regional meetings, and educational and research materials.

The NEA-BPD also offers a twelve-week Family Connections program that teaches people with BPD and their family members coping skills based on dialectical behavior therapy (DBT). This course is taught only in certain cities, and participants are required to pay a fee. The program is also available by telephone. For information, see the organization's website.

The NEA-BPD's extensive website contains information about upcoming conferences, grants, family programs, video and audio resources, and much more. Of special interest is the video and audio archive of presentations from clinicians with expertise on BPD.

Selected Online Resources

Some of the best resources for people interested in BPD can be found on the Internet. Depending on the site, the information on the web can be the most up-to-date. And, of course, the information is instantly accessible.

If you search the phrase "borderline personality disorder," you'll find an overwhelming number of options. Following are some of the most notable online resources that have stood the test of time and offer current, useful information.

Online Support Groups

Something magical happens when a person with a borderline family member meets someone else in the same situation, whether it's in real life or online. Books and clinicians may say, "It's not you, it's the disorder," but it's hard not to feel like a failure when someone you love is insistent that everything is your fault.

When other people say, "That's exactly what's happening to me" and then describe a parallel experience, it becomes much easier to understand the dynamics going on, put aside feelings of hurt and guilt, and start problem solving.

The Welcome to Oz Online Community for Family Members with a Borderline Loved One
www.bpdcentral.com
Welcome to Oz (WTO) was founded by Randi Kreger in 1996. With 16,000 members, it is the largest and longest established family forum. Conversations take place via e-mail. The experiences of WTO members became the basis for *Stop Walking on Eggshells* and *The Stop Walking on Eggshells Workbook*.

Because WTO is large, it can support both large, mixed groups and smaller, specialized groups for people in different types of relationships. These include grandparents (WTOGrandparents), siblings (WTOSiblings), adult children (WTOAdultChildren1), and Christians (WTOChristian). There is also a men-only group (WTOMenOnly) and a women-only group (WTOWomenOnly).

Individuals with a borderline partner can select groups based on the status of their relationship. There are groups for people who wish to remain in the relationship (WTOStaying), those who wish to leave (WTODivorcing), and those who are not sure (WTOTransition). Other groups include WTOCoParenting (includes stepparents) WTOGLBT, and WTOProfessionals (for clinicians who wish to add to their professional knowledge.

Members can subscribe to these groups at www.bpdcentral.com and by sending a blank message to [name of group]-subscribe@yahoogroups.com.

NUTS (parents Needing Understanding, Tenderness, and Support to help their child with borderline personality disorder)
www.parent2parentbpd.org

NUTS consists of parents and grandparents whose children (adult or minor) have BPD, with or without a formal diagnosis. This group, established in 1996, is operated by a dedicated and experienced mother, Sharon, who has appeared several times in this book. There is a small monthly membership fee. Parents discuss a variety of topics, including the effect of BPD on their own emotions and on those of other family members.

Selected Sites on the World Wide Web

BPDCentral
www.bpdcentral.com

BPDCentral was established by Randi Kreger in 1995. It offers a wide variety of information about BPD, including articles, essays, and interviews with experts; excerpts from books and booklets; links and resources; answers to common questions; basic and advanced information about BPD and the effects of borderline behavior on family members; and much more.

Facing the Facts: When a Loved One Has Borderline Personality Disorder
www.bpdfamily.com

This is an extensive site about BPD for family members. It contains a message board, articles and a reliable resource list of links, support groups, and books.

Borderline Personality Disorder Demystified
www.bpddemystified.com

This is a detailed, up-to-date site by Robert Friedel, MD, author of *Borderline Personality Disorder Demystified,* a leading BPD psychiatrist.

Borderline Personality Disorder: Reliable Resources for Family Members

www.bpdresources.net

This site features independent book reviews and interesting excerpts from the books. It also features interviews with the authors.

Touch Another Heart: Empathy and Listening Skills for Emotional Intimacy

www.touch-another-heart.com

This is an interesting, informative site about empathic acknowledgment, which is a key way to improve communication with individuals who have BPD.

www.mytriptoozandback.com

Subtitled "A True Retrospective Story of My Relationship with a Person with BPD," this site is a reproduction of a woman's fifty-page letter to her borderline partner. Her experiences are representative of most people with a borderline partner.

Borderline Personality Disorder from the Inside Out

www.borderlinepersonality.ca

A. J. Mahari, who has appeared in this book many times, is a prolific writer who comes from not only the perspective of a person with BPD but also the perspective of a family member. The site includes links to Mahari's e-books and YouTube videos.

BPDRecovery

www.bpdrecovery.com

This is an extensive site for people with the disorder, which features a message-board community.

Florida Borderline Personality Disorder Association

www.fbpda.org

Middle Path: Awareness, Compassion, and Support for Borderline Personality Disorder

www.middle-path.org

This is a nonprofit online resource for people with BPD.

www.bpdawareness.org
Subtitled "Shades of Grey," this site is dedicated to increasing awareness of BPD. It sells BPD awareness EMBRACElets.

Behavioral Tech, LLC
www.behavioraltech.com
Behavioral Tech, LLC, founded by Marsha Linehan, Ph.D., trains mental health care providers and treatment teams to use dialectical behavior therapy (DBT). This site has a searchable database of U.S. clinicians trained in DBT.

Borderline Personality Disorder Resource Center
www.bpdresourcecenter.org
This site is associated with the Borderline Personality Resource Center (BPDRC) at New York–Presbyterian Hospital. This site provides a great general introduction to BPD.

Schema Therapy
www.schematherapy.com
This site presents information about the treatment method founded by Jeffrey Young, Ph.D.

About Psychotherapy
www.aboutpsychotherapy.com
This is an extensive, far-reaching site about therapy and the therapeutic process.

BPDWorld
www.bpdworld.org
This site offers resources in the United Kingdom.

Association d'Aide aux Personnes avec un Etat Limite
www.aapel.org
This site is from a French organization.

references

Adamec, C. 1996. *How to Live with a Mentally Ill Person*. New York: John Wiley & Sons, Inc.

Al-Anon Family Group Headquarters. 1981. *Detachment*. Virginia Beach, VA.

Beattie, M. 1987. *Codependent No More*. Center City, MN: Hazelden.

Brach, T. 2004. *Radical Acceptance*. New York: Bantam.

Bradshaw, J. 1988. *Healing the Shame That Binds You*. Deerfield Beach, FL: Health Communications.

Brodsky, B., and J. Mann. 1997. "The Biology of the Disorder." *California Alliance for the Mentally Ill Journal* 8:1.

Cauwels, J. 1992. *Imbroglio: Rising to the Challenges of Borderline Personality Disorder*. New York: W. W. Norton.

DSM-IV-TR. 2004. *Diagnostic and Statistical Manual of Mental Disorders*. Washington, DC: American Psychiatric Asociation.

Ellis, T. E., and C. F. Newman. 1996. *Choosing to Live: How to Defeat Suicide Through Cognitive Therapy*. Oakland, CA: New Harbinger Publications.

Engel, B. 1990. *The Emotionally Abused Woman: Overcoming Destructive Patterns and Reclaiming Yourself.* New York: Fawcett Columbine.

Evans, P. 1996. *The Verbally Abusive Relationship: How to Recognize It and How to Respond.* Holbrook, MA: Adams Media Corporation.

Forward, S., and D. Frazier. 1997. *Emotional Blackmail: When the People in Your Life Use Fear, Obligation, and Guilt to Manipulate You.* New York: HarperCollins.

Gibran, K. 1976. *The Prophet.* New York: Alfred A. Knopf.

Golomb E. 1992. *Trapped in the Mirror: Adult Children of Narcissists in the Struggle for Self.* New York: William Morrow.

Gunderson, J. G. 1984. *Borderline Personality Disorder.* Washington DC: American Psychiatric Press, Inc.

Heldmann, M. L. 1990. *When Words Hurt: How to Keep Criticism from Undermining Your Self-Esteem.* New York: Ballentine.

Herr, N. R., C. Hammen, and P. A. Brennan. 2008. "Maternal Borderline Personality Disorder Symptoms and Adolescent Psychosocial Functioning." *Journal of Personality Disorders,* 22(5):451–465.

Johnston, J. A., and V. Roseby. 1997. *In the Name of the Child: A Developmental Approach to Understanding and Helping Children of Conflicted and Violent Divorce.* New York: The Free Press.

Kabat-Zinn, J. 2005 *Wherever You Go, There You Are.* New York: Hyperion.

Katherine, A. 1993. *Boundaries: Where You End and I Begin.* Park Ridge, IL: Fireside/Parkside.

Kreisman, J, and H. Straus. 1989. *I Hate You—Don't Leave Me.* New York: Avon Books.

Kreisman, J, and H. Straus. 1989. *Sometimes I Act Crazy.* New York: John Wiley & Sons, Inc.

Kübler-Ross, E. 1975. *Death: The Final Stage of Growth.* Englewood Cliffs, NJ: Prentice Hall.

Lerner, H. G. 1985. *The Dance of Anger.* New York: Harper Perennial.

Leving, J. M., and K. A. Dachman. 1997. *Fathers' Rights*. New York: BasicBooks.

Linehan, M. 1993a. *Cognitive-Behavioral Treatment of Borderline Personality Disorder*. New York: Guilford Press.

Linehan, M. 1993b. *Skills Training Manual for Treating Borderline Personality Disorder*. New York: Guilford Press.

Links, P. S., R. J. Heslegrave, J. E. Milton, R. van Reekum, and J. Patrick. 1995. "Borderline Personality Disorder and Substance Abuse: Consequences of Comorbidity." *Canadian Journal of Psychiatry* 40:9–14.

Links, P. S., M. Steiner, and D. R. Offord. 1988. "Characteristics of Borderline Personality Disorder: A Canadian Study." *Canadian Journal of Psychiatry* 33:336–340.

McGlashan, T. H. 1986. "Long-Term Outcome of Borderline Personalities." The Chestnut Lodge Follow-up Study. III. *Archives of General Psychiatry* 43:20–30.

McKay, M., J. C. Wood, and J. Brantley. 2007. *The Dialectical Behavior Therapy Skills Workbook*. Oakland, CA: New Harbinger Publications.

McKay, M., P. Fanning, K. Paleg, and D. Landis. 1996. *When Anger Hurts Your Kids: A Parent's Guide*. Oakland, CA: New Harbinger Publications.

Moskovitz, R. A. 1996. *Lost in the Mirror: An Inside Look at Borderline Personality Disorder*. Dallas, TX: Taylor Publishing Company.

Nace, E.P., J. J. Saxon, and N. Shore. 1983. "A Comparison of Borderline and Nonborderline Alcoholic Patients." *Archives of General Psychiatry* 40:54–56.

Nash, M. 1997. "The Chemistry of Addiction." *Time* 149(18):69–76.

Newman, C. F. 1997. "Maintaining Professionalism in the Face of Emotional Abuse from Clients." *Cognitive and Behavioral Practice* 4:1–29.

Novak, J. 1996. *Wisconsin Father's Guide to Divorce and Custody*. Madison, WI: Prairie Oak Press.

Oldham, J. M. 1997. "Borderline Personality Disorder: The Treatment Dilemma." *The Journal of the California Alliance for the Mentally Ill* 8(1):13–17.

Oldham, J. M., A. E. Skodol, H. D. Kellman, S. E. Hyler, N. Doidge, L. Rosnick, and P. Gallaher. 1995. "Comorbidity of Axis I and Axis II Disorders." *American Journal of Psychiatry* 152:571–578.

Preston, J. 1997. *Shorter-Term Treatments for Borderline Personality Disorder.* Oakland, CA: New Harbinger Publications.

Reaves, J., and J. B. Austin. 1990. *How to Find Help for a Troubled Kid: A Parent's Guide for Programs and Services for Adolescents.* New York: Henry Holt.

Roth, K. and F. B. Friedman. 2003. *Surviving a Borderline Parent.* Oakland, CA: New Harbinger Publications.

Santoro, J., and R. Cohen. 1997. *The Angry Heart: A Self-Help Guide for Borderline and Addictive Personality Disorder.* Oakland, CA: New Harbinger Publications.

Siever, J., and W. Frucht. 1997. *The New View of Self: How Genes and Neurotransmitters Shape Your Mind, Your Personality, and Your Mental Health.* New York: Macmillan.

Silk, K. R. 1997. "Notes on the Biology of Borderline Personality Disorder." *California Alliance for the Mentally Ill Journal* 8:15–17.

Stone, M. H. 1990. *The Fate of Borderline Patients.* New York: Guilford Press.

Thornton, M. F. 1998. *Eclipses: Behind the Borderline Personality Disorder.* Madison, AL: Monte Sano Publishing.

Tong, D. 1996. *Ashes to Ashes... Families to Dust: False Accusation of Child Abuse: A Roadmap for Survivors.* Tampa, FL: FamRights Press.

Waldinger, R. J. 1993. "The Role of Psychodynamic Concepts in the Diagnosis of Borderline Personality Disorder." *Harvard Review of Psychiatry* 1:158–167.

Paul T. Mason, MS, is vice president of clinical services at Wheaton Franciscan Healthcare in Racine, WI. Under his leadership, the mental health and addiction care service line has expanded the number of inpatient services and outpatient programs it provides for patients, family members, and loved ones affected by borderline personality disorder (BPD). His research on BPD has been published in the *Journal of Clinical Psychology* and his written work has appeared in the news and print media.

Randi Kreger has brought the concerns of family members who have a loved one with BPD to an international forefront through her website, www.bpd central.com, and the Welcome to Oz online support community. Through Eggshells Press, she offers family members a wide variety of more specialized booklets and other materials. She was also instrumental in the formation of the Personality Disorders Awareness Network (PDAN), a not-for-profit organization. Kreger is author of *The Stop Walking on Eggshells Workbook* and *The Essential Family Member Guide to Borderline Personality Disorder.* She speaks and gives workshops about BPD internationally.